IT Web Services

A Roadmap for the Enterprise

ISBN 0-13-009719-5

HARRIS KERN'S ENTERPRISE COMPUTING INSTITUTE

ENTERPRISE COMPUTING SERIES

IT Web Services

A Roadmap for the Enterprise

Alex Nghiem

Harris Kern's Enterprise Computing Institute

PRENTICE
HALL
PTR

Prentice Hall PTR, Upper Saddle River, NJ 07458
www.phptr.com

A CIP catalog record for this book can be obtained from the Library of Congress.

Editorial/production supervision: BooksCraft, Inc., Indianapolis, IN
Executive editor: Greg Doench
Editorial assistant: Brandt Kenna
Marketing manager: Debby vanDijk
Manufacturing manager: Alexis Heydt-Long
Cover design director: Jerry Votta
Cover designer: Talar Boorujy
Full-service production manager: Anne Garcia

© 2003 Pearson Education, Inc.
Publishing as Prentice Hall PTR
Upper Saddle River, New Jersey 07458

Prentice Hall books are widely used by corporations and government agencies for training, marketing, and resale.

For information regarding corporate and government bulk discounts please contact:
Corporate and Government Sales (800) 382-3419 or corpsales@pearsontechgroup.com

Company and product names mentioned herein are the trademarks or registered trademarks of their respective owners.

Printed in the United States of America
10 9 8 7 6 5 4 3 2 1

ISBN 0-13-009719-5

Pearson Education Ltd.
Pearson Education Australia PTY,. Limited
Pearson Education Singapore, Pte. Ltd.
Pearson Education North Asia Ltd.
Pearson Education Canada Ltd.
Pearson Educación de Mexico, S. A. de C. V.
Pearson Education—Japan
Pearson Education Malaysia, Pte. Ltd.

Contents

Chapter 2

The Basic Web Services Stack 29

Chapter 5

Deployment Issues   107

Chapter 6

Web Services Networks   123

Chapter 9

Emerging Trend: Software as a Service   175

Appendix A

ebXML and Other XML Initiatives   191

Foreword

Jason Bloomberg
Senior Analyst, ZapThink LLC

There comes a point in the lifetime of any technology movement at which the broad acceptance of open standards heralds the golden age for the technology. Standard track gauges brought the railroad industry into its prime; alternating current was the key to electrification; now Web Services offer the same promise to distributed computing. As Alex Nghiem (pronounced *neem*) points out in the Introduction to this book, Web Services are a disruptive technology—their open standards and loose coupling promise to reduce the cost of integration, foster communication among systems across enterprises, and enable the automation of ever more complex, dynamic business processes. Such automation will both reduce the cost of business as well as open up new markets and new ways of serving customers. Make no mistake, Web Services are here to stay, and they will change software and the companies that use it.

No concept in the software world since the dotcom implosion has received as much attention as Web Services. Every software vendor, it seems, has some kind of Web Services product or strategy. Web Services form the battleground where industry titans such as Microsoft and IBM are going head-to-head, surrounded by hundreds of other smaller combatants. However, there are still many CIOs and other technology executives who are unfamiliar with or who do not understand Web Services.

When a concept gets this much attention, hype is bound to follow; Web Services are no exception. The industry sports the full range of hype levels, from serious firms with truly revolutionary products to has-been companies who have rewritten their marketing materials but are still offering the same old legacy applications. That's where books like *IT Web Services: A Roadmap for the Enterprise* can be valuable. You have in your hands a broad, yet reasonably detailed picture of what Web Services are, how they should be used, and how companies are already using them. In many ways, Web Services are an evolutionary step in the development of distributed computing, and Nghiem utilizes this fact frequently; his background in object-oriented analysis and design serves him well when explaining Web Services in the context of distributed computing as it has been done in the past.

If Web Services are more evolutionary than revolutionary, what is it about them that makes them so significant? Open standards are critical, allowing for interoperability among every participating vendor's offerings, but this openness is only part of the story. Web Services are also loosely coupled and allow for dynamic discovery and description. The term loose coupling means that individual Web Services can be changed without breaking the systems that access them. Dynamic discovery and description allow Web Services to be found and invoked while the various distributed systems are running. Combining the concepts of *loose coupling* and *dynamic discovery and description* results in the creation of a roadmap to an agile enterprise vision where distributed systems consist of flexible, dynamic collections of Web Services that adjust to rapidly changing business requirements.

Such a long-term vision for distributed computing promises to transform the software industry, but, as with most visions, it is still several years off. Much work must be done to implement Web Services today and to resolve the many roadblocks that Web Services face, including security, management, transactions, and payments. Today's enterprise technology leaders must focus on the short-term integration improvements offered by current Web Services technologies, as well as plan ahead to capitalize on the future power of Web Services when the roadblocks are no longer there. The timing, in fact, is crucial: jump in too early and struggle with half-baked standards, or delay Web Services implementations and lose the competitive advantage.

What's an IT leader to do? First, keep informed about emerging Web Services technologies; this book can help with that. Second, push your organizations to phase in Web Services wherever practical. And, most important, do what you can to communicate the agile enterprise vision of Web Services to the business leaders in your company. If we learned anything during the dotcom era, it's that businesses must make use of information technology or risk succumbing to market forces.

Acknowledgments

Writing a book is never a one-person effort, and I would like to thank all the people who have made this production and journey possible.

Thanks to my family for providing the love and support.

Special thanks to Don Wolf and Jim Tebbel of B2B Technologies (for contributing the Microsoft .NET portion of Chapter 4), Kyle Brown of IBM (for contributing Chapter 5), and Venkatranga Konda for contributing the review of XMLBus.

Folks who have helped by providing invaluable feedback and guidance include Steve Derezinski, Isaac Adams, Sam Taha, Carl Sturmer, Fred Hart, Randy Pilkenton, and Chris du Toit.

Thanks to all the people who agreed to be interviewed and offered their valuable opinions.

Thanks to the entire salsa team (Alfredo, Randi, Ayako, Koko, and many others too numerous to list here) for offering an environment for learning and for sharing many fond memories of our performances and outings. Special thanks to Michael and Tatiana for offering lots of guidance and keeping the group together.

Finally, a special thanks to Harris Kern, my series editor; Greg Doench, the executive editor at Prentice Hall who believed in the book enough to get it off the ground; and all the folks at Prentice Hall who made this book a success.

Introduction

Today, more than ever, enterprises are faced with great challenges: rising development costs, budget cutbacks, and increasing customer demands, to name a few. Decision makers must determine which projects to fund and are often confronted with an existing technology infrastructure that already includes a hodgepodge of technologies, such as object-oriented technologies, enterprise application integration (EAI), enterprise resource planning (ERP), and customer relationship management (CRM).

Against this backdrop, Web Services emerge promising many wonderful benefits, such as reduced integration costs and a low learning curve. How can a technology planner reconcile these promises with conflicting real-life experiences involving incomplete standards, lack of security features, and other key issues? How should these gaps be addressed? Do Web Services replace existing technologies or do they augment them? Has any firm adopted Web Services successfully? If so, what were the benefits and how was it done? What makes Web Services different from previous attempts of interoperability such as Common Object Request Broker Architecture (CORBA)? And why is it inevitable that Web Services or the like will be adopted on a grand scale?

The answer is that early adopters of Web Services have indeed used the technology successfully to achieve a variety of goals, including providing better customer service (Putnam Lovell Securities), building a digital marketplace with reduced development costs (Pantechnik

1

International), and saving the adopting firm millions of dollars by building a sophisticated procurement platform (Talaris).

An enterprise that is seriously considering using Web Services needs to identify what gaps are relevant and how to address these gaps. Many of the gaps in the standards are rapidly being addressed by emerging technologies or third parties such as Web Services networks.

Understandably, many organizations are reluctant or even nervous about investing in Web Services for the long haul, having lived through too many rosy predictions. With amazing consistency, most of the firms interviewed for this book expressed the concern that Web Services will indeed be ubiquitous for a variety of reasons:

- They are built on existing infrastructure and open standards (Hypertext Transfer Protocol [HTTP], Extensible Markup Language [XML], etc.), which means many firms can launch pilot projects without a huge initial investment. Standards are important not because they are cutting edge—they are important only if they are widely adopted. Web Services are a social phenomenon rather than a technological one (elaborated further below).

- Beyond adopting open standards, vendors are actively working together to ensure interoperability between their technologies. In addition to independent standards organizations such as the Worldwide Web Consortium (W3C), vendors have formed interoperability groups to produce compliance tests. An example of such a group is the Web Services Interoperability Group.

- Every major vendor has announced support for Web Services. One technology executive pointed out that a firm would have to *actively* try to keep Web Services out because the world's largest software company (Microsoft) has embedded this functionality in its Office products.

The best-selling book *The Innovator's Dilemma* coined the term **disruptive technology** to refer to a technology that, once introduced, has the potential to dramatically affect the equilibrium of a market. A disruptive technology has three characteristics:

1. It can pull a large population of less skilled or less wealthy customers into the market.

2. It can get traction *only* if it helps people accomplish something they are already doing in a better or faster way.

3. It can gain a foothold without being as good as an established product.

Let's explore whether Web Services have these characteristics.

Currently, many firms are dealing with high integration costs on too many projects—they have no choice but to buy high-end packages for performing even simple integration. In addition to being expensive, many of these packages require scarce high-end skills. There are entire market segments (small- to medium-sized businesses, predominantly) that cannot afford these types of initiatives.

While they are not appropriate for all integration projects, Web Services can be used in many scenarios that, until now, require a high-end integration package (such as an integration broker or EAI). A consistent message in the industry is that Web Services can *democratize integration* (point 1 above) and make the benefits available to a much larger audience due to a significant drop in costs, thus resolving the criticism in point 1 from the previous list.

To address point 2, firms are already performing integration and, in many cases, are looking for better methods. Again, broadly speaking, integration takes on many forms and involves exchanging information between organizations. Thus, integration can then include transferring files using file transfer protocol (FTP) or email, integrating two back-end systems via EAI, and the like. While Web Services will not replace EAI in the near future, they can automate and streamline many integration scenarios where firms are performing manual tasks. You might be surprised to learn that many enterprises are still exchanging very critical data through a manual FTP process.

The third point is critical to understanding the rate of adoption: many technologists would argue that Web Services are not as capable as existing technologies (EAI, middleware, etc.) and should not be considered. A disruptive technology does not need to compete with existing technologies; it needs to be good enough to address the needs of a market segment that is suffering from a business pain. Again, not all integration problems require a high-end integration package or middleware; in those cases, Web Services provide a compelling alternative.

As an analogy of a disruptive technology, consider the introduction of the personal computer (PC) almost 25 years ago. At the time, many incumbents (including IBM and DEC, who dominated the mainframe and minicomputer market, respectively) did not consider the PC a threat because they could not envision why a business would use such a limited tool. Because the businesses using computers at that time included banks, airlines, the military, and the like, incumbents thought computers needed industrial-strength storage, high throughput, and rock-solid reliability. However, they overlooked a large market: people such as analysts and business owners who performed financial modeling tasks on a daily basis. People like this met all three characteristics of disruptive technology in the earlier list: a large audience of less skilled and less wealthy customers who were already performing their tasks routinely and who did not need a product that competed with the one offered by the market leaders.

Fast-forward 25 years to the present and witness how the entire industry has changed. Companies that were barely formed (Intel and Microsoft) are now among the world's most valuable companies, and one of the two then-market leaders (DEC) is not even around. Many analysts and technology executives are predicting that the introduction of Web Services can have an even bigger impact on the industry than did the introduction of the PC.

Using this book as a roadmap, you should be able to navigate through many of these issues to decide how Web Services should fit into your enterprise's strategy and whether the business benefits are compelling enough to launch a pilot project. At that point, there are many other wonderful references on how to implement Web Services.

▶ Audience

The purpose of the book is to demonstrate the business benefits of Web Services for organizations of all sizes, along with providing the supporting technical background. It attempts to remove much of the noise and hype surrounding this technology and provides a foundation on which to make informed decisions.

It is first and foremost intended as a roadmap for technology planner roles such as chief information or technology officers (CIOs or CTOs), directors of technology or product strategy and software architects. These are the people who are responsible for determining whether this potentially disruptive technology will replace or complement traditional integration technologies such as middleware and EAI.

Others who can benefit from the book include business analysts, who have to decide on whether the claimed benefits—sometimes outrageous ones—provided by Web Services are compelling enough to justify funding a pilot project, as well as investors who are considering whether this market is worth taking a second look at (and investing in).

Web Services are evolving so fast that it is almost impossible to predict where they are headed. Their benefits are illustrated through many extensive one-on-one interviews with executives at leading technology firms and by looking at real-world case studies of early adopters. It is the executives who are making the tactical and strategic decisions regarding technology who will, in many ways, determine the rollout of Web Services. Through the unedited detailed sessions with these executives, you will have a 360-degree view of the marketplace. Then you can reach your own conclusions.

▶ Structure

Chapter 1 starts with some of the business conditions that drive integration at the enterprise level and then provides an inventory of technologies that currently exist to address some of these issues. By discussing the challenges that are present in adopting these technologies (object-oriented technologies, component-based development, EAI, etc.), the chapter illustrates how Web Services came to be.

Chapter 2 discusses what is widely known as the basic Web Services stack, including XML, Service-Oriented Access Protocol (SOAP) (historically called Simple Object Access Protocol), Web Services Definition Language (WSDL), and Universal Description, Discovery, and Integration (UDDI). It then concludes with a discussion on how Web Services will augment (and in some cases replace) the technologies discussed in Chapter 1 and how they will be adopted in multiple phases.

Chapter 3 covers Web Services at the enterprise level and focuses on a key area: messaging. Some key decisions that need to be decided when designing Web Services are whether to use synchronous vs. asynchronous architectures and whether to use a point-to-point or a publish-subscribe model. The pros and cons of these decisions are discussed in detail.

Chapter 4 focuses on two key Web Services platforms: Java 2 Enterprise Edition (J2EE) and Microsoft .NET. Ultimately, Web Services have to be deployed in one of these two platforms. This chapter discusses how the two platforms approach Web Services. It also includes a high-level discussion on how the various J2EE licensees (IBM, BEA Systems, Iona, etc.) differ in their implementations.

Chapter 5 discusses two key areas of concern for large-scale Web Services deployment: security and scalability. The security standards are not yet defined, but the W3C (the international standards body) is evaluating many mechanisms including digital signatures and encryption. The chapter then concludes with a discussion on how to architect Web Services for scalability.

Chapter 6 discusses an emerging market called Web Services networks. These firms provide value-added services including provisioning, guaranteed messaging, and centralized reporting. Two vendors, Flamenco Networks and Grand Central Communications, are profiled, and the chief executive officers (CEOs) of both are interviewed to gain their perspectives on how Web Services will be adopted.

Chapter 7 lists the common architectural patterns that should be considered when adopting Web Services. Each pattern is described with the necessary preconditions for adopting it along with the pros and cons.

Chapter 8 pulls it all together and provides a high-level plan for an organization adopting Web Services.

Chapter 9 discusses an emerging trend that is often confused with Web Services: **Software as a Service** (SAAS). The chapter discusses the pros and cons of adopting such a solution and then provides a one-on-one interview with an SAAS pioneer, Employease.

Appendix A discusses other initiatives including ebXML, Web Services Flow Language (WSFL), and XLANG. A worldwide initiative to provide a standards-based platform to facilitate e-commerce, ebXML includes a catalog of predefined business processes that can either be adopted as is or extended. WSFL and XLANG are emerging but conflicting technologies to address workflow.

Appendix B provides multiple detailed case studies on how enterprises are adopting Web Services to lower integration costs and open new markets. Each of these firms shares the lessons it learned as an early adopter.

Appendix C provides multiple perspectives drawn from detailed interviews with many leading Web Services vendors and startups including SilverStream Software, Iona Technologies, Cape Clear, and Collaxa. Each firm provides some unusual twist in its approach to Web Services.

Appendix D is a detailed product review of the bundled product XML-Bus.

▶ Bundled Software

The bundled CD contains a one-year license to Iona's E2A Web Services Integration Platform: XMLBus Edition. Follow the directions on the CD to install and register the product.

▶ Contacting the Author

I welcome your feedback on the book, and you can reach me at *alexn@bluesamba.com*. Please limit your comments and questions to the contents of the book. If you have questions and comments about the XMLBus bundled product, please forward them directly to Iona Technologies.

▶ Continued Web Support

Addenda to the book and follow-up case studies can be found at *www.bluesamba.com/webservices*.

Business Drivers for Integration

One of the major forces that drove the rapid adoption of the Internet beyond academia and research labs was the invention of the Web browser along with the development of the Hypertext Transfer Protocol (HTTP). Seemingly overnight, companies could publish and share information that traditionally had been locked in proprietary data sources such as legacy systems and databases. The browser provided a near universal display mechanism allowing users to suddenly browse vast amounts of information and run applications without having to learn arcane network protocols or worry about whether the application was installed on their local machine (anybody who has ever had to learn the command line or deal with the limitations of a client-server application can appreciate the two final points).

Shortly after businesses started publishing information (static sites), they then evolved and started conducting business on the Internet; this led to dynamic sites, which are typically linked to databases. Traditionally, commerce has been characterized as either **business-to-consumer (B2C)**, **business-to-business (B2B)**, or **business-to-enterprise (B2E)**. The adoption of the Internet revolved around these different business needs.

In many ways, the Web proved adequate for many businesses when used in the context of B2C. However, it falls far short of the needs of B2B. In some cases, the Web browser can even be a hindrance—many organizations would like to automate business processes without being required to display the information. This direct integration of businesses leads to the term **business-to-business integration (B2Bi)**.

Consider the following scenario. A user visits a site, performs some searches, and then places an order. While this sequence is acceptable for an individual consumer, it falls short in cases where the purchase cycle tends to be repeated frequently (for example, a corporation purchasing a variety of items from multiple sources). The following items are examples of the types of deficiencies faced in B2B interactions:

- Requiring a person to manually perform a process can be time consuming and prone to errors. Automating such processes would certainly streamline a company's operations significantly.[1]
- The information returned from the transaction is a mix of presentation-related data (graphics, formatting instructions, etc.) and business data (product names, codes, prices, etc.); this information is not in a format that can be easily integrated into another system. Consequently, it often requires that a person distinguish what is actually relevant in most interactions. Consider how expensive it is for a purchasing agent to re-enter information into an accounting system that is returned from a purchasing system. This seems rather antiquated by today's standards, but many companies are still performing a lot of their processes manually because there are few, if any, standards for information that is being passed around. What is needed is either a universal format or at least a way to separate business data from presentation data.

In many cases, the functionality offered by one site cannot be merged with another site to provide a more complete solution to the consumer due to technical limitations (lack of standards, integration challenges, incompatible technologies, etc.). As an example of this last point, consider a consumer who would like to book an entire vacation (flight, rental car, lodging, and local activities) online. The consumer (or travel agent) has to visit multiple sites and cobble together a package; then he must ensure that all the relevant criteria (identification, dates, locations, etc.) are matched. Anyone who has planned a vacation has experienced the amount of work involved (no wonder cruise ships are so popular!). This clumsy user experience exists because it is currently too

---

1. In this case, we are talking about automating a business process—purchasing—rather than remembering past purchases for personalization reasons.

difficult for the site operators to break the sites into discrete sets of subprocesses that can be merged or integrated into an experience that is relevant to the consumer (in this case, a total vacation experience). The focus of each site is narrow (the ski school is offering ski instruction, the airline is offering flights, etc.) whereas, as far as the user is concerned, all of these events have to be scheduled and booked to accomplish his overall goal, i.e., to book the entire vacation. Unfortunately, the site that offers skiing instruction has no way of knowing that the consumer visiting the site is the same person who is staying at a local hotel on a particular date.[2] Without that information, the site would have to ask for that information again. Multiply this registration process n times and the poor consumer will feel like taking a vacation after just planning the vacation!

Wouldn't it be much more useful for the consumer if these sites were integrated? On the surface, this seems like a rather straightforward problem, but there is more to the problem than what appears on the surface. Each site is more than just a static site; there are various back-end systems that must process incoming (and outbound) requests, and these systems are plagued by problems that have existed for a long time.

Consider this related example. An airline reservations company (call it XYZ) is trying to expand its market. If XYZ is to acquire a customer, that customer must be able (and willing) to integrate its system to XYZ's back-end system (typically on a mainframe system). However, since the application programming interface (API) to the mainframe system is highly proprietary, the customer must incur the high cost of integration. This high cost to customers limits the number and type of customers that XYZ can attract—typically, only large firms can absorb the high costs of integration, effectively prohibiting XYZ from doing business with many types of marketing channels (such as small businesses). It would greatly benefit XYZ if its systems and those of potential customers could have a common mechanism for exchanging data and functionality. This would significantly reduce integration costs and allow XYZ to effectively perform **application syndication**—just as content can be syndicated to many channels for redistribution, XYZ can potentially syndicate its application to multiple destinations (channels of distribution), which may or may not be Web sites.

---

2. In more technical terms, the sites cannot share the state of the user session. Current technologies allow for saving the state as long as the visitor is on the same site, but maintaining the state between sites is much trickier.

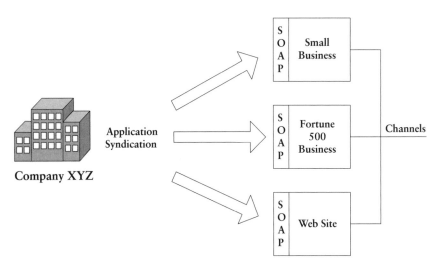

Figure 1–1 XYZ company syndicating its application to multiple channels.

Figure 1–1 illustrates a company syndicating its application to three channels: a small business, a Fortune 500 company, and a Web site. Simple Object Access Protocol (SOAP) facilitates integration and will be discussed further in the next chapter.

And finally, consider a Global 2000 company that has made many acquisitions (or has itself been acquired by another firm). Through a series of external events, it has inherited a number of enterprise systems that need to be integrated to deliver business value to its customers, both internal and external.[3] In many cases, an enterprise is no longer confined inside four walls. Instead, an enterprise now must exist within a larger ecosystem of trading partners, including its employees, customers, suppliers, distributors, and others—the term for this is **extended enterprise**. Figure 1–2 is an example of the extended enterprise.

As a link of a larger chain, the success of an enterprise is often determined by how well it orchestrates its business processes with those of its partners. One of the prerequisites to success is a company's ability to integrate its system with others to make more timely decisions; again, this historically has been prohibitively expensive because of pro-

---

3. According to *EAI Journal*, a Global 2000 company has, on average, 49 mission-critical systems.

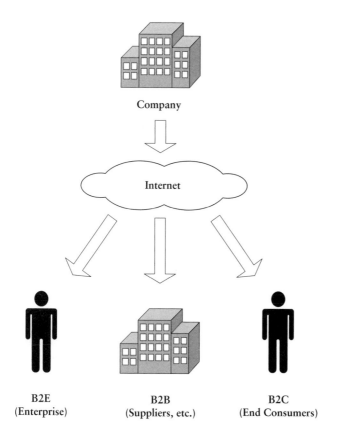

Figure 1–2 An example of the extended enterprise.

prietary technologies and the lack of a common integration approach. According to a survey by a leading analyst firm of over 200 chief information officers (CIOs) at Global 2000 companies, these same CIOs have to pass on three out of five business opportunities because they cannot adequately or quickly perform the integration necessary to capitalize on them.

Web Services offer the promise of addressing many of these challenges faced by enterprises today. The good news is that Web Services are built on many existing technologies. This means that a company does not have to do a complete overhaul of its existing investments.

Before delving into Web Services, let's discuss earlier technologies that attempted to solve some of these same problems. By going backwards a little bit, we can appreciate how some of the technology infrastructure came into being.

▶ Current Technological Limitations

An ongoing challenge of enterprise software development is **interoperability**—how to make two otherwise incompatible systems (due to differences in operating systems, programming languages, database systems, etc.) work together. In the early days of computing, when computer processing unit (CPU) cycles were expensive, the majority of development efforts were focused on optimizing program execution. However, as the world moved to multiple languages, operating systems, and platforms, the largest costs associated with enterprise software development are incurred when integrating two or more incompatible systems.

Another challenge that has existed in software development since its inception is how to achieve **reuse,** defined as the use of existing deliverables, which can be programs, subroutines, requirements, processes, and the like. Achieving reuse would provide many benefits: lower development costs, reduced defects, and time to market. These benefits have been realized by the hardware industry for years, but so far they have not been achievable on a large scale in the software industry.

This chapter discusses multiple technologies and techniques that have been introduced over the years to address the challenge of interoperability and reuse. In later chapters, we'll look at other similarly important issues such as security, authentication, scalability, and transaction control. These technologies include

- Object-oriented technology
- Component-based development (CBD)
- Middleware
- Application servers
- Hypertext Markup Language (HTML)
- Electronic Data Interchange (EDI)

- Packaged applications

- Enterprise application integration (EAI)

All of these topics eventually lead to our primary topic, Web Services.

Object-Oriented Technology

In the early days of personal computing (mid-1970s to mid-1980s) and client-server development, object-oriented technology (OOT) was invented to address some of the aforementioned problems. Providing a metaphor for creating a mental model of software as discrete **objects**, OOT advocated creating large (often complex) hierarchies of classes (from which objects are **instantiated**), and these classes often inherit common functionality and attributes from their parents (known as **superclasses**).[4] OOT is a set of techniques for performing object-oriented analysis (OOA), design (OOD), and programming (OOP). Many of the popular languages still in use today are object-oriented languages; examples include Java, C++, and C#.[5]

OOT did deliver on the promise of reuse but primarily at the coding level (OOT purists will argue that performing OOA correctly also results in business process reuse, but that is largely debatable). However, as it turns out, code reuse requires a substantial amount of investment in initial development (building class libraries, repositories, etc.) and mastery of low-level details. For example, one class can only **inherit** (or reuse the existing functionality) from another class as long as they are both written in the same language and, in many cases, the same release of the same language! Consequently, reuse in OOT is possible; at most, however, it is limited to a departmental level or divisional level, and it requires a fairly well-trained information technology (IT) staff.[6]

As we will see later, Web Services surpass the primary goal of OOT (large-scale reuse between enterprises), but without the single-language restriction and steep learning curve.

4. Technically speaking, OOT was invented in the late 1960s with the invention of Simula, but Smalltalk, which was not invented until the mid-1970s, refined many of the ideas of Simula.
5. HTML is definitely not object-oriented, but perl may be, depending on the passion of the person we are talking to.
6. Few companies have achieved reuse at an enterprise level with OOT.

▶ Component-Based Development (CBD)

As systems grew in complexity, it became more obvious that OOT alone was not sufficient to solve many of the remaining problems. As discussed earlier, one of the shortcomings of OOT was that, in order to achieve reuse, the developers often had to build large hierarchies of classes in the same language (even worse, often it had to be the same release number of the same language). This created a very tight dependency (or, more accurately, **tight coupling**) between fairly small units of work and required an understanding of low-level details.

CBD promotes a slightly less technical view of the world and introduces the concept of components. There are many definitions of the term **component**, but the following definition is adequate for our purposes: a component is a granular piece of software that delivers a set of discrete services that can be invoked via well-defined interfaces.

OOT practitioners would argue that this is similar to the definition of a class, but the difference is that the services provided by a component are *clearly* separated from that component's implementation details. With OOT, the calling program has to be written in an object-oriented language and, with few exceptions, the receiving program has to be written in the same object-oriented language. The component models (for example, CORBA and DCOM, which will be covered later in our discussion of middleware in this chapter), on the other hand, require that the interfaces be cleanly separated from the implementation. This separation allows the calling program to be written in one language and the receiving program to be written in another language.

Another advantage of CBD is that a component can be mapped into a business abstraction such as an order. While it is certainly possible to do the same with OOT, practitioners have found that such a complex abstraction usually results in many **public classes**[7] (which again, have to be written in the same language), adding to the hierarchy of classes mentioned earlier, thus increasing complexity. With CBD, we can create a single-order component with a well-defined interface; this component is the **public face**, and it can route requests to one or more classes behind the scene.[8] The benefits of this approach are twofold:

---

7. A public class is a class that the client may potentially have to learn; this has the chance of increasing the learning curve.
8. Astute readers can argue that the same objective can be accomplished in OOT by implementing a Façade pattern. However, most practitioners of OOT do not create an interface that is separate from the implementation. In Java terms, this means creating an interface and then creating a class that implements that interface.

- The abstraction can be discussed in business terms, e.g., an order.
- The classes from which the component is composed can be written in multiple languages, allowing legacy code to be salvaged.

Note that a component cannot exist in isolation: it needs an **execution context** (i.e., access to a base set of capabilities), and, in most cases, this execution context is provided by an **application server** (discussed further later).

In summary, OOT provides a set of powerful concepts (classes, inheritance, etc.), but it needs to be augmented with CBD to realize the proposed benefits (reuse at the business *and* code levels). At the moment, there is a cottage industry that has emerged to provide components, which can be broadly classified into two major categories: **business components** and **GUI components** (predominantly ActiveX components).

As an approach, CBD is quite sound, but its adoption has been somewhat hindered because the technologies that implement CBD have been quite complex.

Middleware

The term **middleware** is used to refer to the underlying technologies that implement the CBD approach to development. The most popular example of middleware is probably the **Common Object Request Broker Architecture (CORBA)** specifications, which were invented and endorsed by the **Object Management Group (OMG)**, a worldwide nonprofit consortium that promotes interoperability. Another popular middleware platform that works in Microsoft-exclusive environments is **DCOM.** Conceptually, the two technologies are similar, so we will focus on CORBA for now.

One of the design goals of CORBA is to allow applications, written in different languages, to *transparently* communicate with each other, regardless of where they are located. As an example, if program A needs to communicate with program B, ideally it should not need to know where program B is physically located or even what language program B is written in.

To achieve these and other goals, the CORBA specifications define an **object request broker (ORB)**, a program that resides on both the server and the client. For example, assume that a Java client wishes to communicate with a C++ server. First the developer needs to determine exactly which methods need to be invoked on the server. These methods are then specified in a syntax called **interface definition language** (**IDL**). IDL is a programming-language-independent language that deals with issues like mapping the appropriate data structures from the various languages; for example, an object is stored differently in C++ than it would be in Java.

The developer then compiles the IDL code via an IDL compiler, which produces the source file for a **skeleton,** a server-side representation of the remote client. This process is then repeated on the client side. The compilation produces the source file for a **stub**—a client-side representation of the remote server. Both the skeleton and stub are referred to as **proxies,** or local representations of remote objects. The skeleton and stub are language specific for reasons that will be made obvious later. In most cases, the stub and skeleton are incomplete; the developer has to add application-specific code to these templates. Figure 1–3 illustrates this process.

Rather than communicate directly with the server, the client sends a request to the stub. The stub is responsible for **marshalling** the

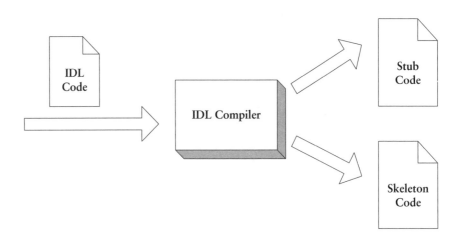

Figure 1–3   Compiling IDL.

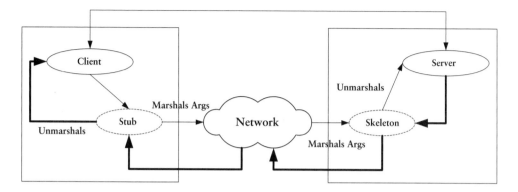

Figure 1–4 Marshalling and unmarshalling arguments.

arguments (the process of deconstructing the data so it can be sent across the network) and then forwarding this request to the appropriate recipient.

On the server side, the skeleton **unmarshals** (i.e., reconstructs) the request and forwards it to the appropriate object on the server (the actual recipient of the message). Once the request is received and processed, the results are returned to the skeleton, then back to the stub, to finally arrive at the original requester (client).[9]

Figure 1–4 illustrates this multistep process.

CORBA has enjoyed good success, but only in limited circles because the skills necessary to implement a CORBA-based system are quite scarce due to the complexity (IDL syntax is human readable but does require considerable experience). Additionally, it turns out that many interoperability problems do not need the full strength of CORBA at all (the CORBA specifications are extremely comprehensive, defining transaction control, security, real-time extensions, and so on).

To make matters more challenging, many customers have adopted both DCOM and CORBA. While the two technologies are conceptually similar, they differ greatly in implementation details and protocols. Consequently, the two cannot coexist without additional integration work, but integrating CORBA with DCOM (or vice versa) is one of the

9. CORBA does not require that the client or the server be written in object-oriented languages. Also, do not interpret that CORBA is a 2-tier environment because of the terms client and server; many CORBA systems are architected in an *n*-tier fashion. See the next section for a more thorough discussion on *n*-tier architectures.

most difficult interoperability problems to solve and therefore expensive. It is usually accomplished via a **CORBA-DCOM bridge**, a software layer which translates a call from one format to the other.

Web Services, as we shall see, provide a reasonable alternative to many interoperability problems that historically were implemented only with CORBA or DCOM. Web Services also allow integration between CORBA and DCOM more easily than using a bridge.

Application Servers

Client-server development is characterized by a client application that handles much of the processing logic and a server program that processes database requests. Unfortunately, this architecture requires expensive client machines because all the processing happens on the client side. For programs to be deployed to a larger audience (i.e., the Web), it is not feasible to always expect the users to own high-end client machines. Hence, there needs to be an alternate way of designing applications.

Distributed computing broadly refers to the technique of implementing applications by decomposing tasks and assigning these tasks to smaller machines rather than using a single processing computing source (such as a mainframe). However, the term has evolved to be almost synonymous with *n*-tier development (*n* being 3 or more). Client-server development is usually referred to as **2-tier development** (the client is one tier and the server is the other). Figure 1–5 illustrates a typical *n*-tier architecture.[10]

In 3-tier development, the third tier is often referred to as the **middle tier**; this tier houses the business process logic[11] that ideally should be independent of the underlying database logic and user interface (UI). To fully utilize the investment in business logic, the functionality can be shared by multiple applications. In order to accomplish that goal, the middle tier provides a set of infrastructure capabilities to handle issues like session management, resource management, concurrency management, and messaging.[12]

---

10. In more sophisticated architectures, the business logic may include yet another tier—the business process tier.
11. The business logic is usually implemented as server-side classes.
12. An application server provides many of the same services as a CORBA ORB.

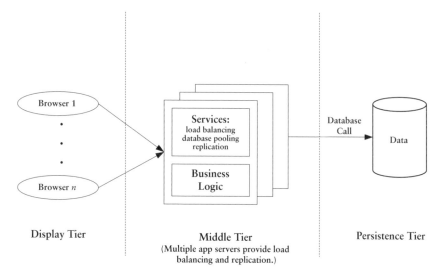

Figure 1–5 A typical *n*-tier architecture.

Rather than implement these sets of capabilities for every business application, it is common to purchase them in the form of an **application server**. With an application server, developers can then focus on writing business logic rather than infrastructure code, which is the most difficult to write.[13] Anecdotal evidence has shown that projects can save from 30% to 60% in delivery time by using an application server. The concept of an application server was popularized with the increasing use of Java as a server-side implementation language. Application server vendors include BEA Systems, IBM, and Iona, to name a few.

This section discusses the basic services provided by an application server. For a more technical discussion on the APIs typically provided by an application server, see the J2EE section of the next chapter.

The client program communicates with the application server, which in turn communicates with the database. Multiple copies of the application server replicated among many physical servers can provide load

---

13. The language in which the business logic is written is dependent on which application server is used. As an example, JavaSoft defines the J2EE standard, and using a J2EE-compliant application server requires that the business logic be written in Java (C++ is also supported via the Java Native Interface [JNI] package).

balancing and resource pooling, which prevent performance degradation and improve stability as the number of users escalates.

Since the business logic is centralized on one or more servers (rather than distributed across many client machines, as is the case with a client-server architecture), this architecture provides the following benefits:

- With the processing happening primarily on the server, the client machine becomes primarily a display device. Consequently, the client machine can be a lower-end machine because it is now primarily responsible for displaying information rather than processing business logic (which is more CPU intensive). This, in turn, reduces hardware purchases and operating system dependencies (of course, we now have browser dependencies).

- Deploying or updating an application does not require installing an application on each user's machine. The client machine often requires only a browser. The middle tier executes the business logic and the client machine simply displays the data. Hence, distributed computing often leads to a **thin-client** architecture.

- There are potentially fewer compatibility issues because many of the software installations and updates are on the server side, which can be handled in a centralized fashion.

However, nothing in life is free—both distributed computing and thin clients have significant disadvantages:

- Building distributed applications is notoriously more difficult than building client-server applications. Debugging and tuning these types of applications are not trivial because there are more points of failures and errors.

- The UIs on thin-client applications are rarely as sophisticated as those on client-server applications. These UIs tend to be browser based, and the browser imposes limitations on what is possible. However, a client-server application can interact directly with the native windowing environment as well as the native operating system. For example, few (if any) thin-client applications support a sophisticated drag-and-drop metaphor, whereas this is a very common metaphor in most client-server applications.

- The performance tends to be slower on a thin-client application than on a client-server application. With a client-server application, the client application can perform sophisticated operations without depending on the server; a thin-client application tends to be able only to display the results of processing that has happened on a server (the processing is typically initiated by the client to the server over a network). The network latency tends to be the bottleneck of a thin-client architecture, whereas the processing power of the client machine tends to be the bottleneck in a client-server architecture.

Even with these limitations, a thin-client architecture is the more viable architecture for applications that have to be deployed to a large audience desiring minimal installations and hassles, as is the case with Web applications.

As we will see later, Web Services share many of the advantages of a thin-client architecture (location independence and centralized management); however, some of the challenges (such as performance tuning, debugging, and a consistent graphical user interface [GUI]) are potentially magnified.

HTML

The explosive adoption of the Internet was strongly aided by the invention of the browser, which displays information by interpreting instructions and data in HTML documents (a process known as **rendering**). While HTML is easy to learn and lightweight, it is a poor language for business integration primarily because HTML is a markup language that mixes business data with formatting instructions (which are specified by using a predefined set of **tags**).

Automating the retrieval business information stored in an HTML document requires an extraction program that can differentiate between the formatting instructions and business information. While this may sound trivial on the surface, the real difficulty lies in the fact that HTML does not allow the author of the document to specify the format of the business information. Without this, the extraction program cannot reliably extract the desired information. This limitation exists because the HMTL language defines tags only for displaying information, and the language is nonextensible.

HTML does provide the use of frames to facilitate integration, but it is more at the GUI level and not at the process or data level. Many of the shortcomings of HTML are addressed by Extensible Markup Language (XML), one of the cornerstone technologies of Web Services that will be discussed in the next chapter.

Electronic Data Interchange (EDI)

EDI was one of the earliest (if not the earliest) attempts at solving some of these interoperability challenges and lack of business process standards. Invented when bandwidth was expensive, EDI was designed for quick transmission. Therefore, EDI messages are often compressed and codes are used to represent complex values.[14] Unlike XML messages, which are self-describing through its metadata, EDI messages are often cryptic and require considerable training to decipher.

As businesses evolve, they often need to add new data formats and fields. Unfortunately, trying to accomplish those tasks with EDI was extremely difficult.[15] This inflexibility often led to many implementations that deviated from the proposed standards (X12, EDIFACT, etc.), thus slowing down the adoption rate. Additionally, when EDI was invented, there was no global public network like the Internet, and many firms had to invest in building or renting expensive **value-added networks** (**VANs**). These deliver EDI messages to **mailboxes**, which are designated entry points for the messages to an organization. EDI is still very prevalent, but only among the largest of companies—e.g., Wal-Mart and GM—due to its high fixed costs.

Figure 1–6 illustrates a typical EDI architecture.

---

14. EDI message transmissions are often charged by the character.
15. On the other hand, XML documents can easily be transformed into various formats, including EDI, through multiple means including Extensible Stylesheet Language Transformation (XSLT) or another programming language.

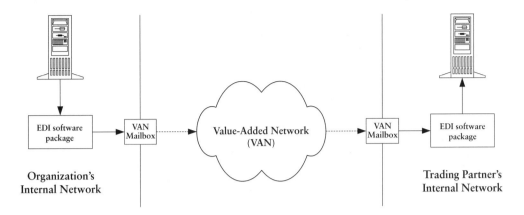

Figure 1–6 A typical EDI architecture.

Packaged Applications

As these different technologies were adopted throughout the enterprise, many firms were operating under the looming deadline of Y2K. Instead of building new applications or continuing to support existing ones, many firms instead bought packaged applications and tried to standardize their business processes into the structure imposed by these applications.

One of the main challenges of these packaged applications was the mass customization needed by each company in order to fully utilize the product. In addition, this customization was in a language that was proprietary to each package. These products either focused on the back-office operations (**enterprise resource planning** or **ERP**) or customer-facing operations (**customer relationship management** or **CRM**). These applications were written originally as large client-server applications, but many of them have since moved to an *n*-tier architecture.

Enterprise Application Integration (EAI)

As companies started to adopt multiple ERP and CRM systems across the enterprise, it became apparent that these systems could not be integrated directly due to different implementation languages, data models, APIs, and other issues. For example, an enterprise may wish to keep its human resources (HR) database synchronized with its forecasting system (the company needs to hire more people to accommodate any increase in sales). Without integration, this would require either re-entering the information or exporting a flat file that is then uploaded to the destination.

Thus, a set of solutions was invented to address these integration issues: enterprise application integration (EAI). EAI is characterized by point-to-point integration (for a more thorough discussion of this term, see Chapter 3) and is most often used to normalize data from a source to a destination.[16]

Unfortunately, EAI often requires the purchase and customization of adapters, which are custom libraries needed to merely connect to the various ERP and CRM systems. To make matters worse, instead of being provided by the ERP or CRM vendors, the adapters are provided by third-party firms that do not have access to the underlying architecture of the systems being integrated. Consequently, the adapters are expensive (due to a limited market) and often trail the release of the systems they are meant to integrate, causing further integration headaches.

In addition to data transformation, EAI technologies often include transaction support, versioning, and, in some cases, fault tolerance. As a whole, EAI is characterized by complex APIs (the adapter has to map the underlying API into a more accessible API for the application); this is often adequate as long as the company has some control of the two endpoints. This is not an issue when the integration is behind the firewall, but it *is* an issue when many companies do not have the luxury of dictating the platforms of their trading partners. Thus, EAI is often a challenge when dealing with integration issues beyond the firewall.

Fortunately, many of the ERP and CRM vendors have recognized the difficulties associated with using EAI exclusively and are now beginning to offer Web Services support in their products. That is, rather than connecting to the system through the vendor's API (which is often proprietary), the vendor is now offering a higher form of API that is Web Services compliant. As of this writing, SAP has taken the lead and announced that it is fully committed to making its product line com-

---

16. EAI can also be used to perform integration at the method level or at the business process level. The approach is more related to the architecture and approach than to the technologies.

pletely accessible from Web Services. The implications of this will be made more clear in the next chapter, which discusses Web Services, and in Chapter 4, which discusses a related technology—the Java Connector Architecture.

▶ Summary

As the Internet has grown in popularity, many companies have adopted it, first for sharing information and later for conducting business, which requires back-end integration. Many technologies including object-oriented technologies, client-server applications, CBD, application servers, HTML, EDI, packaged applications, and EAI have attempted to solve the increasing demands of integrating disparate systems. Each of these technologies, while adequate for its time, is insufficient by itself to address the growing complexities of the enterprise because of inadequate functionality, complexity, or lack of standardization. As we will see, Web Services will not replace these technologies but instead will build on and coexist with many of them to provide a cleaner and simpler form of integration.

The Basic Web Services Stack

Many of the challenges presented in the previous chapter revolve around interoperability challenges on multiple operating systems and/ or middleware packages. These include high integration costs, lack of industry standards, and high deployment costs. Web Services have the potential of addressing many of these issues, and this chapter discusses the cornerstone technologies that are essential for Web Services. These include Extensible Markup Language (XML), Service-Oriented Access Protocol (SOAP), Web Services Definition Language (WSDL), and Universal Description, Discovery and Integration (UDDI). Chapter 3 then follows with emerging standards around security, scalability, and so on. This chapter concludes with a discussion on how Web Services can augment the technologies discussed in Chapter 1.

Before delving into the underlying technologies, let's take a broad view of the various roles of a Web Services architecture, which is also sometimes referred to as a service-oriented architecture.

▶ Service-Oriented Architecture (SOA)

An **SOA** is called service oriented because the central idea is that a client (which can be a person or a computer) needs a particular set of services to be fulfilled. Of course, before the client can request the service, it needs to find the provider (which previously published the service); this location service is provided by a **service broker,** who typically operates a repository. Upon request, the service broker returns a document that allows the client to first locate and then **bind** to the provider. Thus, the three key roles in an SOA are

- Client
- Service broker
- Service provider

Figure 2–1 illustrates the roles and the sequence of events in an SOA.

The role of the broker may not be immediately obvious, especially for a small set of services. However, keep in mind that a client may ask for multiple services, each of which may have a different provider. Registering the services in a central registry that can be searched by clients provides them with the flexibility needed to perform queries based on a dynamically changing set of criteria—they do not have to statically bind themselves to the provider. Without a registry, the client would have to hard-code the location of the service provider, which can obviously lead to maintenance difficulties.

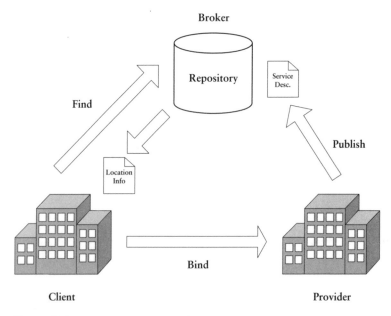

Figure 2–1 The roles in an SOA.

Chapter **2** I The Basic Web Services Stack

SOAs have been present for a number of years, but, again, they have been used with proprietary protocols and technologies. For example, both CORBA and DCOM provide a naming service and a location service. With the advent of Web Services, the idea has been more widely adopted because of the use of standards-based technologies. The most fundamental standard of all is a common language for describing data—this is the role of XML.

▶ Extensible Markup Language (XML)

To say that XML has been popular with the industry press is an understatement. At the moment, every major vendor has announced support for XML in one form or another, and innovative uses for XML are emerging almost daily.

But what is exactly is XML? It is not a programming language like Java, C++, or C#; that is, it cannot be used to write applications per se. Rather, it is a **meta-language** that can be used to create self-describing, modular documents (data), programs, and even other languages, commonly referred to as **XML grammars**.[1] These documents are often used for data exchange between otherwise incompatible systems.

XML is incredibly diverse and includes a host of other technologies including **XPointer, XLink,** and Resource Description Framework (**RDF**). Our intent here is not to give an in-depth discussion of XML, but to provide enough background information to help you understand the implications of how XML is being used in the context of other technologies such as SOAP, WSDL, and UDDI—the foundation of Web Services. Strictly speaking, Web Services can be implemented by using only XML, but for the purposes of our discussion, we are defining Web Services to be built on XML, SOAP, WSDL, and UDDI over a transport protocol such as HTTP. This definition will become clearer as our discussions progress.

The **Worldwide Web Consortium (W3C)**, an international standards body, began working on XML in mid-1996 and released XML 1.0 in 1998. XML was heavily inspired by the **Standard Generalized Markup Language (SGML)**, but, in many ways, XML is more readable and

---

1. An example of an XML grammar is wireless markup language (WML), a popular language for creating (appropriately enough) wireless applications. WSDL and UDDI are also XML grammars.

simpler. The real value of XML is not in its innovativeness as much as its industry acceptance as a common way of describing and exchanging data (and, as we will see later with WSDL and SOAP, XML can also be used to describe applications and invoke them as well).

XML Syntax

As a markup language, XML uses tags to describe information (the tags are highlighted in bold in the following example).

```
<?xml version="1.0" encoding="UTF-8"?>
<Order>
    <Customer>
        <name>John Doe</name>
        <street>1111 AnyStreet</street>
        <city>AnyTown</city>
        <state>GA</state>
        <zip>10000</zip>
    </Customer>
</Order>
```

A tag, enclosed in brackets (<>), is a label or a description (e.g., **street** in our example) of the data that follows, which is called an **element** (the element for **street** in our example is **1111 AnyStreet**). The element is delimited by a similar tag preceded by a slash (**/**), to indicate the end of the element. In our example, the element **1111 AnyStreet** is terminated by the closing tag **</street>**.

The first line in our example is a convention used to signal the XML parser (the program that has to parse the XML document) that the incoming document is an XML document. Also, the **Customer** element has several child elements:

John Doe
1111 AnyStreet
AnyTown
GA
10000

You may have already noticed one advantage of XML—since it is a text-based language, XML is fairly verbose and therefore human readable. However, this advantage can also be a disadvantage: because they are verbose, XML documents can quickly become very large for complex data sets. There are other points worth noting about XML:

- **XML is extensible.** Unlike HTML, which has a fixed number of tags, XML allows the developer to define any number of tags—whatever is necessary to solve the problem. In our example, the document represents an abstraction of a customer and includes fields to describe the customer.

- **XML is hierarchical.** Elements can have subordinate elements under them. In the example, the **Customer** element contains several child elements.

- **XML is modular.** By allowing documents to reference other documents, XML provides for modular designs and promotes reuse.

- **XML does not include built-in typing.** This data enforcement and validation is provided through document type definitions (DTDs) and XML schemas, two concepts that will be discussed in further detail later.

- **XML does not make any assumptions about the presentation mechanism.** This is unlike HTML, which does make these assumptions. In fact, XML has to be coupled with another technology (such as **XSLT** or **Cascading Style Sheets**) to be displayed. This separation stems from one of XML's primary goals of being a way of exchanging data; oftentimes data is exchanged between systems and hence may not need to be displayed at all.

- **XML is programming language independent.** Since XML is not a programming language per se, it can be used as a common mechanism for data exchange between programming languages and, as we will see later, a common way of connecting applications as well (via SOAP).

- **XML provides validation mechanisms.** Through the use of DTDs and XML schema, XML documents can be validated to determine whether the elements are correct (i.e., whether the values are within a specified range).

Some of the main XML concepts that are especially relevant to Web Services include parsers, namespaces, DTDs, and XML schemas.

XML Parsers

Processing an XML document requires the use of an XML parser, a program that can decompose the XML document into its individual elements. There are two major categories of XML parsers: **Document Object Model (DOM)** and **Simple API for XML (SAX)**.

DOM is a language-neutral API for accessing and modifying tree-based representations of documents such as HTML or XML documents. Developers can use language-specific DOM parsers to programmatically build and process XML documents.

DOM parsers have two major shortcomings:

- The entire XML document is represented in memory; this can lead to performance issues if the XML document is exceedingly large.
- Since the API is language independent, it is quite generic; therefore more steps are often required to process an XML document than would be the case if it were optimized for a particular implementation language. This has led to language-specific variants such as the **JDOM** parser, which is tuned for the Java language.

The SAX parser is an event-based parser and can be used only for reading an XML document. A SAX parser works from event registration. The developer registers event handlers, which are then invoked as the XML document is processed. Each event handler is a small block of code that performs a specific task. The main advantage of a SAX parser over a DOM parser is that the former does not require the entire document to be in memory—the XML document is processed as a stream of data, and the event handlers are invoked. While SAX is easier to work with than DOM, there are some disadvantages:

- Once the XML document has been read, there is no internal representation of the document in memory. Thus, any additional processing requires the document to be parsed again.
- A SAX parser cannot modify the XML document.

Thus it is important to understand the needs of the application before selecting an XML parser.

Well-Formed and Valid XMLs

XML documents must conform to a certain set of guidelines before they can be processed. This leads to two terms that are used to describe the state of a document: well formed and valid.

A **well-formed** XML document is one that follows the syntax of XML and that can be *completely* processed by an XML parser. If there are syntax errors in the document, then the parser rejects the entire document. As far as an XML parser is concerned, there is no such thing as a partially well-formed XML document.

A **valid** XML document is a well-formed document that can also be verified against a DTD, which defines constraints for the individual elements—the order of the elements, the range of the values, and so on. A **validating** XML parser is one that can validate an XML document against a DTD or XML schema, which are described next.

DTDs and Schemas

XML offers two mechanisms for verifying whether or not a document is valid. A DTD is an external document that acts as a template against which an XML document is compared. The XML document references this DTD in its declaration, and the XML parser (assuming it is a validating parser) then validates the elements of the XML document with the DTD. A DTD can specify the order of the elements, the frequency at which elements can occur (for example, an order can contain $0-n$ line items), etc.

While a powerful concept, DTDs have many shortcomings.

- The concept of a DTD predates that of XML (it originated from SGML) and does not conform to XML syntax. This increases the learning curve and can lead to some confusion.

- A DTD does not support data types; this means it is impossible to specify that a given element must be bound to a type. Using the order example under "XML Syntax" earlier in this chapter, there is no way to specify that the line item count needs to be a positive integer.

- An XML document can reference only one DTD; this limits how much validation can occur.

- A DTD cannot enforce data formats; i.e., there is no way to specify that a date must be of the mm/dd/yyyy format.
- DTDs were invented before the standardization of namespaces and consequently do not support namespaces, which can lead to many element name collisions. For more on namespaces, see the next section.

Because of these limitations, applications that have to process XML documents include a lot of error checking functionality. Additionally, SOAP, one of the cornerstone technologies of Web Services, prohibits the use of DTDs in the document declarations.

To address the shortcoming of DTDs, the W3C produced the **XML schema specifications**. XML schemas provide the following advantages:

- The XML schema grammar supports namespaces.
- XML schemas include a predefine set of types including string, base64 binary, integer, positive integer, negative integer, date, and time, along with acceptable ranges and data formats.
- XML schemas also allow for the creation of new types (simple and complex) by following a well-established set of rules.

XML Namespaces

An enterprise system consists of dozens if not hundreds of XML documents. As these XML documents are merged from other sources, inevitably there will be duplicate element names. This can cause problems because each element must have a unique name. XML resolves this name collision issue through the use of **namespaces** (Java provides a similar feature through **packages**). Each element is prefixed with a namespace and therefore has to be unique only for that given namespace rather than globally. In practice, the prefix is usually the name of the company, although any Uniform Resource Locator (URL) will do.[2] Thus, an element name is composed of two parts: the namespace and the name of the element. By qualifying the name of each element with a qualifier, the likelihood of a name collision is greatly reduced. Consider the file system, for example. For a given

2. Technically, the identifier is usually a Uniform Resource Identifier (URI). For our purposes, we will ignore the distinction between a URI and a URL.

directory, a filename must be unique. However, there can be multiple identical filenames as long as each exists in a different directory. In a sense, the directory provides the namespace and qualifies the filename to resolve filename conflicts.

Service-Oriented Access Protocol (SOAP)

One of the challenges of performing integration using traditional middleware is the lack of a universal protocol. By being XML based and not tied to any particular language, SOAP has evolved to become the primary de facto standard protocol for performing integration between multiple platforms and languages.

SOAP originally meant **Simple Object Access Protocol,** but the term has been unofficially redefined to mean **Service-Oriented Access Protocol** because SOAP is not simple and certainly not object oriented; the latter point is important because not all languages are object oriented.

This flexibility in the protocol allows a program that is written in one language and running on one operating system to communicate with a program written in another language running on a different operating system (i.e., a program written in perl running on Solaris can communicate with another program written in Java running on Windows 2000). There is at least one SOAP implementation for each of the popular programming languages including perl, Java, C++, C#, and Visual Basic.

Advantages of SOAP

Before discussing the characteristics of SOAP, let's examine why it has become so popular.

- **SOAP is a fairly lightweight protocol.** Some of the earlier distributed computing protocols (CORBA, RMI, DCOM, etc.) contain fairly advanced features such as registering and locating objects. At its core, SOAP defines only how to connect systems and relies on additional technologies to provide registration features (UDDI) and location features (WSDL).
- **SOAP is language and operating system independent.** In this respect, SOAP is unlike many other middleware technologies

(such as RMI, which works only with Java, and DCOM, which works only on Microsoft Windows and NT).

- **SOAP is XML based.** Instead of relying on proprietary binary protocols (as is the case with CORBA and DCOM), SOAP is based on XML, a ubiquitous standard. As previously noted, XML is fairly readable.

- **SOAP can be used with multiple transport protocols.** These include HTTP, Simple Mail Transfer Protocol (SMTP), file transfer protocol (FTP), and Java Message Service (JMS). Most of the examples in this book will focus on HTTP since it is the most commonly used protocol with SOAP-based systems.

- **SOAP can traverse firewalls.** SOAP needs no additional modifications to do this. Contrast this with CORBA- or DCOM-based systems, which require that a port be opened on the firewall. This is a key requirement for building distributed systems that have to interact with external systems beyond the firewall. (This is also a disadvantage, as we will see later.)

- **SOAP is supported by many vendors.** All major vendors including IBM, Microsoft, BEA, and Apache provide support for SOAP in the form of SOAP toolkits (the IBM and Apache SOAP toolkits are two of the most popular).

- **SOAP is extensible.** The header values (specified in the **Header** element) in the XML document can be used to provide additional features such as authentication, versioning, and optimization. These features are discussed further in the next chapter.

Disadvantages of SOAP

On the down side, SOAP does have some disadvantages.

- **There are interoperability issues between the SOAP toolkits.** It seems ironic that there would be interoperability issues with a technology that promotes interoperability, but this is mostly attributable to the infancy of the SOAP specifications. These have been identified and documented, and the various vendors have been quite cooperative in resolving these differences.

- **SOAP lacks many advanced features.** Much has been written about the advantages of SOAP as a lightweight protocol, but there are a host of missing features such as guaranteed messaging and security policies.

Many of these issues can be addressed through third-party technologies such as Web Services networks, which are discussed in further detail in later chapters.

SOAP Basics

SOAP is built on a messaging concept of passing XML documents from a sender to a receiver (also called the **endpoint**). The XML document becomes known as a SOAP document and is composed of three sections: **Envelope, Header,** and **Body.** Figure 2–2 illustrates the structure of a SOAP document.

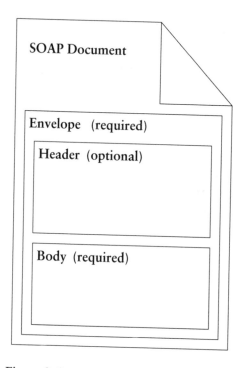

Figure 2–2 The structure of a SOAP document.

The SOAP standards define three major parameters:

- **Envelope body structure.** The envelope contains information such as which methods to invoke, optional parameters, return values, and, where something did not execute successfully, optional exceptions (known as SOAP **faults**).
- **Data encoding rules.** Since SOAP has to support multiple languages and operating systems, it has to define a universally accepted representation for different data types such as float, integer, and arrays. More complex data types (such as Customer) require custom coding, although some toolkits, such as GLUE, inherently provide this mapping.
- **Usage conventions.** SOAP can be used in a multitude of ways, but they are all variations of the same actions: a sender sends an XML document, and the receiver, optionally, returns a response in the form of an XML document (this is the case of a two-way message exchange). As mentioned previously, the XML document may contains faults if errors occurred during processing.

By allowing receivers to be chained together, SOAP-based architectures can be quite sophisticated. Figure 2–3 shows five common architectures that are used with SOAP-based systems—Fire and Forget, Request Response, Notification, Broadcast, and Workflow/Orchestration.

Any link in the processing chain that is not the endpoint is referred to as an **intermediary.** The SOAP specifications allow an intermediary to process a SOAP message partially before passing it to the next link in the processing chain (which can be another intermediary or the endpoint). You will see an example of this in the discussion of the SOAP header later in the chapter.

Migrating from XML to SOAP

Migrating from XML to SOAP is a fairly straightforward procedure. The migration includes these steps:

- Adding optional **Header** elements
- Wrapping the body of the XML document in the SOAP body, which in turn is included in the SOAP envelope
- Declaring the appropriate SOAP namespaces

Chapter **2** | The Basic Web Services Stack

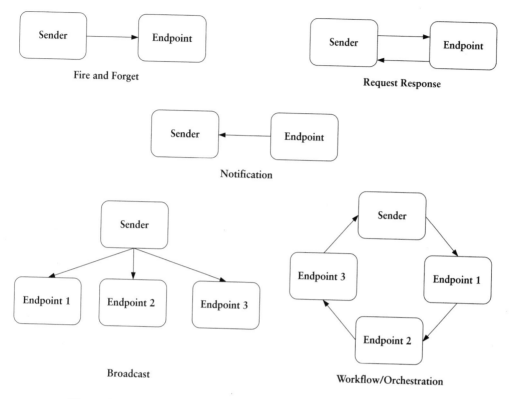

Figure 2–3   Common SOAP architectures.

- Adding optional exception handling
- Specifying the protocol that should be used

For example, converting our earlier XML document to SOAP involves adding the following parts (highlighted in bold; for the sake of simplicity, the HTTP fragment has been stripped away):

```
<?xml version="1.0" encoding="UTF-8"?>
<SOAP-ENV:Envelope
    xmlns:SOAP-ENV="http://schemas.xmlsoap.org/soap/envelope"
    xmlns:xsi="http://www.w3.org/1999/XMLSchema-instance"
    xmlns:xsi="http://www.w3.org/1999/XMLSchema">
<SOAP-ENV:Header>
    . . . [optional header information]
</SOAP-ENV:Header>
<SOAP-ENV:Body>
<Order>
```

```
<Customer>
    <name>John Doe</name>
    <street>1111 AnyStreet<street>
    <city>AnyTown</city>
    <state>GA<state>
    <zip>10000</zip>
</Customer>
</Order>
<SOAP-ENV:Body>
<SOAP-ENV:Envelope>
```

The next sections describe these additional parts.

SOAP Envelope

The SOAP envelope is the container for the other elements in the SOAP message. A server-side process called a **SOAP handler** can use the availability of the SOAP envelope (along with the *http://schemas.xmlsoap.org/soap/envelope/* namespace declaration) to determine whether the incoming XML document is a SOAP message or not. The handler can be part of the application server, or it can be an external product such as Cape Clear CapeConnect. SOAP handlers are explained in more detail later in the section on adding SOAP support.

SOAP Header

As part of their extensibility design goal, the architects of SOAP provided the **Header** element to allow SOAP messages to be extended generically while still conforming to the SOAP specifications. If a SOAP **Header** element is present (and there can be more than one **Header** element present), it has to be the first child of the **Envelope** element. Each **Header** element can in turn have child elements.

Two examples of using header information to provide extensibility include

- embedding authentication information
- specifying an account number for use with a pay-per-use SOAP service

A SOAP intermediary can use this header information to determine whether the incoming message is properly authorized before forwarding it (to either another intermediary or the endpoint).

Exception Handling

In cases where a SOAP handler cannot decipher a message, a SOAP fault is generated, identified by the **Fault** element. Its child element, **faultcode**, identifies the category of errors that can happen. SOAP 1.1 defines four values for the **faultcode** element:

- **VersionMismatch.** The recipient of the message found an invalid namespace for the SOAP envelope element.
- **MustUnderstand.** The recipient encountered a mandatory Header element it could not understand. Remember, header elements are optional.
- **Client.** The fault was in the message being received. Possible causes: missing elements, malformed elements, and the like.
- **Server.** The fault occurred on the recipient side, i.e., a server error.

Note that an application is free to extend these values using a (.) notation. For example, a value of **Client.Login** can be used to specify that there was a problem with a client login.

In addition to the **faultcode** element, there are two other elements that can be used to provide further clarification on the fault:

- **faultstring.** This element provides a readable explanation on why the fault occurred.
- **detail.** The value of the **detail** element indicates that the problem occurred while processing the **body** element. If the **detail** element is not present, then the fault occurred outside of the body of the message.

Adding SOAP Support

One of the advantages of adopting SOAP is that the support can be built on top of existing technologies. Figure 2–4 shows a typical J2EE Web-based architecture without support for SOAP.[3] Adding SOAP support to such a system typically requires the addition of a SOAP

---

3. This deployment shows the servlet engine separated from the application server, a format that provides more scalability. A simpler, albeit less scalable, deployment would be to use the servlet engine that is built into the application server.

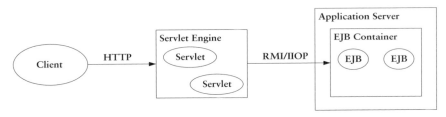

EJB = Enterprise Java Beans
IIOP = Internet Inter-Orb Protocol

Figure 2–4 Typical J2EE deployment.

handler (if the application server cannot support SOAP requests), which parses incoming SOAP requests and then calls the appropriate native method in the implementation language. Recall that SOAP is a protocol, not a programming language; hence, the request must be mapped to an entry point in an executing application. The entry point can be a method in a class (for object-oriented systems such as Java, C++, or C#) or a function name (for systems such as perl, which are not object oriented).

Common SOAP handlers include CapeConnect from Cape Clear, Iona's XMLBus (see Appendix D for a more detailed discussion), and Apache Axis. In summary, a system is said to be SOAP compliant if it can take an incoming SOAP request, forward it to the appropriate endpoint, and package the result back in a SOAP response.

Figure 2–5 illustrates the addition of a SOAP handler to the J2EE environment shown in Figure 2–4.[4]

While SOAP provides many useful features, it is still incomplete because it does not address this issue: how does an endpoint unambiguously describe its services? Likewise, another outstanding issue: how does a requester locate the endpoint? These two features are provided by two other key technologies—WSDL and UDDI.

---

4. Many of the application servers have announced SOAP support, which means the SOAP handler may be part of the application server as well.

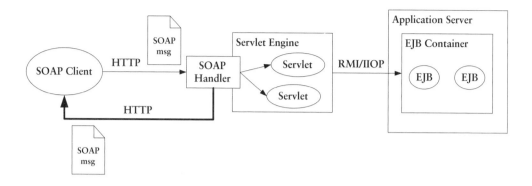

Figure 2–5 Adding SOAP support to J2EE environment.

Web Services Definition Language (WSDL)

To enable a client to *use* a Web Service effectively, there first has to be a mechanism for *describing* that Web Service. At first glance, this may seem difficult, but the challenges are many. We can provide a description in prose format (such as a **README** file), but it would not be practical to describe all the different ways a Web Service can be used in prose. We can also list some examples of how the Web Service can be used effectively, but, again, that may not adequately describe all the combinations for which a Web Service can be invoked.

The problem of succinctly and unambiguously describing a Web Service is similar to the challenge faced by compiler writers—the conventional solution is to use a grammar tree to describe the syntax of a language. While quite effective, a grammar tree is rarely decipherable for those without a strong background in compiler theory.

WSDL was created in response to the need for unambiguously describing the various characteristics of a Web Service. As an XML grammar, WSDL is not easy to learn, but it *is* considerably less intimidating than a programming language (such as C or C++).

A WSDL document is a well-formed XML document that lists the following characteristics for one or more Web Services.

Publicly accessible functions.[5] A WSDL lists all the operations a client can expect a Web Service to support.

- **Input and output parameters along with associated types.** In order to invoke each operation, the client needs to know the expected parameters for each input operation and the expected output of each operation. Again, this is identical to a normal function declaration. In order to support portability between languages and operating systems, all data types are defined in XML schema format.

- **Binding and address information for each Web Service.** To allow loose coupling between a requester and a Web Service, WSDL specifies where the service can be found (usually a URL) and the transport protocol that should be used to invoke the service (remember that a Web Service can be used with multiple protocols).

In essence, WSDL defines a contract that a provider is committed to supporting, and, in the spirit of separating implementation from interface, WSDL does not specify how each Web Service is implemented. As a point of comparison, WSDL can best be likened to CORBA's IDL.

Most of the existing toolkits (GLUE, IBM Web Services Toolkit [WSTK], BEA Web Services Workshop, Cape Clear CapeStudio, etc.) have built-in functionality to automatically parse and generate WSDL files (although, due to the immaturity of the tools, the generated files still require some manual tweaking). Even so, it is still worthwhile to understand the structure of a WSDL document.

WSDL Syntax

The WSDL specifications list six major elements:

- The **definitions** element is the root element containing the five remaining elements; it defines the name of the service and declares the namespaces used throughout the document.

---

5. The astute reader will notice the use of the term "functions" rather than "methods." SOAP is not object-oriented and does not support object-oriented terminology; therefore, WSDL is the same.

- The **message** element represents a single piece of data moving between the requester and the provider (or vice versa). It declares the name of the message along with zero or more **part** elements, each of which represents either a single parameter (if this is a request) or a single return value (if it is a response). If there is no part, then the request requires no parameter or there is no return value, depending on whether the message represents a request or a response. Note that each message element declares only the name (which is used by the **operation** element below), value(s), and the type of each value; it does not specify whether the message is for input or output—that is the role of the next element.
- The **portType** element represents a collection of one or more operations, each of which has an **operation** element. Each operation element has a **name** value and specifies which message (from the **message** element) is the input and which is the output. If an operation represents a request/response interaction (a method invocation with a return value), then the operation would include two messages. If an operation represents only a request with no response or a response with no request (e.g., an automatic notification from the provider with no request from the requester), it would include only a single message. In Java terms, a portType can best be thought of as an interface; an operation can best be thought of as a single method declaration; a message can best be thought of as a individual piece of an operation, with each message representing (if the operation is an input) a parameter name and the associated type or (if the operation is an output) return value name and the associated type.
- The **types** element is used to declare all the types that are used between the requester and the provider for all the services declared in the WSDL document.
- The **binding** element represents a particular portType implemented using a specific protocol such as SOAP. If a service supports more than one protocol (SOAP, CORBA, etc.), the WSDL document includes a listing for each.
- The **service** element represents a collection of **port** elements, each of which represents the availability of a particular binding at a specified endpoint, usually specified as a URL where the service can be invoked.

Invoking Existing Web Services: A Sample

To invoke a Web Service, we can either write a SOAP client or use an existing generic one. The *www.soapclient.com* site provides a Web interface that allows us to enter the WSDL file and invoke the service. Before we can launch the service, we need to find the WSDL file. In this case, we can find some sample WSDL files at *www.xmethods.net*, a public repository of Web Services. For our example, we will invoke a Web Service that can print the traffic conditions of a specified California highway. Use the following instructions:

- Visit the *www.soapclient.com/soaptest.html* site.
- Type *www.xmethods.net/sd/2001/CATrafficService.wsdl* in the WSDL address field.
- Select **HTML** instead of **XML** for the output.
- Click **Retrieve**, which loads the WSDL file from across the Internet.
- In the textfield, type **101** (for Highway 101) and click **Invoke** to invoke the service.
- The resulting screen should print text that explains the current conditions for Highway 101.

This example illustrates how straightforward it is to invoke a Web Service from a browser. The user, in most cases, will not even be aware that Web Services are being used to return the values. Of course, the user can just as easily be a program, in which case the program would programmatically pass the appropriate parameters.

▶ Universal Description, Discovery, and Integration (UDDI)

The vision behind **UDDI** is to provide a distributed repository that clients can search (during design time and runtime) to find Web Services. Originally launched as a collaboration among Microsoft, IBM, and Ariba in September 2000, the UDDI consortium has since grown to include hundreds of members.

UDDI can be thought of as two major concepts:

- **The specifications.** These standards describe how such repositories should work and include three major concepts: white pages, yellow pages, and green pages. These will be described further below.

- **The implementations of the specifications.** Microsoft and IBM are UDDI operators of two public repositories, called **business registries,** which are the first public implementations of the UDDI specifications. A company can register at one repository and be confident that the entry will be replicated to the other repository (currently, the entries are replicated every 24 hours). However, for security reasons, any updates must be performed at the repository where the service was first registered. Of course, like everything else that is related to Web Services, the entries in the UDDI repositories are XML data. As mentioned, the business registries are examples of public registries; we will discuss private registries in detail below.

UDDI Categories

A UDDI repository contains entries about businesses, the services these businesses provide, and information on how those services can be accessed. Modeled after a phone book, a UDDI directory has three categories:

- **White pages** contain basic information about a service provider, including the provider's name, a text description of the business (potentially in multiple languages), contact information (phone number, address, etc.), and other unique identifiers such as the Dun & Bradstreet (D&B) rating and the D&B D-U-N-S Number.

- **Yellow pages** include the classification of either the provided service or the registered company using standard taxonomies. Examples include

  - Standard Industrial Code (SIC)

  - North American Industrial Classification System (NAICS): a classification scheme specific to the United States, Canada, and Mexico

- Universal Standards Products and Services Classifications (UNSPSC): an open global standard used extensively by catalog and procurement systems

- Geographic taxonomies: location-based classifications; for example, US-CA indicates a business in California

- **Green pages** contain the technical entries for the Web Services—the address of the Web Service, the parameters, etc.

The entries in a UDDI directory are not limited to Web Services; UDDI entries can be for services based on email, FTP, CORBA, RMI, or even the telephone.

UDDI Data Model

The UDDI data model includes an XML schema that provides four major elements:

- The **businessEntity** element represents the owner of the services and includes the business name, description, address, contact information categories, and identifiers. Upon registration, each business receives a unique **businessKey** value that is used to correlate with the business's published service. The categories and identifiers can be used to specify details about a business, such as its NAICS, UNSPSC, and D-U-N-S codes—values that can be useful when performing searches.

- The **businessService** element has information about a single Web Service or a group of related ones, including the name, description, owner (cross-referenced with a unique **businessKey** value of the associated **businessEntity** element), and a list of optional **bindingTemplate** elements. Each service is uniquely identified by a **serviceKey** value.

- The **bindingTemplate** element represents a single service and contains all the required information about how and where to access the service (e.g., the URL if it is a Web Service). Each binding template is uniquely identified by a **bindingKey** value.

The service does not have to be a Web Service; it can be based on email (SMTP), FTP, or even the fax.

- The **tModel** element (shortened from "technical model" and also known as the **service type**) is primarily used to point to the external specification of the service being provided. For a Web Service, this element (more specifically, the **overviewURL** child element) should ideally point to the WSDL document that provides all the information needed to unambiguously describe the service and how to invoke it. If two services have the same tModel key value, then the services can be considered equivalent (thus allowing the requester potentially to switch from one service provider to another). Here is a useful metaphor: a tModel that can be thought of as an interface for which there can be multiple implementations, presumably from different companies since it does not make sense for a firm to implement more than one service for a given tModel (just as it would not make sense for a single class to implement the same interface in different ways).

UDDI Usage Scenarios

As mentioned earlier, a service-oriented architecture involves three roles: client, provider, and service broker. To illustrate the flexibility of the UDDI model, we'll use the example of the MegaBucks Consortium.

MegaBucks Consortium (a financial consortium) wants to create a standard way of valuing small retail businesses and then publish this information so that its member firms can implement Web Services to conform to that standard. In this example, the consortium operates a private registry (see the next section on types of UDDI registries for more information on private versus public registries). To allow its members to access this standard, the consortium needs to

- Produce a WSDL file to define the specifications to which a valuation service should adhere. The provider of the valuation service would most likely be a member of the financial consortium.
- Publish the WSDL file at a public location (for example, *www.megabucks.org/valuation.wsdl* on its server, or any publicly accessible location).

- Create a tModel to represent the valuation service specifications (these specifications are described in the WSDL file mentioned in our first bullet point).
- Publish the tModel in its registry. As part of the publishing process, the registry issues a unique key for the tModel (5000X, for example[6]) and stores the URL of the WSDL file in the overviewURL child element of the tModel element.

Figure 2–6 illustrates this sequence of events.

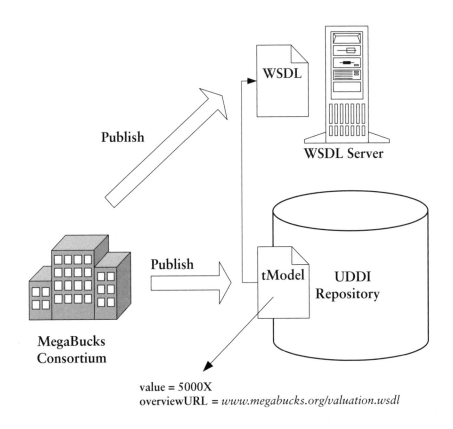

value = 5000X
overviewURL = *www.megabucks.org/valuation.wsdl*

Figure 2–6 Creating a tModel.

---

6. The value of a tModel key is considerably more complex than this, but this simplification is adequate for our purposes.

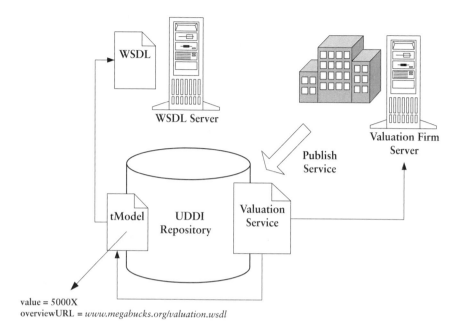

value = 5000X
overviewURL = *www.megabucks.org/valuation.wsdl*

Figure 2–7 Using the tModel.

A firm that wants to publish a Web Service to comply with this standard (presumably a member of the MegaBucks Consortium) needs to do the following (see Figure 2–7 for the sequence of events outlined in the bullets):

- Publish its business to the private registry operated by MegaBucks Consortium.
- Publish the Web Service with a bindingTemplate, access point of which is the URL of the firm's Web Services implementation and whose tModel's value (5000X) is that of the tModel published by MegaBucks Consortium. In essence, this member firm is advertising that its valuation service complies with a set of specifications (captured in the tModel) established by a consortium (in this case, Mega-Bucks Consortium).

As mentioned earlier, multiple firms can publish Web Services that implement the same tModel.

A firm that actually wants to invoke the valuation service (e.g., a holding company that buys other businesses) first has to know the value that represents the valuation service (in this case, 5000X) and must use this value to locate the Web Service either statically (by browsing the operator nodes via the Web) or programmatically. If the search results in more than one service, then the client can use other criteria (price, location, etc.) before selecting a provider.

In our example:

- MegaBucks Consortium is a publisher (because it is publishing a service—the tModel) and a service broker (because it is hosting a repository that requester firms are searching).
- The member firm—the one that is providing the actual valuation service—is the provider.
- The holding company is the client.

Figure 2–8 illustrates the requester locating the valuation service and invoking it.

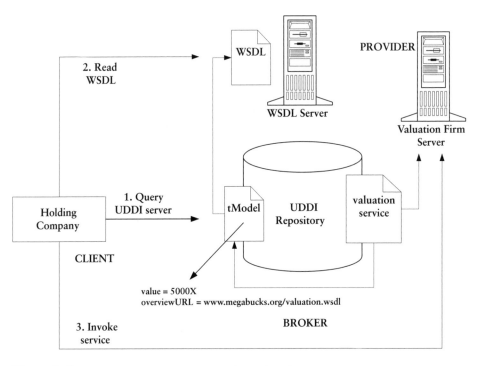

Figure 2–8 Locating and invoking a Web Service.

Types of UDDI Registries

UDDI registries can be categorized into two major groups:

- **Public.** Anyone can publish an entry in a public registry, which has no process to ensure the validity of its entries. (The business registries operated by IBM and Microsoft are examples of public registries.) Because an entry is not validated, there may be questions as to whether the business actually exists, whether the services are even provided, and whether the services are delivered at an acceptable level. For these and other reasons, many believe that public registries will not be feasible for a long time.

- **Private.** A private registry is a more likely scenario for the majority of the firms because each firm can enforce certain criteria on an entry before it is published to the repository. There are different variations of private registries including

  - **EAI registry.** This is useful for large organizations that want to publish commonly used services by various departments or divisions. Without a central repository, these services are often duplicated. An example would be a service for accessing the human resource legacy system.

  - **Portal UDDI.** The registry is located behind a firewall. Therefore, the external users can search for entries, but only the operators of the portal can publish or update the entries in the portal. In a sense, this is the model of the portals today. Users can browse and invoke services (such as stock quotes), but they cannot add new services (although they can personalize the views).

  - **Marketplace UDDI.** Only members of the marketplace (typically a closed environment) can publish and search for services. This type of registry is appropriate for vertical industries. The marketplace operator can establish qualifying criteria before an entry is added to the repository and can then provide additional fee-based services such as certification, billing, and nonrepudiation.

▶ Web Services and Other Technologies

Now that we have explained the basics of Web Services, it is worth reviewing whether Web Services will coexist or whether they will replace many of the technologies we've discussed. Remember, a WSDL document advertises the methods that can be invoked, and SOAP provides the mechanism for invoking the methods. However, there is still a need to have back-end applications take the SOAP request and perform the processing. This functionality is still provided by some applications, which can be written in a client-server or *n*-tier architecture. The following scenarios elaborate how existing technologies can be affected by the adoption of Web Services.

- **Application servers, middleware, and object-oriented technologies.** Recall that application servers are written predominantly in Java; it follows that applications using application servers must be written in Java as well. Without SOAP, Java applications must use either RMI (which allows communications only with other Java programs) or CORBA (fairly expensive and difficult to learn) for integration to legacy systems. Most popular application servers now provide SOAP support. Furthermore, through SOAP, applications built with an application server (i.e., Java applications) can now communicate with programs in other languages, regardless of the language in which they are written (provided that language has SOAP support). However, keep in mind that, in many cases, CORBA is still the only viable solution for connecting systems speaking different languages and/or on different operating systems because it defines many features (real-time extensions, etc.) that are not available with Web Services. The key is to determine what needs to be done and address the missing functionality. In many cases, a viable option is to use third party products, such as Web Services networks, to address some of the gaps in the existing standards. We'll talk more about Web Services networks in Chapter 6.

- **ERP, CRM, and EAI systems.** ERP and CRM systems provide the core functionality for many firms and will continue to do so even with the emergence of Web Services. In some cases, Web Services may replace the simpler integration scenarios between CRM and ERP currently addressed by the lower-end EAI solutions. However, as of now, the base Web Services do not address many of the advanced features found in the higher-end EAI solutions—transaction control, message integrity, queuing, to name a few. For an in-depth look at the types of cases in which it can be beneficial to use Web Services in place of traditional integration, see the case studies in Appendix B. For a more thorough discussion how EAI and Web Services will coexist, see the JCA section of Chapter 4.

- **EDI.** There are conflicting points of view about whether Web Services will make EDI obsolete; quite a few believe that EDI will be around for a long time. First, a lot of money has been invested in EDI by major corporations such as Wal-Mart and General Motors. Furthermore, EDI provides a data exchange mechanism and a set of predefined business processes. As of this writing, without the adoption of ebXML or something similar, Web Services do not address the issue of business processes. For more information on ebXML, see Appendix A.

▶ Phases of Adoption

In most surveys conducted by leading analyst firms (Gartner Group, Forrester, IDC, and others) with IT decision makers, many respondents have consistently ranked Web Services as a technology that will be adopted in their enterprises. However, the adoption will not happen in a single large wave. According to these same firms, the adoption will happen in the three distinct phases described in the next three sections (for other perspectives on the phases of adoption, see Appendix C, which includes in-depth interviews with executives at Web Services firms).

Phase I (2002–2003+)

In this phase, organizations will adopt Web Services as a more affordable way of performing application integration behind the firewall; they will launch pilot projects to gain some hands-on experience. A natural point of entry will be when a firm chooses to use Web Services instead of conventional middleware to integrate **enterprise information portals** (**EIPs**) from multiple disparate data sources. Because most firms already have a portal strategy and/or deployment, this would be a low-risk incremental strategy to save on integration costs. The lack of Web Services transactional standards will not be a huge deterrent here since many information portals are not transactional in nature.

Figure 2–9 illustrates how Web Services are used with an enterprise portal.

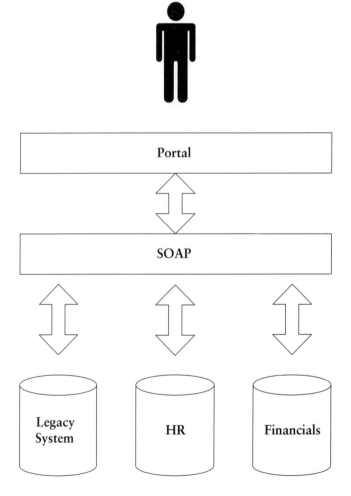

Figure 2–9   Portal integration via SOAP.

Phase II (2003–2005)

As the standards mature (especially regarding security, messaging, and transaction control), organizations will start integrating business processes and applications beyond the firewall. Workflow standards will also mature to the point where organizations can build sophisticated, collaborative systems with trading partners. For a more thorough discussion of workflow standards, see the Silver Stream interview in Appendix C.

Phase III (2006+)

By this time, the repositories should contain a critical mass of publicly available Web Services. This will allow business analysts to start building complex applications by statically assembling these available Web Services, which were once the exclusive province of developers. This may even include using software agents—programs that can act on behalf of a user—to dynamically change the behavior of the system by dynamically reconfiguring the workflow to react to changing business conditions.

▶ Summary

The term Web Services defines a set of lightweight protocols and standards (SOAP, WSDL, and UDDI) that facilitate integration. Adding a thin layer on top of standard XML, SOAP provides a lightweight protocol for exchanging data, invoking applications remotely, and handling exceptions. SOAP does not provide the functionality itself, but instead provides a platform- and language-neutral way of forwarding an incoming request (frequently an HTTP request, although FTP and SMTP are also supported) to the appropriate method or function in an existing application and then returning the value to the requester.

WSDL provides a way for service providers to advertise the list of operations they are willing to support. WSDL is quite verbose and is often generated by tools rather than being written by developers.

UDDI provides a set of specifications for companies to use when registering their services. Major companies, including IBM and Microsoft, are also hosting public repositories, which are currently not being audited. For most organizations, it is more practical to build private registries that can be updated and searched only by trusted parties.

In many cases, Web Services will not replace the existing technologies (application servers, EDI, EAI, etc.); they will instead coexist with them. The next chapter discusses outstanding issues that need to be addressed in rolling out Web Services at an enterprise level.

Enterprise-Level Web Services

Among the most widely known Web Services available to the public are the currency converter and the stock quote. However, these are just two of many publicly available Web Services that are listed in XMethods (*www.xmethods.net*) and SalCentral (*www.salcentral.com*), the two directories listing public Web Services. While these Web Services can be useful, it is highly unlikely that anybody would pay for them since they are far too granular to an enterprise (and even to an individual consumer).

Broadly speaking, Web Services can be classified into two major categories:

- RPC-oriented Web Services (synchronous)
- Document-oriented Web Services (asynchronous)

▶ RPC-Oriented Web Services (Synchronous)

An example of a synchronous Web Service is a credit card validation Web Service. Using SOAP, the client program invokes the credit card verification Web Service and blocks until it receives a return value. The synchronous model is also known as the RPC (Remote Procedure Call) model, so named because, at the implementation level, one program is calling another *remote* program (or more specifically, one *procedure* is calling a *remote procedure*; it is considered remote because it is not on the same machine as the calling procedure). The exact mechanism varies by language—it can be RMI, CORBA, or sockets. Typically, the client program calls the service and passes a small number of parameters. At the completion of the call, the server returns the appropriate values.

The synchronous model works for a granular service with a short response time, but many B2B transactions involve multiple parties and/or processes and can cover a much longer span of time (hours, days, weeks, or even months).

▶ Document-Oriented Web Services (Asynchronous)

Unlike RPC, which relies on frequent invocations with limited data passing (to minimize network traffic per invocation), this model advocates passing a document between the requester and provider. In most cases, this is the preferred way of integrating at the enterprise level for the following reasons:

- Loose coupling
- Asynchrony support
- A business-level interface

Loose Coupling

With traditional integration methods (such as CORBA or DCOM), integration tends to happen on a point-to-point basis, and the two endpoints (or, more specifically, the applications at each endpoint) have intimate knowledge of each other, which creates dependencies. For example, if the dependency is a particular database product, then changing the database product would most likely cause the system to fail.

Loose coupling advocates using a public contract when applications exchange public XML messages (this is the purpose of the WSDL document) while leaving the implementation details to each application.

This, then, separates the interface from the implementation details and hence creates a much weaker dependency between the endpoints. Loose coupling is more resilient to the inevitable changes that will occur than is tight coupling.

Another advantage is that the sender and the receiver(s) do not have to be available at the same time. In a later section, we will examine how a sender can send messages to multiple recipients.

Asynchrony Support

A complex interaction can cover a long time span and often consists of applications and manual processes. At any given time, a particular resource may not be able to respond immediately because it is unavailable or busy; the bandwidth may not be available for the two systems to be reliably connected; or the request may take a long time to complete (in this case, the receiving application should send an acknowledgment to the requester to broadcast that it has successfully received the message).

For example, contrast a phone call with an email message. The phone call is synchronous because it requires both parties to be available (and both phones to be functional) for an exchange of information to take place (that is, both sides have to be synchronized). However, an email message is asynchronous—one party can send an email and then carry on with other business without waiting for a response. The email recipient can be offline at the time the message is sent, but will eventually receive the message when online. For asynchrony to function properly, it requires the support of a solid messaging infrastructure that can guarantee that messages will be delivered. Asynchronous systems are often called **message-based systems**; however, as we will see later, guaranteed delivery is not yet part of current Web Services standards.

If the asynchronous model is so superior, why would anyone use the synchronous model? The short answer is that it is much more difficult to implement an asynchronous model; furthermore, in many cases, asynchrony is not needed. Consider a scenario where a customer's credit card needs to be validated. In this case, the customer is not allowed to continue until the credit card has been validated; thus the synchronous model is sufficient and, in fact, preferred.

A Business-Level Interface

A third characteristic of an asynchronous Web Service is a business-level interface. As mentioned earlier, CORBA and other forms of middleware (J2EE and DCOM) already supported the concept of loose coupling, but their model was flawed because it encouraged designing a distributed system as though invocations to a remote system were transparent. That is, all invocations were handled without regard for network latency, often the biggest bottleneck in a distributed system. A program, during execution, makes a great number of invocations (passing along associated parameters), and the performance of a system is directly dependent on the total of these invocations.

A classic way of designing systems is to pass only the minimum data necessary during each invocation, resulting in many round-trip invocations. This model results in a fine-grained interface that is much more granular than may be originally surmised; that is, the list of operations that can be invoked is long because each one performs a very granular function, usually getting or setting data.

Consider, for example, a Create-a-Customer business scenario. From the business analyst's perspective, creating a customer is a single business process; however, because of the way traditional middleware works (i.e., fine-grained interfaces), the public interface—the one that is exposed to the outside world—lists all the low-level operations. This exposure of low-level details often leads to tight coupling (a potential maintenance problem), and it can also lead to performance problems. Figure 3–1 illustrates some problem areas with this model. While the many round-trip invocations may be manageable on a local area network (LAN), it will not be effective on the Internet because of unpredictable delays between the caller and recipient. For example, a local invocation (on the same machine) can complete in microseconds; a remote invocation between two machines connected on a LAN can complete in milliseconds; a remote invocation between two machines connected across the Internet, however, can take seconds, which is potentially thousands of times slower. Recall that the performance of a system is tied directly to the total of the invocation time, and it becomes fairly obvious that this model is not well suited for the Internet. Instead of viewing the architecture as a series of connected *applications*, we need to view it as a series of connected *businesses* and define the interfaces at that level.

Identifying a business-level interface is not as simple as it may appear. To minimize round-trip invocations, the two parties need to mutually

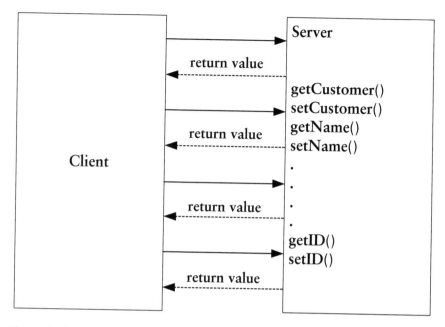

Figure 3–1 A typical low-level interface.

agree on a business process (say, the Create-a-Customer scenario); then they must define an associated document structure that allows the recipient to process the information without requiring round-trip invocations. This document structure can (and should) follow industry-specific standards (for example, the HR industry defines a standard structure called HRXML); this can minimize the work of defining the structure and facilitate interoperability. The challenge, then, is to build a workable process model along with the associated documents to interact with the various parties.

▶ The Importance of Messaging

One of the prerequisites of an asynchronous system is an infrastructure for reliably delivering messages from the sender (i.e., the invoking application) to the recipient. Among other things, this functionality is provided by **messaging-oriented middleware (MOM)**. Popular examples of MOMs include IBM's **MQSeries** (which owns the lion's share of the market and is available on over 35 platforms), **SonicMQ** from Sonic Software (popular among the J2EE market), and **Microsoft Message Queue (MSMQ)** (popular among the Microsoft market, obviously).

Different MOMs offer different functionality but, at minimum, they need to provide

- Guaranteed delivery
- Only-once delivery
- In-order delivery

As MOMs evolved, different features were added, which created another category—**integration brokers**. Usually built on MOMs, integration brokers provide the following additional features:

- Transformation
- Content-based routing
- Workflow modeling
- Adapters
- Message warehousing
- Management

Examples of popular integration brokers include **MQSeries Integrator** from IBM, **eGate** from SeeBeyond, and **ActiveEnterprise** from TIBCO.

While it may not be immediately obvious, these integration brokers are still necessary even if Web Services are used. Broadly speaking, Web Services define how two or more systems should communicate, but they do not provide the services listed previously, which are critical to a robust enterprise system. Because Web Services will have to coexist with these technologies, for the foreseeable future, it is worthwhile to understand their capabilities.

Once a message (which may or may not be SOAP based) has been received, the integration broker typically handles the message, optionally transforms it, and then routes it to the right recipient internally, which is often a legacy or ERP system.

As we will see later, there is an emerging set of vendors who are addressing these shortcomings specifically for Web Services in the form of a Web Services network.

Guaranteed Delivery

Guaranteed delivery specifies that a message, once sent, is guaranteed to arrive at the recipient. If the recipient is unavailable, then the messaging system needs to queue this message and continue trying. The MOM provides a store-forward mechanism that stores the message in a persistent storage (either a file system or a database) and then forwards the message at the appropriate time. Most MOMs can be configured so that, after a certain number of tries or an amount of elapsed time, the MOM can conclude that the remote system is unreachable; then it will log an error. This is similar to most email systems, which try to deliver a message up to a certain number of attempts or for a certain amount of elapsed time; at some point, if the receiver is unreachable (potentially because of an erroneous email address or an invalid domain), the email system simply sends an error message to the sender.

Only-Once Delivery

Only-once delivery is an often overlooked feature, but it is critical because duplicate messages result in additional network traffic, and, in some cases, erroneous results. Consider the situation where a sender sends a message to deduct $500 from a bank account. The messaging system needs to ensure that only one such occurrence is sent to the recipient; otherwise there will be a very irate bank customer.

In-Order Delivery

Email is a messaging model, but it does not ensure that outbound messages are received in the order they were sent. A robust MOM must ensure in-order delivery because, in many cases, the order can affect the state of the recipient because the messages can be individual steps of a transaction. Let's use our example of a series of bank transactions. The balance is originally $1,000, and the sequence of messages is this: deposit $2,000, and then transfer $2,500. If the transfer message is received before the deposit message, then there would be insufficient funds to cover the transfer. Again, we would have an irate customer.

Figure 3–2 Sample Data Transformation Process.

Transformation

A feature more common in integration brokers than in pure MOMs, transformation is the process of taking a message in one format and then converting it to another format (see Figure 3–2 for a sample data transformation process). This is common when there are differences in data formats or when the message must be decomposed to the appropriate level of granularity. For example, the incoming message may contain two name fields (**First** and **Last**). Unfortunately, the recipient system (a database, an ERP system, etc.) has a structure that needs the name to be in one field (**Name**). In this case, there has to be a mechanism for mapping the incoming fields to the appropriate destination field. This is a common occurrence in data-level integration with EAI.

The mappings between the systems are typically stored in a mapping repository that tracks the source system, the format of the incoming messages, the destination system, and the desired format of the destination system.

Content-Based Routing

In many cases, the integration broker has to determine which recipient to route the incoming message to. This is usually specified at design time through a GUI. While useful, this basic routing may not be adequate for many firms. Content-based routing is more powerful because it can route messages based on topics (see the discussion on publish-subscribe integration later on in this chapter), header, or payload.

Chapter **3** I Enterprise-Level Web Services

Consider the example of a financial company that caters to individuals with varying levels of net worth. The firm wants to route messages to designated salespeople who handle orders above a certain amount (e.g., $50,000). In addition, because these are large orders, the firm wants these salespeople to have the customers' trading history, risk profile, and recommendations for similar securities. To make all this happen, the integration broker must be able to look at the fields of the incoming message, perform additional processing (pull up trading history, risk profile, etc.), and then include this in the message to the broker. This content-based routing results in a more optimal solution than simply routing the bare message to the broker. With the additional context, the broker should be able to provide better customer service.

Workflow Modeling

Most integration brokers provide some form of workflow modeling tool that visually captures the mappings of message and routing. This produces a model that is stored in a repository to be updated (and versioned) as necessary. Unfortunately, there is no standard format for the workflow models created by these tools; this results in incompatibilities. To learn more about workflow, see the SilverStream interview in Appendix C.

Adapters

In most enterprises, a number of legacy applications already exist that were either acquired (through third parties or literally through an acquisition) or built as the company matured. Of course, these applications typically have their own APIs, which are not compatible with others. Similar to a database driver, an **adapter** is a software module that allows a connection to be established to a particular system, be it an ERP system, legacy system, or other type of system. Adapters are typically written by third-party software companies or consulting firms that have built this knowledge through multiple engagements (in many cases, the software companies started as consulting firms). It stands to reason that the popular adapters are the ones that connect to popular systems such as ERP packages (SAP, PeopleSoft, etc.) and eCRM packages (Siebel, Clarify [purchased by Nortel], etc.). Before the integration broker can communicate with the destination system, in many cases it has to load the adapter and use it to establish a connection. The J2EE specifications define the **Java Connector Architecture (JCA)**, a platform-independent mechanism for connecting to an external system. JCA is analogous to the **Java Database Connector (JDBC)** driver concept, a database-independent API for connecting to data sources (relational databases and flat files). For more on the JCA, see Chapter 4.

Message Warehousing

Some of the integration brokers offer as an option a message warehouse, a persistent storage that holds the messages that have flowed through the message broker. This persistent storage can be used to perform additional functionality such as message mining and message integrity.

- Similar to a data warehouse, the message warehouse allows the administrator to perform message mining to determine trends or performance metrics. As an example, the frequency of a refund message (matched to the Refund Goods business process) may indicate the declining quality of sold goods. Likewise, a light load of messages between two systems may indicate that the business relationship is not generating the expected revenues. The message warehouse can also be used to perform audits to potentially enforce the terms of a service-level agreement.
- As a persistent storage, the message warehouse stores all the messages that have been sent or will be sent, if the destination system is down. This message logging can then be used to manually reconcile any discrepancies or exceptions, if necessary, between the source and the destination system.

Management

Usually the weakest area of most integration brokers, the management feature is typically offered in the form of a console. The console allows the administrator to start and stop processes, view performance statistics, and set alerts in case of exceptional conditions—for example, if the number of messages per second falls below an acceptable range.

This feature will be explored further in the discussion on Web Service networks.

▶ Models of Integration

Before a suite of technologies (application server, integration broker, and/or Web Services) is selected, one of the key integration decisions that still needs to be addressed is obviously which systems need to be integrated and how they are to be integrated. Integration models can be grouped into two categories, regardless of the implementation technologies.

- Point-to-point integration
- Publish-subscribe integration

In either case, the key roles are those of the **sender** and the **receiver**. In many cases, the role is only for a given message because, especially with point-to-point integration, the current sender may be a receiver in another message exchange.

Point-to-Point Integration

Also known as one-to-one integration, point-to-point integration is simpler than the publish-subscribe model. Point-to-point integration is used when a source has to send a message to a single target (i.e., a one-to-one relationship). For example, an organization may need to update an HR database with information from an ERP system. In this model, the destination is a queue, provided by the integration broker, in which the producer can place messages (a given message is placed on an individual queue).

The sequence in the point-to-point model is as follows:

- The sender places a message on the queue.
- The integration broker then forwards this message to the appropriate receiver (optionally, the broker can do additional

processing on the message before forwarding, including transforming it).

- The receiver receives the message and processes it as appropriate.

While adequate for simple integration, this model is quickly unmanageable for larger integration because of the $n(n-1)$ connections rule (also referred to as the n-squared problem). For example, assume that four different systems have to be integrated. This means that the total number of connections can be 12 or under (a bidirectional connection counts as two connections). In practice, this rarely happens, but it does illustrate how quickly this integration model can become unmanageable with even a small number of systems (see Figure 3–3 for illustration). Hence, this model should be adopted *only* when the number of systems that need to be adopted is fairly small.

Another drawback of this model is that it is fairly fragile. By its nature, point-to-point integration is used for synchronous communications. If the receiver is down, the entire system can fail (or, at the very least, hang) because of the tight coupling between the sender and the receiver.

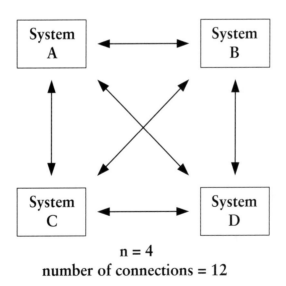

n = 4
number of connections = 12

Figure 3–3 Point-to-point integration.

Publish-Subscribe Integration

The publish-subscribe model, as its name implies, is useful for integrating one system to many systems. Instead of directly hardwiring one system to another, the destination in this model is a topic to which subscribers can subscribe. A subscriber (i.e., receiver) is free to subscribe as many topics as desired.

When a publisher (i.e., sender) publishes a message to a topic, all subscribers to that topic receive the message. The canonical example of this model is a financial institution where financial analysts want to be notified in real time about events affecting the companies they cover. Figure 3–4 illustrates such a scenario.

The system administrator is responsible for specifying the list of topics to which subscribers can subscribe, and the publisher can add or delete topics dynamically. Many integration brokers also allow the use of nested topics, which form a hierarchy; this provides for a finer control over which messages are sent to the subscribers. For example,

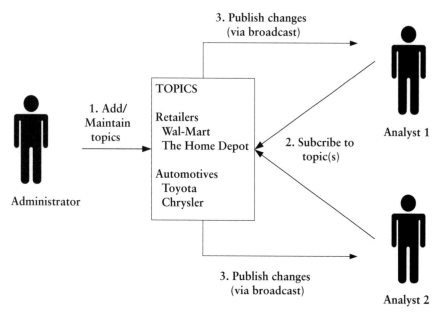

Figure 3–4   Publish-subscribe integration.

assume that the message hierarchy for stocks is based on industries, which are categorized as follows:

- Retailers
  - Wal-Mart
  - The Home Depot
- Automotives
  - Chrysler
  - Toyota

A subscriber to the Retailers topic would also receive messages involving Wal-Mart and The Home Depot (subtopics under the Retailer topic). A topic is identified through a dot notation (similar to an Internet address); in this case, the notation is Retailers.TheHomeDepot.

The sequence for the publish-subscribe model is

- The system administrator specifies which topics the subscribers can access.
- The subscriber registers a callback (a message handler to be invoked when a message is broadcast).
- The publisher creates a message and sends it to a topic.
- The integration broker delivers the message to the appropriate subscribers, which results in invoking the appropriate callback of each subscriber. Each subscriber is then free to perform unique processing on the message.
- Once all the subscribers have been notified and each subscriber has acknowledged receiving the message, the integration broker removes the message from the topic.

This model provides for durable subscribers, a fact that allows for subscribers who are often offline. A key example of this model: wireless devices, which often do not have the luxury of being constantly connected. The integration broker stores messages persistently and then forwards them to the wireless devices when they come back online.

▶ Summary

There are two broad categories of Web Services: synchronous (RPC) and asynchronous (document-centric). While it is simpler, the RPC model tends to lead to tight coupling, thereby making it less resilient to change. The asynchronous model provides many benefits including loose coupling, asynchrony, and a business-level interface.

One of the key technologies for an asynchronous architecture is a messaging infrastructure. Messaging systems and a related technology—integration brokers—provide many features not currently addressed by Web Services; these include transformation, content-based routing, workflow modeling, adapters, message warehousing, and management.

In the next chapter, we discuss the two main Web Services platforms—Java 2 Enterprise Edition and Microsoft .NET.

Web Services Platforms

[The .NET section of this chapter was authored by Don Wolf and Jim Tebbel of B2B Technologies.]

To review, Web Services are a set of emerging technology standards (SOAP, WSDL, UDDI, and XML) to help promote interoperability between systems, including both legacy applications and applications that have yet to be developed. Regardless of what languages the legacy systems are written in or what platforms they are executing on, we still need to decide on an integration strategy. We also have to determine which Web Services platform(s) to use for performing that integration. In this chapter, we'll focus on the two most popular Web Services platforms—J2EE and Microsoft .NET. First we discuss the J2EE platform (including APIs specifically for working with Web Services) and those vendors supporting the J2EE platform (Sun Microsystems, IBM, BEA Systems, and Iona); then we look at the .NET platform. The chapter concludes with a high-level comparison between J2EE and .NET.

▶ The J2EE Platform

Originated from Sun Microsystems, **Java 2 Enterprise Edition**, or J2EE, is a set of specifications and a platform for building enterprise-level applications. Sun produces a reference implementation of the

J2EE specifications, and other organizations are then free to improve upon these specifications, although implementations must pass a series of compliance tests to be considered J2EE compliant. These specifications and technologies have been widely adopted by many organizations in the industry, including IBM, BEA Systems, Oracle, HP, and Iona. Each of these companies has in turn developed products that comply with the J2EE specifications, thus enabling an organization to mix best-of-breed products from multiple vendors. Most of these products are in a category called **J2EE application servers.** For more information on application servers, see the section on J2EE Web Services Integration later in the chapter.

A vendor is not obligated to support the entire J2EE API; some vendors produce niche products that support a subset of the J2EE API (an example of this is Sonic Software, which produces a messaging platform that supports Java Message Service [JMS], a subset of the J2EE specifications). The most notable exception to the vendors supporting the J2EE standard is Microsoft, which is producing its own Web Services platform called .NET. However, as we will see, through Web Services, J2EE systems can now integrate with .NET systems.

Changes to the J2EE specifications are handled through a collaborative effort called the **Java Community Process (JCP)** to ensure portability and compliance to the standards. Since its launch, more than 200 companies have contributed to various specifications in the J2EE standards. A change or addition of a new feature is initiated by a **Java Specification Request (JSR)**; in fact, many of the technologies related to Web Services are currently in various stages of acceptance and are tracked by different JSRs.

The main goal of J2EE is to produce a platform for building portable, scalable, secure, and robust enterprise-level applications. J2EE is a large framework of related Java classes designed to handle many of the lower level details necessary for facilitating the creation such applications.

The underlying implementation language of J2EE (as its name implies) is Java. Many of these aforementioned goals (portability, scalability, security, and robustness) are inherently present in the Java language.

- **Portability.** Java is portable through the use of the Java Virtual Machine.

- **Scalability.** Scalability is defined in two manners: development and deployment. Because Java is object oriented, Java applications tend to be more manageable than those written in procedural languages. There is nothing inherent in the Java language to handle deployment scalability, although many of the products we will be discussing do address this issue.
- **Security.** Java applications execute in a controlled security context and typically cannot modify system resources (such as the system clock).
- **Robustness.** Java has a well-defined set of exception-handling mechanisms to handle exceptions during runtime.

The J2EE APIs

Even though J2EE defines many technologies, for our purposes, we will concentrate on the following:

- **Servlets** are server-side Java programs that process incoming HTTP requests from the clients and are supported through servlet engines. Popular examples include Tomcat from Apache, JRun from Allaire, ServletExec from NewAtlanta, etc.
- **Java Server Pages (JSPs)** can contain HTML and Java code, providing a mechanism for displaying results that will be returned to a user. JSPs are an extension of the servlet model. The first time a JSP is requested, the servlet engine compiles it into a servlet. The servlet engine then invokes the servlet and returns the value to the client.
- **Enterprise Java Beans (EJBs)** represent a component model for capturing business logic and can be one of four categories:
  - **Stateless Session Bean** is an abstraction representing the session of a user with a server. A stateless Session Bean stores the state of the session but only for the current method invocation.
  - **Stateful Session Bean** is similar to a stateless Session Bean except it stores the state of the request between method invocations. The prototypical example of a stateful Session Bean is a shopping cart: the contents of the cart need to be remembered between method invocations. Generally speaking,

stateless systems (that is, systems that make use of stateless Session Beans) are more scalable than stateful ones. For a more thorough discussion on this issue, see Chapter 5.

- **Entity Bean** is an object representation of persistent data, which can be stored in a number of mechanisms but most often in relational databases. While the life span of Session Beans (stateless and stateful) is the same as that of the client session(s), the life span of an Entity Bean is determined by the life span of the associated data. Working with Entity Beans requires dealing with issues such as **container-managed persistence (CMP)** and **bean-managed persistence (BMP)**.

- **Message Beans** were introduced in EJB 2.0 and are used with JMS (see JMS section below). A Message Bean is a consumer of asynchronous messages.

- **Remote Method Invocation (RMI)** is used for invoking methods in remote Java objects. Like many distributed computing technologies (such as CORBA), RMI uses proxies to accomplish this functionality.

- **Java Naming Directory Interface (JNDI)** provides a unified interface to multiple naming and directory services such as Novell Directory Services and Lightweight Directory Access Protocol (LDAP). Since JNDI uses RMI as its underlying technology, it can be used to register, locate, and bind only to Java objects.

- **Java Database Connector (JDBC)** provides a unified interface for dealing with multiple data stores with a primary focus on relational databases. Connecting to a database requires the installation of a database-specific JDBC-compliant database driver. By interfacing with a database through JDBC (instead of directly with the database), an application is loosely coupled with the database, thus allowing the underlying database to change with minimal impact to the application.

- **Java Connector Architecture (JCA)** is described in more detail in the section below.

- **Java Message Service (JMS)** is also described in its own section.

Figure 4–1 shows all the major parts of the J2EE architecture.

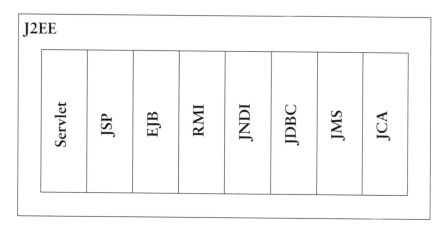

Figure 4–1   The J2EE architecture.

Java Connector Architecture (JCA)

JCA defines a platform-independent interface for dealing with enterprise systems such as ERP systems and mainframe systems (JCA defines both of these as **enterprise information systems [EISs]**). To facilitate integration, the JCA defines a set of APIs called **contracts**. There are two different types of contracts:

- A **system-level contract** between an application server and a resource adapter
- An **application-level contract** between an application component and a resource adapter

The advantages of these contracts to the EIS vendor, the application server vendor, and the application developer are as follows:

- **EIS vendor.** Having these contracts facilitates integration because, instead of providing a resource adapter for *each* J2EE-compliant application server (BEA WebLogic, IBM WebSphere, etc.), the vendor need only provide a single resource adapter that can be plugged into *any* application server (provided that the application server is J2EE compliant). The resource adapter is a system-level software library, provided by the EIS vendor;

the application server accesses the resource adapter to connect (and manipulate) the EIS. In many ways, a JCA resource adapter is similar to a JDBC driver; in fact, a JDBC driver can be thought of as a specific example of a resource adapter, one that works specifically with relational databases.

- **Application server vendor.** Each application server can now support multiple EISs, regardless of the EIS vendor.
- **Application developer.** Instead of learning the idiosyncrasies of each EIS, the application can interface with the EIS through a consistent API (the **Common Client Interface [CCI]**) rather than multiple APIs.

At first glance, while it might seem that the JCA would not be needed with the emergence of Web Services, the reality is that there are many EISs that can be connected only through special adapters because they have not been (and may never be) accessible through Web Services. Thus, for the foreseeable future, the JCA and Web Services will coexist. The JCA provides the "last-mile" integration to the legacy system. See the section on J2EE Web Services integration to see how Web Services and JCA can work together.

Java Message Service (JMS)

As we discussed earlier, one of the cornerstone technologies of enterprise systems is a messaging platform. JMS defines a platform-independent API to multiple messaging systems and is currently supported by IBM's MQSeries, Sonic Software's Sonic MQ, and others; these vendors are known as **JMS providers**. Java client applications that use JMS to exchange messages are called **JMS clients**. JMS supports both models of integration: the point-to-point model and the publish-subscribe model.

Similar to JDBC, JMS defines the base API necessary to interact with multiple providers (in this case, messaging systems), but it leaves many individual features for the vendors to differentiate themselves. These include

- Security
- Load balancing and fault tolerance
- Error notification

- Administration
- Wire protocols

Java XML Pack

J2EE also offers the Java XML Pack, which includes the following additional APIs specifically for working with Web Services (see the following sections for discussion of these APIs).

- Java API for XML Processing (JAXP)
- Java API for XML Messaging (JAXM)
- Java API for XML Registries (JAXR)
- Java API for XML-Based RPC (JAX-RPC)

The Java XML Pack is part of the **Java Web Services Developer Pack (Java WSDP)**, which includes a host of other things such as a Java Registry Server (a UDDI-compliant registry).

Java API for XML Processing (JAXP)

JAXP is a document-oriented API; through a plugability layer, it allows any XML-compliant parser to be used from within an application. (As discussed previously, XML parsers support either the SAX API [for efficiently parsing XML documents through the use of event handlers] or the DOM API [for building and modifying XML documents through a tree structure].) JAXP also supports namespaces and XML schemas as well as **XML Stylesheet Language Transformation (XSLT)**, which provides both a display mechanism for XML documents and a way to transform XML documents from one format to another.

Java API for XML Messaging (JAXM)

JAXM facilitates developing programs that produce and consume SOAP messages. It provides methods for working directly with the SOAP constructs such as creating SOAP messages and adding contents to the SOAP messages.

An application that uses JAXM is known as a **JAXM client** or a **JAXM application**. By default, a JAXM application supports only synchronous messaging. To support asynchronous messaging, a JAXM application must use a JAXM provider.

Additionally, the API provides functionality for industry initiatives such as ebXML. For more on ebXML and other XML initiatives, see Appendix A.

Java API for XML-Based RPC (JAX-RPC)

JAX-RPC provides an API for building Web Services and clients using RPCs and XML. Although it uses SOAP for messaging, the application does not actually deal with the actual parts of the SOAP message (as is the case with JAXM). JAX-RPC supports both static invocation and dynamic invocation. Dynamic invocation is useful in cases where services can be discovered only during runtime.

Java API for XML Registries (JAXR)

JAXR defines a uniform way of accessing different types of registries. Currently JAXR supports both the ebXML registry and UDDI registries. It includes functionality for publishing, searching, modifying, and deleting entries in the registry. JAXR also includes sample JAXR clients for browsing well-known registries, including those from Microsoft and IBM.

J2EE Web Services Integration

Before looking at each specific vendor, let's look at how to perform integration using an application server. Recall from our earlier discussion that an application server provides common server-side services—such as load balancing, fault tolerance, and database pooling—that are needed by all applications but not provided by the J2EE specifications. Each application server from a J2EE vendor (BEA, IBM, Sun, etc.) implements these services in different ways and with varying levels of performance; however, at a conceptual level, they are all doing the same thing.

An application server usually includes a servlet engine and an EJB container (but, to add to the confusion, not all application servers have built-in servlet engines, and not all application servers can host EJBs). As of this writing, all the major application server vendors have announced support for SOAP and varying levels of support for WSDL and UDDI.

In order to effectively support Web Services, a servlet must be able to process an incoming SOAP request (usually via HTTP) and then route the request to the appropriate destination (JMS message, EJB, another servlet, etc.). Once the SOAP request has been processed, the application then uses other facilities in the application to continue processing. This may include connecting to a legacy system using JCA and/or connecting to a relational database using JDBC. This result is then packaged into an XML document and returned via SOAP to the client. Figure 4–2 illustrates this sequence.

The following section discusses the major J2EE vendors including Sun Microsystems, IBM, BEA Systems, and Iona. See Appendix C for discussion of two other J2EE vendors, SilverStream and Cape Clear.

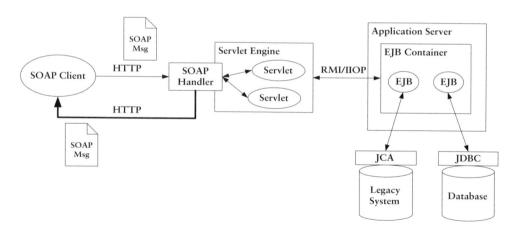

Figure 4–2 SOAP integration with JCA and JDBC.

Major J2EE Vendors

This section discusses the foremost J2EE vendors and the products they have developed.

Sun Microsystems

As the creator of the Java language and the J2EE specifications, Sun is a key player in the Web Services market. Sun's vision is embodied in **Sun ONE (Open Network Environment)**, a standards-based platform for building **Services on Demand** that can be offered any device including computers, personal digital assistants (PDAs), and wireless devices. The platform is a set of specifications and related products including Java, **Forte Tools, Solaris,** and **iPlanet Server Suite**. With the exception of Java, these products are discussed in more detail below.

Solaris Operating System Unlike the majority of vendors, Sun is both a hardware and a software company. The operating system that powers its hardware is Solaris, a 32-bit and 64-bit industrial-strength Unix implementation with significant market share, which runs on SPARC and Intel systems.

Forte Tools With the acquisition of Forte, Sun considerably expanded its own suite of development tools. The Forte tools allow developers to build native Web Services and wrap existing Java code using Web Services protocols.

iPlanet Server Suite Originally an alliance between Netscape and America Online, iPlanet has been folded back into Sun. Among other things, the product line includes an LDAP server, a Web server, the **iPlanet Integration Server** (in two editions, **EAI Edition** and **B2B Edition,** which were called **Forte Fusion** and **iPlanet ECXpert** respectively), and the **iPlanet application server,** a J2EE-compliant application server.

IBM

Another strong supporter of the J2EE platform and a key Web Services player is IBM. In fact, IBM has been an early pioneer in establishing or helping to establish many of the key Web Services standards including SOAP and UDDI. IBM has been exceedingly thorough in adding support for Web Services throughout all of the company's product lines, including the WebSphere product line, the DB2 database, Lotus products, and MQSeries. Additionally, IBM offers the Web Services Toolkit and contributes to the open source product, Apache Axis.

Some of these products are discussed in further detail below.

WebSphere Product Line

The term **WebSphere** is often used to refer to the **WebSphere Application Server,** a J2EE application server that has a substantial share of the market. This industrial-strength application server supports all the Web Services standards and runs on IBM's many operating systems including AIX and AS/400.

Other products in the WebSphere product line include but are not limited to

- WebSphere Business Integrator (includes business process modeling features)
- WebSphere Portal (includes personalization features)
- WebSphere Studio (a development workbench)
- WebSphere Host-on-Demand products (for connecting to mainframe applications)

Many existing IBM customers can adopt Web Services by simply using one of the many products in the WebSphere product line.

Apache Axis

IBM has long been a strong supporter of the open-source movement and contributes actively to Apache Axis, an open-source Web Services platform (Axis is the latest release of the Apache SOAP Project). Axis originally stood for **Apache Extensible Interaction System,** but most developers now refer to it as project Axis or simply Axis. The name stems from the use of chaining handlers to extend the functionality of the core Axis engine.

IBM also contributes the following open-source Web Services products: **UDDI4J,** a Java class library for accessing a UDDI registry; and **WSDL4J,** a tool for representing WSDL documents as Java objects.

Web Services Toolkit (WSTK)

WSTK is a freely available toolkit that includes developer tools for developing Web Services and a runtime environment for deploying Web Services (including a lightweight version of the commercial WebSphere application server called **Embedded WebSphere** and a WSDL generator, which generates WSDL from existing software assets such as Java classes and Enterprise Java Beans).

BEA Systems

Another active supporter of the J2EE standard is BEA Systems, an enterprise software company that is best known for its WebLogic product line. Other products include **Tuxedo**, a transaction processing monitor at the core of many high-end transaction-oriented systems, and **WebLogic Java Adapter for Mainframe** for supporting CICS and IMS systems.

The WebLogic product line includes the following products: **WebLogic Server, WebLogic Integration Server, WebLogic Personalization Server** and **WebLogic Workshop**. These products are described further below.

WebLogic Server (WLS)

WLS is probably the best-known J2EE application server. This is due to a combination of factors, including BEA's early aggressive support of J2EE (including establishment of some key standards), WLS's comprehensive features, its scalability, developer support, and savvy marketing. WLS is also well known because BEA has an original equipment manufacturing (OEM) program—other software companies such as Interwoven and BroadVision build their products on top of BEA's WLS. In fact, with so many OEM customers, BEA often refers to WLS as a platform. It supports all the current Web Services standards, and BEA has actively committed to incorporating new standards as they emerge—BEA is currently spearheading **Business Transaction Protocol (BTA)** to address a major gap in the existing Web Services standards (for more information, see Appendix A).

WebLogic Integration Server

Built on the WLS, this product adds higher-level features, including business process modeling and deployment. It includes two major pieces: a visual authoring environment, the **Integration Studio,** for laying out business processes and a process execution engine.

WebLogic Personalization Server

Built on the WLS, this product offers personalization based on user preferences, prior history, and customizable business rules. With WLS as its base, this product supports all the Web Services standards as well.

WebLogic Workshop

Originally named **Cajun,** BEA's newest product, WebLogic Workshop, is intended to facilitate Web Services development with WLS. It was developed with the recognition that J2EE programmers include system-level programmers (people who are familiar with the intricacies of the more challenging APIs such as JMS and EJBs) and application developers or even visual programmers (such as business analysts). The premise is that system programmers develop components (and register them in a well-known repository); application developers and business analysts then visually assemble these components.

This tool provides a visual authoring environment and a runtime environment. Existing resources (EJBs, JMS messages, etc.) are visually represented as controls that can be connected to perform **conversations** (sequences of asynchronous messages). The business analysts are likely to spend most of their time in the visual authoring environment.

To hide some of the underlying complexity of J2EE for the application developers, Workshop makes use of the **Java Web Service (JWS)** format—a standard Java source file (supporting the **Service** interface) that can include predesignated tags for establishing functionality such as asynchronous conversations and serialization/deserialization (marshalling and unmarshalling).[1] During runtime, the Workshop runtime environment (executing in conjunction with WLS) generates the necessary code (EJBs, etc.) to implement the functionality described by the tags.

---

1. This approach is very similar to the approach taken by Collaxa, which provides tags for handling orchestration. For more information on Collaxa, see Appendix C.

In this manner, an application developer or even business analyst can develop sophisticated applications without having to learn the underlying J2EE environment.

While there is some concern that the JWS format is a proprietary standard (and that using it ties the application to WLS), BEA has initiated a JSR process to adopt the JWS format into a Web Services standard. As of this writing, BEA has not announced any plans of making the Workshop technology available on other application servers.

Iona Technologies

With the possible exception of IBM, Iona has been in the interoperability market longer than any firm listed here. Iona is best known as the market leader of CORBA middleware products, the **Orbix** product line. In addition to enhancing the Orbix product line, Iona has been aggressively diversifying with the introduction of several products including **Enterprise Integrator** (for B2B integration) and **iPortal Application Server** (a fully J2EE-compliant scalable application server).

Furthermore, Iona is a pioneer in the Web Services market with several products centered on Web Services products including the **E2A** (End to Anywhere) **Web Services Integration Platform** (**Collaborate Edition, Partner Edition,** and **XMLBus Edition**). Most of our discussion will focus around the E2A XMLBus Edition.

E2A XMLBus Edition

XMLBus, the low-end Web Services integration product of the E2A Web Services product line, provides several tools for building, debugging, monitoring, and testing Web Services. It also provides a process flow engine for chaining existing Web Services to create a workflow. For a more thorough discussion of XMLBus, see Appendix D, which provides a full review. The book includes a year's subscription to a fully functional XMLBus developer license, without the workflow engine.

▶ The Microsoft .NET Platform

Probably more than any organization, Microsoft has been most successful in branding and raising awareness about Web Services through its .NET marketing strategy and its inclusion of these capabilities into its ubiquitous Windows operating system and Office products. In these sections, we will provide a high-level overview of .NET, including an introduction to the various facets of the .NET platform; describe the technical underpinnings of .NET, illustrating the power of the new development environment and tools; and then we will discuss what these subjects mean to a business evaluating .NET.

.NET's Main Component Areas

When developers talk about .NET, they are most often referring to the .NET development tools, but .NET is more than that. The main components of .NET fall into these areas:

- Enterprise servers
- Commercial Web Services
- Development tools

Enterprise Servers

Microsoft sells several enterprise applications. These products include the following (this list includes *only* those products used for building e-commerce and Web Services solutions):

- **Application Center 2000** for managing groups of servers for high-availability Web applications.
- **BizTalk Server 2002** for EAI and B2B integration; BizTalk Server 2002 ships with the SOAP Toolkit 2.0 Service Pack 2 (SP2), which enables business process orchestration and Web Services.
- **Commerce Server 2000** for e-commerce solutions.
- **Host Integration Server 2000** for mainframe connectivity.
- **Internet Security** and **Acceleration Server 2000** for security and Web page caching.
- **SQL Server 2000** as the database.
- **Windows .NET Server** as the operating system.

Commercial Web Services

Microsoft has also embarked on the creation of several well-known commercial Web Services that developers worldwide may employ in the creation of applications. These include **Passport** and **.NET My Services** (formally known as **HailStorm**).

Microsoft Passport Microsoft Passport is an authentication service that identifies end-users, making it useful for identifying end-users accessing Web sites and applications. If Passport gains industry-wide adoption, end-users will no longer be required to have individual user IDs and passwords for each Web site and each application they access. While it is useful for *identifying end-users*, Passport is not a good mechanism for *authenticating access to Web Services* because the clients of Web Services are rarely (if ever) end-users—the clients of Web Services are more likely to be internal and external computers or applications.

Through **.NET Passport Single Sign In Service**, a member can use the same user ID and password on any participating Passport site. When members sign in, Passport can deliver their ZIP code, country, and city. Members have control over other information provided. .NET Passport Express Purchase service speeds online purchasing by letting consumers use billing and shipping data from their Passport Wallet without re-entering at each different site.

The idea of a single sign-on service for participants in the Passport network is similar to being able to use a bank's ATM card in a different bank's machine. Visa and MasterCard were launched in the mid-1960s to provide common, interchangeable credit cards between banks and retailers; before these caught on, credit card holders had to have separate cards issued by each retailer or gas station they used. The potential benefit of Passport cannot be denied, but what are some of the concerns?

- Users need assurance that they retain control over what information is given, either automatically or with their explicit consent.
- Passport spoofing—i.e., putting the Passport logo on a site in an effort to steal user IDs and passwords—must be prevented.

Both of these concerns can be addressed. Under Passport, users *do* retain control over the information they give and when they give it.

However, there is much misinformation in the popular press about this.

Passport-enabled sites work by redirecting the user to *login.passport.com* to log in. Upon successful login, the user is returned to the original site, carrying with him his Passport identifier (not a user ID). The user can verify by looking at his URL that he is at *login.passport.com*; however, this requires the user to move the cursor to the location bar and position it at the start of the URL.

At present, Passport Wallet requires the user to store a credit card number, and many people will object to that. If Passport could save only a user's shipping address and make it available, that might be more acceptable. Many of us do not want to give a credit card number until we are ready to buy.

Microsoft .NET My Services Microsoft .NET My Services is a platform for centralized storage, protection, and the sharing of individual profile data, allowing developers to design applications that are user-centric. Users have complete and flexible control over what they put into their profile and with whom it can be shared. The current plan is to incorporate user data such as names, nicknames, special dates, contacts and address books, online presence indicators, email, calendar management, document storage, application settings, URL management (e.g., Favorites), credit card numbers, and general purpose lists. .NET My Services also provides authentication services by employing an advanced version of the .NET Passport service.

Microsoft originally planned to store all this information but, due to industry resistance, has since refocused on marketing the technologies to third parties; they, in turn, can provide the centralized data management to their customers.

Development Tools

The final aspect of .NET is in fact the greatest achievement of the .NET strategy—the delivery of the .NET Framework and .NET development environment. Let's dissect that statement:

- All of the enterprise servers (with the exception of the Windows .NET server) already existed prior to .NET. They are simply application servers rebranded under the .NET platform.

- The commercial Web Services are essentially products of the new .NET Framework and .NET development tools; without the new development tools, they would be only mildly interesting.

- Non-PC device support services, like the commercial Web Services, are truly valuable as consumers of those Web Services that are products of the .NET Framework and .NET development tools.

The .NET Framework and .NET development tools make it extremely easy to build Web Services. By automatically implementing the infrastructure, these offerings allow developers to focus on building business solutions instead of learning the intricacies and subtleties of the XML protocols that make up Web Services, thus leading to more rapid application development (RAD). But being able to build Web Services quickly and easily is not the only feature of Visual Studio.NET to consider. Using Visual Studio.NET enables developers to build systems that are more maintainable,[2] better in terms of performance,[3] and easier to deploy;[4] these systems also can be written in any of 20 languages.[5] Let's look at how that can be accomplished in the next section.

Visual Studio.NET

Visual Studio.NET provides a greatly enhanced development environment that is sure to improve developer productivity. Gone are the separate development environments for Visual Basic (VB) and the other Visual Studio.NET tools like C++ and Interdev. Visual Studio.NET improves on the best features of its predecessors with a common environment for all languages, including third-party languages. In addition to browsing server resources, a developer can now browse Web Services.

2. ASP developers can testify to the fact that ASP lends itself to spaghetti code in two ways: it allows the mixing of presentation logic, business logic, and database logic together on a single page; and it is most often a combination of three languages: HTML, JavaScript, and VBScript. Visual Studio.NET takes steps to improve this.
3. Again, using ASP as an example, the pages are script based and not compiled, so they are slow. All Visual Studio.NET pages are compiled.
4. No more component object model (COM) component registration headaches! No more dynamically loadable library (DLL) hell!
5. That number is growing as more language vendors move to implement their languages under .NET.

Visual Studio.Net includes the Microsoft .NET Framework; the Integrated Development Environment (IDE); and compilers for VB.NET, C#, C++.NET, and JScript.NET. However, as mentioned, since Visual Studio.NET provides a common environment for all languages, developers are not limited to these languages—20 or so other languages, including Forth, Eiffel, and Python, soon will be available from other vendors.

.NET Framework

At the core of Microsoft .NET is the .NET Framework. This foundation provides benefits such as the **Common Language Runtime (CLR)**, inheritance, debugging, memory and thread management, and security. Other core components of the .NET Framework include ADO.NET and ASP.NET.

The CLR provides a standard type system that all .NET languages can use. In the .NET Framework, all variables—even the primitive types such as integer and Boolean—are objects that have their own methods. Since all languages are using standard types, it is possible to inherit classes written in any other .NET language. Developers can write in the language they know best. Since all languages are using the CLR, code to accomplish a specific task can be rewritten in any language and it will look remarkably the same with minor differences in syntax. While the .NET Framework is included with Visual Studio.NET, it is also part of Windows XP and will remain a part of future Microsoft operating systems.

Managed code—a new term for C++.NET and C# users—is any code that uses the .NET Framework. In C++.NET and C#, developers have the option of writing managed code or of writing traditional C++ Windows code that calls Win32 APIs or uses the Microsoft Foundation Library. All other .NET languages can write only managed code. Managed code provides greater safety against memory leaks and results in improved reliability. Figure 4–3 shows that managed and unmanaged applications exist in the .NET Framework.

How are applications developed for the .NET Framework? Any module can be developed simply by using any editor (such as Notepad) and then can be compiled with the appropriate language compiler. Compilation by the language compiler does not result in native code. Rather, compilation takes whatever .NET language is being used and translates

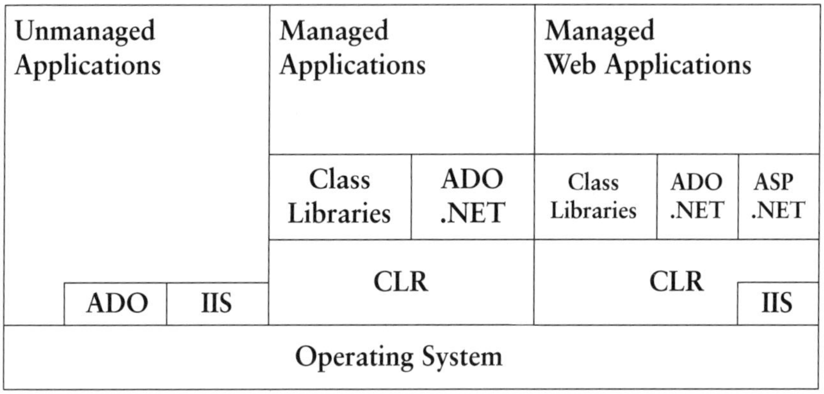

Unmanaged Applications		Managed Applications		Managed Web Applications		
		Class Libraries	ADO .NET	Class Libraries	ADO .NET	ASP .NET
ADO	IIS	CLR		CLR		IIS
Operating System						

Figure 4–3 The .NET architecture.

it into **Microsoft intermediate language** (**IL**). Metadata is generated during compilation and packaged with the IL into a **Portable Executable** (**PE**) file.

The metadata makes the code in the PE file self-describing and eliminates the need for type libraries or an interface definition language (IDL). When loaded by the operating system, the PE file is then compiled to native code by a **just-in-time** (**JIT**) compiler. By contrast, Java compiles to byte-code, which is then interpreted by the Java Virtual Machine.

By designing .NET so that all the different languages compile to IL, Microsoft has accomplished several things:

- All languages have equal access to the CLR.
- Projects compiled for the .NET Framework will be portable to any processor or operating system to which the .NET Framework has been ported.

.NET on Other Platforms

While .NET was initially released by Microsoft for the Windows family of platforms, there are several initiatives to move .NET to other platforms:

- Miguel de Icaza, the creator of GNOME, is working on Mono, which will be an open source port to Linux.
- The DotGNU Portable.NET project goal is to provide a suite of free software tools to build and execute .NET applications.

It remains to be seen how many of the CLR class libraries will be implemented outside of the Windows environment. Cross-platform portability of any project is dependent on all of the languages, class libraries, and other components used. These initiatives can be successful if developers are able to use the same .NET skills to develop for multiple platforms, even if a particular solution in its entirety is not portable to all possible platforms.

Security

The .NET Framework supports code access security and role-based security through the CLR. Role-based security is the familiar Windows NT security model. Each user's login is assigned to one or more security roles. Applications can check for a particular role in effect and permit or deny access based on roles. Code access security allows code to be trusted based on its origin and identifying information. It offers protection for the code against malicious misuse.

Before the advent of Web Services, role-based security met most needs. However, the introduction of Web Services as an easy way to perform RPCs over HTTP is just one of a number of the reasons additional security is necessary. In addition to code access security, Microsoft is working with VeriSign to make digital signature technology available in .NET Web Services.

Meet C#

C# is the first language built from the ground up for the .NET platform. Like C++, this new language is a fully object-oriented language, but C# offers protection against memory leaks and holes. Furthermore, with syntax similar to Java, C# is easier to use than C++. Microsoft seems to be placing more emphasis on C# by choosing it as the language for implementing many of the .NET tools, including the IDE. In early beta releases of .NET, C# was regarded as the most mature of the .NET languages.

Visual Basic Goes to the .NET

Visual Basic.NET is a radical departure from the VB of years past. VB.NET is now fully object–oriented, and classes no longer have to be declared in separate modules. The class structure now closely resembles that of a C++ class. These are great improvements, but they come at a price: in order to comply with the .NET Framework, VB.NET in some respects may break compatibility with older versions. Some of the changes include:

- VB.NET is now an object-oriented language supporting inheritance, constructors, destructors, and overloaded methods (methods with the same name but with different parameters). VB was capable of interface inheritance only in prior versions, whereas VB.NET can inherit fully from classes written in VB.NET as well as the other .NET languages, and it can override base class methods.

- Free threading can be used for long-running tasks to keep the rest of an application responsive.

- The VB runtime functions are now part of the richer CLR class library.

- VB.NET now supports namespaces, which minimizes the occurrence of name collisions.

Say Goodbye to DLL Hell

Prior to .NET, much of the development on the Microsoft platform was based on building reusable component object model (COM) components. These had their accompanying type libraries, class IDs, and interface IDs. Each COM component was compiled to a dynamically loadable library (DLL) and had to be registered with Windows. When COM components were overwritten, sometimes bad things happened to good applications, and the users would find themselves in "DLL hell." .NET promises to save us from this fate.

In Visual Studio.NET, one or more classes can be compiled into a class library. Classes within the library can be called in a similar way to invoking a class from a COM component. Class libraries can further be compiled into an assembly, which also has a .DLL extension. However, it is not a COM component. There is no registration required for an assembly, and information about the assembly is never stored in the registry.

ASP.NET

Perhaps the biggest attraction for Visual Studio.NET is ASP.NET. Application service providers (ASPs) worked on the request response model of traditional HTML, and ASP.NET is still bound to those same constraints. ASP.NET brings an event-driven programming model to Web programming. Some key differences include the following:

- Instead of being interpreted, ASP.NET pages are now fully compiled, which provides faster response and greater scalability.
- Web forms have a well-defined event model and encourage the separation of user interface from logic. Code can now be placed behind forms files, eliminating the spaghetti code that results from mixing script and HTML elements. In many ways, Web forms bring productivity gains to the Web similar to what VB first brought to Windows.
- Server controls allow programming of HTML elements. These can automatically persist data and simplify the passing of information between the client and the Web server. These controls are browser aware and will automatically detect and generate appropriate code for each browser. Server controls can be bound to a database.
- State management is much improved, to the point that state is maintained even when a Web server crashes.
- In Visual Studio.NET, debugging ASP.NET pages is easy to set up, and it works consistently. While it *was* possible to debug ASP code in Interdev, the majority of ASP programmers could never get it to work.

Much has changed since the introduction of Active Server Pages and Visual Interdev in early 1997. Let's look at a few of the things Microsoft has accomplished with the .NET Framework and Visual Studio.NET.

- Developers familiar with other programming languages can now be productive under the .NET platform.

- First-class integration and support for XML and SOAP are available.
- Easy-to-write and -use XML-based Web Services enable RPC over HTTP(s) via XML and are not limited to .NET components.
- There is increased Web scalability via compilation to native code.
- Languages are designed specifically for the Internet.
- A new, more productive model for Web programming is available—Web forms.

Business Impact of .NET

Let's examine the investments that businesses have to make in .NET to be effective.

Basic Costs of .NET

The basic costs surrounding this new development tool can be broken down into three categories:

- Software licensing
- Hardware
- Training

The hardware investment is negligible so we will not discuss it here.

Software Licensing Visual Studio.NET comes in three varieties:

- Visual Studio.NET Enterprise Architect
- Visual Studio.NET Enterprise Developer
- Visual Studio.NET Professional

The difference between these versions is in the number of features each has to offer. For example, the Enterprise Architect comes with Visio-based database modeling and Unified Modeling Language (UML) application modeling, as well as a development license for BizTalk

Server; the other versions do not. At a minimum, enterprise developers will want to invest in the Developer edition.

Training The largest cost involved with Visual Studio.NET is the investment in educating the developers. The learning curve is steep; some have compared the move from previous versions of Visual Studio to Visual Studio.NET as similar to the move from developing DOS applications to developing Windows applications. To alleviate some of the pain, Microsoft provides subsidized training in several ways:

- In major metropolitan areas, Microsoft sponsors one- and two-day free or very inexpensive (less than $500) training workshops.
- The Microsoft Developer Network (MSDN) Web site contains a variety of free resources including online training seminars that cover many aspects of .NET.
- MSDN subscribers receive quarterly shipments that contain many free resources on CD.

Based on similar major shifts in the past, expect a six-month learning curve for the developers. Visual Basic has changed so drastically that some people have advocated renaming it, since it is not basic any more!

Additional Factors to Evaluate

Besides the basic costs, there are other factors to consider when evaluating the move to .NET:

- Learning curve
- In-development solutions
- Production solutions
- Client-server applications
- New architectures
- Language choice
- Migration paths from other languages

Let's explore some of the things to evaluate when moving to .NET.

Learning Curve With the .NET Framework and Visual Studio.NET tools, Microsoft went back to the drawing board and rebuilt the entire suite of tools and APIs (MFC, ATL, Win32). As a result, every aspect of building solutions has changed. Even simple things such as accessing the file system, updating the registry, and processing errors have to be relearned. So it is a good idea to start on a simple, non-mission-critical project to allow developers to familiarize themselves with the new tools.

In-Development Solutions Most development organizations have several projects in the works at any one time, all of which are at different phases in the development cycle. For projects in the early stages prior to development, embrace the .NET Framework and Visual Studio.NET tools, especially if the learning curve can be absorbed without major impact. Generally it is far too costly to switch development tools in the middle phases of a project.

Production Solutions For business solutions that are already in place, a decision needs to be made whether or not to migrate them. If the applications are stable, stand-alone systems with little or no future enhancements, it may be best to leave them as is because the migration path is not an easy one. Again, since every aspect of the Visual Studio.NET tools has changed, most code will require substantial, manual recoding by developers. But all is not lost: there is an upgrade wizard that performs some of the mundane work automatically.

If the intent is to migrate solutions to the new .NET platform, then first target those systems that will be integrating with newer .NET applications because there is a performance penalty for calling old *unmanaged* components from .NET *managed* code.

Client-Server Applications Many applications built today are Web-based applications; all that must be installed on the client is a browser, so the operating system has no bearing on these applications. However, if a team is building client-server applications, both the clients and the servers need to reside on the latest operating systems. This is because only a subset of the .NET Framework will operate on older operating systems; to use the full suite of .NET Framework features, clients must be on Windows 2000 or Windows XP.

New Architectures Because .NET introduces a host of new architectures, it is important to evaluate and choose the best architecture for the business solution. Web Services introduce a new element to development that should be considered on every project: Is there a need for other systems to integrate with the new system? If so, then use Web Services to expose an object model or interface. If the current systems are using DCOM as the communication mechanism between software components, then the components should be rearchitected to use Web Services.

In addition to Web Services, there are new development techniques for ASP.NET pages (separating presentation logic and business logic) and new frameworks for data access (ADO.NET employs an XML-based, disconnected data source model).

VB developers can now employ all the facets of OOP that they have been missing out on for years. With the addition of inheritance, developers must reconsider the structure of objects and their relationships to each other.

So, when embarking on a new development project, be cognizant of these new architecture choices and apply them appropriately.

Language Choice One of the appealing aspects of .NET is that a developer can code in any language available. However, it is not practical to develop software using five or more different languages, so standardize on one or two languages and develop everything using them. Also, while it may seem natural for a firm that has standardized on VB to migrate to VB.NET, this may be not be the best choice because of the drastic changes in the language. If an organization using VB has considered migrating to a different language, now is the best time to do it, because it may be almost as difficult for VB developers to learn VB.NET as it would be to learn a completely new language. Microsoft's new language, C#, will appeal to C++ and Java developers since the syntax is very similar (after all, they all derived from C).

Migration Paths from Other Languages Some organizations have significant investments and expertise in the Java platform, but would like to round out their technology options. For these organizations, Microsoft provides a tool, the **Microsoft Java Language Conversion Assistant,** that automatically converts existing Java-language source code into C#. In fact, Java programmers can continue to develop in Java and then convert their code to the .NET platform using this tool.

There are many other factors that make .NET attractive, although platform and language choices are always hotly debated. .NET is an obvious and welcome step for those with Microsoft experience, but what about the rest of us? Here are some of the things that will make .NET attractive even to non-Microsoft users:

- Support for multiple languages through IL
- Compilation to native code, regardless of source language
- A common runtime library common to all .NET languages and platforms (Windows, Web, etc.)
- An advanced and improved development model, particularly for Web pages with ASP.NET
- Superb integration of a rich set of included tools; easily extensible for third-party vendor tools and components

▶ Summary

Many, if not most, enterprises will have both .NET and J2EE, and, practically speaking, they can interoperate through Web Services. However, it is still worthwhile to summarize how the two platforms differ in their approaches. Some of the major differences are listed below (this list is by no means exhaustive; it is intended to highlight some major differences):

- J2EE is, first and foremost, a set of specifications from Sun Microsystems, not a product. Major technology firms, including Sun Microsystems, IBM, and BEA Systems, then build products (typically, application servers) that conform to the specifications. These application servers provide many features—such as load balancing and database pooling, to name just two—not found in the base J2EE specifications. All of the firms that build the products conforming to the J2EE specifications have announced support for Web Services.
- NET, on the other hand, is a product suite from a single vendor—Microsoft—that supports many Web Services standards.
- J2EE provides development in a single language that is portable across multiple operating systems through Java and the Java Virtual Machine.

  .NET supports multiple development languages—VB.Net, C#, etc.—through its CLI and CLR. However, .NET is available only on operating systems from Microsoft (Windows 2000 and NT although, as mentioned earlier, there are efforts to port .NET to an open-source environment).

In short, J2EE considers Java both as a platform across multiple operating systems and as a language, whereas Microsoft considers the operating system to be the platform and sees the languages as simply a development tool.

- .NET provides built-in support for building and debugging Web Services. Since this integrated development model is not part of the J2EE specification, J2EE vendors need to explicitly integrate their platforms with commercial IDEs such as Borland's JBuilder.

- .NET offers integration through BizTalk Server, Microsoft Message Queue (MSMQ), and others, whereas J2EE defines these similar capabilities in JMS, JCA, and so on.

In the next chapter, we will focus on issues that have to be considered when deploying Web Services.

5

Deployment Issues

[This chapter was authored by Kyle Brown of the WebSphere team at IBM in North Carolina.]

The basic Web Services stack provides the bare minimum for connecting systems to each other. However, there are a number of other issues that need to be resolved including security, scalability, and workflow. This chapter discusses the various initiatives around security and how to architect for scalability. Appendix A discusses the initiatives around workflow including Web Services Flow Language (WSFL) and XLANG.

▶ Web Services Security

Security is a subject that all developers think they understand. Nevertheless, we read stories daily about Web sites being hacked or defaced or computer systems being compromised. Yet, at the same time, we have the attitude that "it can't happen to me." Either we put our trust in systems that in fact may not be trustworthy, or we blithely go about our business, convinced that security is someone else's problem and that there are other people in our organization who will make our systems secure. However, while the reality is that few developers really understand enough about security, building secure systems is the job of *all* developers, not just a privileged and knowledgeable few.

107

In the past we could rely on the obscurity of protocols used in passing data over the Internet, or even over a corporate intranet, to keep us secure. The plethora of communications protocols in use (DCOM, CORBA, RPC, and the Systems Network Architecture [SNA] protocols) encouraged this—it's not easy to casually browse information encoded in an arbitrary binary protocol. However, Web Services changes everything. First, consider the impact of sending data across the network as XML: Now, for the first time, instead of encoding data in a binary format, business-critical information is being passed in human-readable, text form. Not only is the data in human-readable form, but the semantics of the data are available and human readable as well. For instance, it might be considered an acceptable risk to let an arbitrary string of numbers flow over a network.

```
41282293111100001002
```

However, it is a different matter entirely when the data has semantics encoded in it.

```
<credit-card-number>4128229311110000</credit-card-number>
<expiration-date>10/02</expiration-date>
```

Moreover, it is easier to spy on HTTP than it is to spy on other distribution technologies. For one thing, HTTP is an extremely well-known protocol—nearly every programmer in the world knows at least the basics of how HTTP works. This is very different from the situation with, say, DCOM or CORBA—even an experienced distributed systems programmer could be oblivious about what form the bits used to flow over the wire. Additionally, the strength of the global Internet lies in its ability to allow HTTP messages to flow from nearly any browser to almost any server and back, despite the fact (or perhaps more *because of* the fact) that the bits of each request and response are invisibly retransmitted, reformatted, and redirected by potentially dozens of intermediate proxies, caching servers, and routers.

Because of the nature of the protocol, Trojan horses and easily exploitable security holes in routers and HTTP servers can make it almost child's play for a hacker to gain access to the contents of HTTP requests and responses. For this reason, developers must take security seriously when developing Web Services. The same features that make the systems easy for developers to build and extend can also make them easy targets for unscrupulous people with the same skills.

So, what is security, really? Well, for the most part, security comes down to answering a few basic questions about the system.

1. Can we know for certain who is making a request of our Web Service? This is often called the problem of **authentication**. We do not want just any Tom, Dick, or Harry to access our mission-critical Web Service. We want to know exactly who makes each request, and we want to make sure that they are who they say they are.

2. Can we be certain that no one other than the Web Service and its clients will be able to read the messages flowing over the network? That is, do we know that our conversation is confidential? Normally, the use of **encryption** allows us to answer this question affirmatively.

3. Should the person or program making this request be allowed to make this request? This is often called the problem of **authorization**.

In addition, there are a few related questions that are also important:

1. Can we be sure that the message received by one party in a transaction is, in fact, the message sent by the originator? That is, can we be sure that no one has altered the message along the way, or can we be certain of the **integrity** of the message?

2. If we are participating in a business transaction, can we be assured that, if our partner in the transaction receives a message, he will not be able to deny later on that the message was received? For example, let's say that Party A is the winning bidder on an item being sold by Party B at an auction. Party A sends Party B the payment information via a Web Service. Then suppose that Party B decides to sell the item to a third party for more money. Party B could simply say that he never received the payment information, thus relieving him of the obligation to sell the item to Party A. This is called the problem of **nonrepudiation**.

The key to making Web Services secure involves making sure that these questions have been carefully thought through and that we have the right answers to them for the particular situation.

Authentication

Authentication consists of two processes: **identification** and **validation**. Identification means that a party making a request has to provide some proof of identity—a credential. This credential is often in the form of a user ID and password pair (something only that person would know) or a certificate (something that only that person would have access to) being provided. Validation consists of the other partner in the transaction validating a match between the user ID and password and a previously stored pair or verifying the certificate or other credential with a trusted third party (like a certificate authority).

So, how do we perform authentication for Web Services? How do we authenticate the users of the Web Service so that we do not (for instance) have random people off the street submitting orders to an e-marketplace?

At one level, Web Services do not provide anything in the way of authentication. There are no special standards for Web Services authentication, and there is no special software with which we can lock down our Web Services to allow entry to only authorized users. However, in many cases we can take advantage of features built into the HTTP protocol and the J2EE containers into which our Web Services are deployed in order to achieve the same ends.

In the most common scenario for Web Services user authentication, we take advantage of the authentication mechanism that is built into the HTTP 1.1 protocol. This is often called **basic authentication**, and the basic procedure works like this:

1. A client requests a secured URL.

2. The server responds back with an HTTP response code (401) indicating the need for authentication. (In a browser, this request for authentication is handled by popping up a standard dialog box asking for a user ID and password.)

3. The client resubmits the request with the authentication header filled in.

4. The server validates that the user ID and password match a value in a directory or database (a user registry) and then, if the user is authorized to view this page, returns the HTTP response for the page request.

The key here is in the authentication header. This is a standard part of the HTTP protocol, and all it really contains is an encoded (but not encrypted) version of the user ID and password. Thus, if we are going to use HTTP basic authentication, we should perform this series of steps over an HTTPs connection (the secure version of HTTP) so that the information flowing over the network is encrypted.

How does this work for Web Services? Support for HTTP basic authentication is a requirement for all J2EE-compliant Web containers. Thus, if we are building our Web Service in a J2EE container, then support on the server side should already be built in. We can simply secure the URLs for the Web Service using the server's standard security mechanisms. However, we still need to handle the insertion of the authentication header into the HTTP request on the client side in order to take advantage of this server-side support. Luckily, Apache Axis and most other Web Services toolkits handle this for us and hence will support the basic authentication method. In the client code, we simply set the user ID and password on the Call object that invokes the Web Service.

Encryption

When data is encrypted, it simply means taking a message and scrambling it in some way so that it can be unscrambled and read only by the party for whom the message is intended. Most modern schemes for encrypting data are based on a technique called **public key encryption,** which starts with the assumption that we have two keys. One key (**the public key**) is distributed widely to people we wish to communicate with; the second key (**the private key**) is never shared. Data that is encrypted with the public key can be decrypted by using only the private key. Likewise, if we encrypt data with a private key, we can decrypt it using only the public key.[1]

---

1. In fact, this is based on the mathematics of prime numbers. The basis of public key encryption is that it is fiendishly difficult to factor a number that is the product of multiplying together two very large prime numbers. So, if we encrypt a message using the product (the public key), we can decrypt it only if we know one of the two factors of the product (the private key). Since it's so difficult to find the factorization of the product (we would have to try all of the billions of possible factors to see if the product divides evenly), we can assume the secret is safe.

In the context of Web Services, there are two ways of encrypting requests being made of our Web Services and responses provided back by the Web Services.

1. The network protocol over which the applications send messages may support encryption as a standard feature. This is true of the secure version of HTTP, which we will cover first.

2. The messages themselves can be encrypted before being transmitted over the network. This is the domain of XML Encryption, which we will examine later in the chapter.

HTTPs

In order to understand how HTTPs works, we must remember that the HTTP protocol is built on top of the Transmission Control Protocol/Internet Protocol (TCP/IP) software stack. In particular, HTTP works using TCP sockets, a standard way of transmitting information in packets over a network. **Secure Sockets Layer (SSL)** is a common technique for securing TCP/IP communication using public key cryptography. HTTPs is the secure variant of the HTTP protocol and is built on top of SSL. HTTPs is not hard to understand if we grasp the basics of public key cryptography. The basic HTTPs handshake looks like this:

1. The client sends a request to the server to connect.

2. The server sends a signed certificate back to the client.

3. The client verifies that the certificate signer is in its acceptable certificate authority list.

4. The client generates a session key to be used for encryption and sends it to the server encrypted with the server's public key. The client takes the public key from the certificate it received from the server in step 2.

The server then uses its private key to decrypt the session identifier.[2]

Once an HTTPs session is established, the HTTP request information can be encrypted using the server's private key, and the client can decrypt the HTTP responses using the server's public key.

---

2. An additional option would be to have the client send a certificate to the server as well, which allows the client to be authenticated in the same way the server is authenticated in step 3.

The good news for companies wanting to deploy Web Services over HTTPs is that most Web servers and application servers already handle HTTPs as a matter of course. Thus, if our Web Service is built using the facilities provided by a standard Web server or Java application server, then all of this has been already handled for us. In fact, most companies already have the appropriate infrastructure in place to handle HTTPs on the Web sites, so it is not difficult to simply extend these capacities to handle Web Services.

However, while it is easy to set up HTTPs on the server, it is not always as easy to set up the client side of the conversation. Here things are complicated by the fact that the client code must be able to handle the verification of the server certificate as well as the encryption and decryption of the messages. To handle this, the client code must contain a cryptography suite; while these are available for nearly all popular client languages, setting them up and verifying their operation can be time consuming and require more specialized knowledge than is needed for Web Services in general.

XML Encryption

While protocol-level encryption schemes like HTTPs can provide confidentiality and integrity in most cases, it is not sufficient in all Web Services implementations. For instance, not all protocols have encryption—if we implement a Web Service over SMTP, for example, then we run the risk that the mail server (and any intermediate mail servers) may not implement SSL. This is a primary reason for the evolution of the XML Encryption standard, which allows for the encryption of a single element in a document, a set of nested elements in the document, or anywhere up to the entire XML document. Why would we wish to encrypt some but not all of the data in a document? One reason might be that intermediaries can process different parts of a message, so we may want to secure those parts. We will continue to discuss the aspects of XML Encryption later on in this chapter.

Authorization

Authorization is the process of controlling access to resources. The basic process of authorization involves an **access control list**, which is a way of specifying a mapping system between users and resources that shows which users have access to which resources.

The basic problem is that there are no special Web Services standards or APIs for authorization. That is because Web Services standards address the way in which systems communicate, not the way Web Services themselves are implemented. The fact that Web Services have no standards for authorization is in fact one of their strengths—it allows interoperability between different platforms and languages. However, for issues like authorization, it is a drawback as well. Since we cannot dictate the implementation of a Web Service, we cannot dictate how the services will be authorized. For instance, different platforms (like J2EE and .NET) handle authorization differently.

Consider how J2EE handles authorization and the effect a J2EE implementation of a Web Service would have on the use of the Web Service. J2EE bases its authorization model on the notion of a **role**. Basically, each J2EE component (a servlet or an EJB, for instance) is associated with a set of abstract, developer-defined roles. These abstract roles are granted access to run the methods of a particular EJB or to use a particular servlet. At deployment time, these abstract roles are mapped to actual groups of users that are stored in a user repository (like an LDAP repository or a Windows domain, for instance).

Let's begin by looking at a particular scenario to see how this affects the way in which a Web Service is used. Assume that a particular user wants to invoke a Web Service from a client application. If the server is implemented using Apache Axis, for example, then the HTTP request will first be handled by the **rpcrouter** servlet. At this point, the developer could choose to set up a set of roles that can access the **rpcrouter** servlet. This is a very large-grained level of authorization because it basically says that members of this set of groups can use any Web Service, while no other users can use them at all.

A more fine-grained way of providing authorization is available if we choose to implement the Web Service with an EJB. In this way we can restrict the set of users of a particular Web Service by placing security restrictions on that EJB.

However, note that, if we are *not* using a J2EE container to host the Web Services, then there are no standard ways to do authentication.

XML and SOAP Security

Given the fact that in most cases encryption can be handled by the underlying protocol used for Web Services, why do we need to discuss additional security layers on top of what is provided for us? The answer to that involves the SOAP specifications, which allow intermediaries to process parts of the SOAP message. Since a SOAP message is simply an XML document, there are many scenarios that could be applied, a few of which are listed here:

1. A SOAP message could be cached by a caching proxy server like IBM's Web Traffic Express or Akamai. Thus, responses to popular requests could be returned by the proxy server rather than having to be completely processed by a Web Service. In this situation, it is important to know that the message that was cached was *really* the message originally sent.

2. A SOAP message might be passed from one protocol to another (like from HTTPs to HTTP). Thus, any protocol-level encryption would be lost in the switchover.

3. It is possible that different business partners (or different parts of the same company) might process different parts of a SOAP message. In that case, while it might not be necessary to encrypt the rest of the message, we might want to encode any sensitive information (like credit card information) to prevent its misuse.

For these reasons and a host of others, it has become necessary to begin developing standards (and software to implement those standards) for digitally signing SOAP messages and for encrypting all or part of a SOAP message. There are two W3C standards that are emerging as primary standards for encrypting SOAP messages:

1. The W3C Candidate Submission on XML Digital Signatures
2. The W3C Working Group Proposal on XML Encryption Syntax and Processing

While neither of these proposed standards have yet reached approval by the W3C, the broad industry support that both have generated will result in rapid movement toward their completion as W3C standards as well as their general acceptance by the industry. In the next section we will examine these standards and briefly discuss other emerging standards and proposals that will affect developers working in this area.

Message Integrity and XML Digital Signatures

Many XML documents that are used in business processes must travel over a public network. One of the key things we want to ensure is this: that the document arriving at a business partner's Web Service can be confirmed as being the same document that was originally transmitted from the client program; that is, we need to ensure the integrity of each document. For instance, let's say we are building an electronic market-place for car parts. Car manufacturers could place orders for parts, and different suppliers could then bid on fulfilling those orders. We can't have some unscrupulous character intercepting orders meant for GoodGuy Motors and then changing their contents so that the parts are shipped to the BadGuy Engine Works factory, while the bills are then sent on to the GoodGuy Motors financial office!

To address this need for message integrity, digital signatures have evolved. A **digital signature** is a value that can be computed using a cryptographic algorithm, which is then appended to the data being sent. The recipient can then use the signature to ensure that the message received has not been altered in any way. Again, this is done through the magic of public key cryptography. The sender takes the entire message or a portion thereof and uses a private key to derive the value of the signature. Thus the recipient can then use the public key to check the value of the signature against the contents of the document and determine if it has been altered.

The W3C proposal for digital signatures provides a way to digitally sign either all or a part of an XML document. Several vendors have joined together to submit another note to the W3C[3] on using the XML digital signature standard within SOAP headers.

There is a great deal of other work being done in this area. The W3C SOAP digital signature note is the basis for a Java Community Process (JCP) proposal called **JSR 105**. This will eventually result in a standard Java interface for handling SOAP digital signatures. In the meantime, there are currently several proof-of-concept digital signature implementations available from a number of vendors.

3. A W3C note is an early step in the standardization process; it does not represent an accepted standard, but a proposal for a standard.

XML Encryption Standard

To see how the XML Encryption standard works, look at the following example (drawn from the W3C protocol document); it shows how to encrypt a credit card number while leaving the rest of the SOAP message unencrypted.

```
<?xml version='1.0'?>
<PaymentInformation xmlns='http://mysite.com/payments'>
<credit-card-number>
<EncryptedData Type="http://www.w3.org/2001/04/xmlenc#Element"
xmlns="http://www.w3.org/2001/04/xmlenc#">
<CipherData>
<CipherValue>A23B45C56</CipherValue>
</CipherData>
</EncryptedData>
</credit-card-number>
<expiry-date>
10/02
</expiry-date>
</PaymentInformation>
```

The XML Encryption standard is fairly simple. Encrypted data is held within the **EncryptedData** element, which contains both references to the namespace and element type, as well as the actual encrypted data (held within the **CipherData** element). We can choose to encrypt a single element (as we have done above), or we can encrypt a set of nested elements, up to the entire XML document.

Why would we choose to encrypt some data in a document, especially when protocols like HTTPs already provide encryption of all the data in the data stream? For the reasons described earlier (such as the fact that intermediaries can process different parts of a message), we may want to secure some parts of a message, but not others. For instance, a validation routine may need to kick out all payments trying to use an expired credit card before it is passed on to a credit card processing system. In this way, we could run the validation checks in a nonsecured part of our network (perhaps even outsourcing validation checking if volume warranted it), while keeping the critical customer information secure. In addition, encrypting and decrypting data is a time-consuming process that can affect performance and should not be used unnecessarily.

▶ Web Services Scalability

Whenever a new distribution technology arises, one of the first questions asked by serious developers is how well it scales. A technology that might work fine in a small-scale proof-of-concept implementation may not scale up to the level of the hundreds of machines and thousands of users needed by modern high-volume Web sites. Luckily for budding Web Services developers, the answer to how well Web Services scale is a positive one. Given the right conditions, Web Services can scale as well as any currently available technologies.

This question really comes in two parts: How scalable is the protocol that is being used and how scalable is the networking topology upon which the system is built? To answer this question for Web Services, let's begin by discussing scaling options for the commonly used HTTP protocol.

Web Services over HTTP

HTTP is what is referred to as a **stateless** or **connectionless** protocol; that is, there is no notion of a connection between a client (browser) and a Web server. Each HTTP request is independent from other requests—this becomes important when considering how well the protocol scales. Since each request is independent, then a different Web server can handle each request from each user. If we know that a particular Web server running on a particular machine can handle a certain number of requests, it is very easy to determine how many machines are needed to handle a predicted load. Simply divide the total number of expected requests by the capacity of each machine. If we plot a graph with the number of requests on the y-axis and with the number of machines added on the x-axis, we will see that the curve is linear. This is a desirable feature and one of the key benefits of placing SOAP requests over HTTP.

Most large Web sites now use a technique often called **load balancing** to divide requests across multiple Web servers. The idea behind this technique is simple: Since each HTTP request is independent of the previous one, each incoming request can be assigned to the different Web servers in a network according to a very simple algorithm (like a random or round-robin policy). Figure 5–1 illustrates the common topology for load-balancing Web servers.

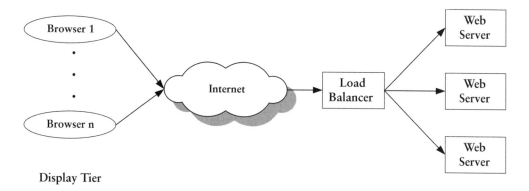

Display Tier

Figure 5–1 Load balancing across multiple Web servers.

A side effect of using a load-balancing technique is that, while the number of Web servers behind the load balance can vary theoretically from one to an unlimited number, the Web site only presents a single IP address to the Internet. Since hosting companies charge by individual IP addresses, this is very cost effective for the company hosting the Web site. Currently, there are a number of different load-balancing products available that work with HTTP. Cisco Systems' Local Director is quite popular, as are the F5 Product from Big IP Technologies and IBM's Edge Server.

In general, load balancing is all that is needed for many Web Services installations to achieve linear scalability for most applications. Most commercial (and open-source) Web Services implementations using HTTP as a transport do so with a J2EE-compatible servlet model. In short, this means that a servlet running in a J2EE-compliant Web container invokes the Java implementation of the Web Service.

Either the Web container can be implemented as part of the Web server (often called the **in-process model**), or it can be implemented as a process that is separate from a Web server (the **out-of-process model**). Thus, it does not matter if a particular application server vendor implements its Web container as a Web server plug-in or within the application server itself. Logically, there will be a process that implements the Web container function, and either that process or another will implement the Web server function.

The number of processes required to handle a Web Service request can grow linearly as the number of requests for the Web Service grows. There are two ways to deal with the increasing number of processes.

- **Scale the hardware vertically.** Add more processors in a single machine to handle the increased processing requirements.
- **Scale the network horizontally.** Add more machines to handle the load, with each machine running a number of Web container processes.

There are some programming practices that can limit this linear scalability. In particular, while it is not easy, it is certainly possible to develop a Web Services application that is **stateful**, one that requires a constant connection between one client process and one server process, although this should be avoided whenever possible. For instance, developers should not try to take advantage of features of a Web container such as **HttpSession** while implementing Web Services. Likewise, developers should not rely on storing user information in Java Singletons[4] or other programming tricks that limit the scalability of the final application.

To achieve scalability, Web Services should follow these guidelines:

1. All of the information necessary to process a request should be either in the SOAP message (either the header or the body) or in a globally accessible store like a UDDI repository or a relational database. Do not store information about the status of a series of requests (or a flow) in static variables, such as **HttpSession**, or other repositories that might limit processing to a single Java Virtual Machine.

2. Always try to follow this order in implementing Web Services:
   a. Obtain all the necessary information about the request from the SOAP headers and SOAP body.
   b. Obtain any shared resources necessary to complete the processing of this request (JDBC connections, JMS connections, etc.).
   c. Process the request and formulate the response.
   d. Release any shared resources acquired in step b.
   e. Return the response.

---

4. A Singleton is a design pattern that allows for only the single instance of a given class.

3. Always test the applications on a network configuration that approximates the final network configuration (but with a reduced scale) as early as possible in the development life cycle. Early testing with multiple Java Virtual Machines can often quickly pinpoint performance and scalability limiting factors that otherwise would not be found until late in the development cycle, when it would be more expensive and difficult to correct the problems.

▶ Summary

Security is a key issue in deploying all technologies including Web Services, especially when it involves integrating with trading partners which, by definition, are beyond the firewall. Unfortunately, there is still no standardized way of implementing security with Web Services, although the W3C is evaluating some key submissions including XML Digital Signatures and XML Encryption.

While HTTPs requires an entire session to be encrypted, XML Encryption allows part or all of a SOAP message to be encrypted. This is needed because HTTPs is a protocol-level encryption and may be lost if the SOAP message is passed between multiple protocols (recall that SOAP can be implemented in multiple protocols such as SMTP and FTP).

Another key issue in deployment is how to architect for scalability. Since Web Services ultimately rely on underlying technologies (in the case of J2EE, this technology would be an application server), the techniques for achieving scalability are similar: architect using stateless servers and also adopt load balancing tools along with load balancing techniques.

In the next chapter, we discuss other means of achieving scalability and enforcing security: the Web Services networks.

Web Services Networks

As discussed in Chapter 5, many of the standards involving the extended Web Services stack are in various stages of maturity and acceptance. However, there are other key features required even beyond those currently being discussed by the W3C. These include versioning, auditing, nonrepudiation, service level agreement definition, fault tolerance, guaranteed delivery, load balancing, and performance enhancements (such as streaming and compression of XML documents).

Vendors are emerging to fill this void; this market category is called **Web Services networks**. The two best-known firms in this category are Grand Central Communications and Flamenco Networks. While they are both trying to solve the same problems, conceptually their approaches are markedly different.

The value proposition of a Web Services network is that there are a certain number of infrastructure issues that have to be resolved in order to effectively deploy and manage Web Services. These common business problems include

- **Provisioning.** In delivering Web Services to the enterprise, a common challenge is how to turn the service on for an authorized user and turn the service off (e.g., when the user is transferred or terminated).

- **Audit trail.** An audit trail provides a journal to resolve exception conditions or to confirm commitments of one or both parties.

With an audit trail, the two parties can more easily perform nonrepudiation if a problem occurs.

- **Service-level agreement (SLA) terms.** In order to enforce an SLA, there must be metrics that record the reliability and performance of the two endpoints. These metrics need to be provided in reports that the administrator can view whenever necessary.
- **Versioning.** As an enterprise signs up more users, a common challenge is how to handle multiple versions of a deployed service; that is, an existing service may be limited to only x users, and a firm now needs to roll out a newer version of an existing service to handle the extra users.
- **Guaranteed delivery.** As discussed earlier, this feature ensures that a message is guaranteed to be delivered to the recipient.
- **Security enforcement.** Users should be able to access only those services for which they are authorized.
- **Centralized management and reporting.** Some of the biggest challenges in an enterprise are administration issues. Thus, administrators should be able to administer the network policies (provision customers, set security policies, etc.) from a central location as well as generate on-demand reports.

Both Grand Central and Flamenco Networks charge on a per-connection basis. To help seed the market, they both waive fees to firms with a low number of connections (under five). A connection is defined as two endpoints (firms) that are exchanging messages.

Furthermore, each vendor is identifying additional requirements it feels necessary for an enterprise to successfully adopt Web Services; it is here that the two vendors diverge in their implementations.

▶ Grand Central

Overview

Grand Central's premise is to reduce the cost and complexity of establishing integration relationships with partners and customers. Clients can easily connect business processes through Grand Central's Web Services network and deploy and administer Web Services for a lower cost because the supporting infrastructure is shared among many customers. In some ways, Grand Central can be viewed as a value-added network (VAN) for Web Services, analogous to the VANs provided for EDI.

Grand Central provides several value-added features; we will look at these next.

Value-Added Features

Protocol Mediation

Grand Central's approach aims to solve the problems that earlier technologies have failed to address. As a result of this failure, these earlier technologies have not reached critical mass (e.g., EDI) because they require that both parties be on the same technology stack, be it network protocol, language, operating system, etc. While Web Services technologies do address the issue of language and operating system independence, the assumption still exists that, because SOAP is being used as a transport mechanism, the two endpoints can parse SOAP messages.

According to Grand Central, this may not always be the case. Therefore, the network does *not* assume that both (or, for that matter, either) endpoints can handle SOAP messages. Thus, two trading partners can keep their existing technologies, and Grand Central allows them to communicate through protocol mediation. This mediation is accomplished through Grand Central's investment in building a certain number of adapters, connectors (SOAP to EDI, for example), and gateways (FTP, etc.).

Likewise, the administrator can specify a different security policy per Web Service, thus controlling authorization at a fairly granular level. For example, a trading partner may publish one Web Service for general consumption (which requires simple user name and password) and another Web Service for a more limited audience (which requires additional authentication).

Workflow

Before sending a message to the ultimate destination, the Grand Central network can provide additional routing and processing. Consider a situation in which a loan processing Web Service requires a credit check with three credit agencies (which may not be Web Services) before it can proceed to another step. The Grand Central network can be configured so that the invoked Web Service can communicate with the three credit agencies through any number of mechanisms including, but not limited to, Web Services. Depending on the result, the loan approval Web Service may approve or reject the applicant.

Data Transformation

In many cases, trading partners have different data formats; this can lead to different semantics as well. For example, with Putnam Lovell Securities (an investment bank based in San Francisco) as one of its earliest clients, Grand Central decided to add support for Research Information Exchange Markup Language (RIXML, a standard in the financial industry) so that outbound messages could be formatted in this industry-standard format. As it adds more clients, Grand Central intends to add more data transformation services.

In addition, there is support for other data transformation such as HTML to XML; this is accomplished through **screen scraping** (i.e., capturing the output of a screen and then mapping it to another format).

Registry

In some cases, clients may wish to publish Web Services to a limited audience; in other cases, clients may wish to publish the service to a larger audience. In the latter situation, the client can broadcast the availability of the service to all registered Grand Central clients.

Grand Central Summary

On one level, Grand Central can be viewed as an outsourced integration broker with additional features such as reporting and provisioning (in fact, much of the functionality provided by Grand Central is implemented using IBM's MQSeries). However, the network goes beyond that by providing a repository of Web Services (with all the additional functionality such as protocol mediation and security policies) that future clients can reuse. In other words, if a firm has defined a business process and added it to the repository rather than replicating the functionality for each newly added trading partner, it can quickly get a return on investment (ROI) by asking other trading partners to join the Grand Central network.

Early evidence seems to support Grand Central's claims of significantly reduced integration and deployment costs. Early client Putnam Lovell Securities estimated it saved well over $200,000 in licensing fees and development costs on a modest project. For the Putnam Lovell Securities case study, see Appendix B.

▶ Flamenco Networks

Overview

Flamenco Networks' approach is markedly different than Grand Central in that the firm does not really offer a physical network. Instead, it offers a software product that provides a peer-to-peer platform for sending and receiving messages between designated endpoints and a data center to monitor the health of the network that is created by the software.

Flamenco Networks' premise is that a peer-to-peer model is inherently scalable because it mimics the underlying architecture of the Internet. To use Flamenco Networks, each user at each endpoint installs a local proxy that transparently routes messages back and forth. The sequence is as follows:

- The sender sends the message to the local proxy, which marshals the arguments.
- The proxy then routes the message to the remote proxy.
- The remote proxy unmarshals the arguments and then forwards the message to the ultimate recipient.
- The recipient processes the message and then returns the value. This entire sequence is repeated in reverse order to deliver the results back to the sender of the message.

This sequence is almost identical to those used by other distributed environments such as CORBA and RMI, but this architecture uses the underlying Web Services standards including SOAP (rather than IIOP) for the transport mechanism and WSDL (rather than IDL) for the service description.

The proxy also provides the additional functionality presented in the next section.

Additional Functionality

Compression

A commonly cited advantage of XML documents is that they are self-describing, but this tends to make them verbose and hence very large. Additionally, while ASCII is human readable, it is not the most compact form for storing text. Thus, the proxy compresses any incoming (or outgoing) XML documents before encrypting them. In many cases, the compression rate ranges from 50% to 80%.

Streaming

For asynchronous systems, the intent is to send documents rather than many round-trip method invocations (as is the case with an RPC model). This can cause a one-time delay for a large document. To provide better throughput, the proxy automatically provides streaming in 32KB chunks.

Persistent Messages

To provide guaranteed delivery along with once-and-only-once delivery, the messages are first stored in a local custom-written, lightweight XML database. No message is deleted until it has been received and acknowledged by the receiver.

This database also contains other information including the current IP address of the endpoint. Through the local database, the platform supports disconnected users (who often connect via dialup, resulting in dynamically assigned IP addresses). After the disconnected user has been reconnected to a network, first the proxy wakes up and sends a message to the Flamenco Networks data center with its new IP address. The data center updates this information centrally and then pushes this new IP address out to all the other proxies who were connected to this proxy at the old address.

Self-Healing Network

While the messages are routed in a peer-to-peer fashion, diagnostic statistics are batched and routed to the data center every 3 minutes for data gathering purposes. The data center is also responsible for determining the health of the proxy (including whether it is an outdated version) and then transparently upgrading it as necessary. Each message contains a **universally unique ID** (**UUID**) to allow post processing (such as billing and SLA enforcement). The firm has hinted about partnering with external firms to explore the data mining opportunities this information presents.

Security Features

The Flamenco proxy can make use of a number of security mechanisms, the strongest of which is based on RSA 1024 nonsymmetric-key-based encryption with signed X.509 certificates. SSL, due to its handshaking nature (keys need to be exchanged and evaluated for every message), can be quite time consuming for machine-to-machine message-based communication. Due to the unique patent-pending architecture of Flamenco Networks, the X.509 certificates for each endpoint and public keys are exchanged (using SSL) during the connection-building process from the centralized information site. The message is then sent securely using the RSA process.

Migrating to Flamenco Networks

To migrate to Flamenco Networks, the subscriber installs the proxy (written in Java) on the local machine. The proxy then contacts the Flamenco Networks data center to register and updates itself if there is a newer version available.

The administrator then brings up the administration console and specifies the URL of the endpoint (this endpoint also requires installation of the Java proxy as well because it is a peer-to-peer platform). From there, the exchange of messages happens as outlined above.

The firm recognizes that many clients want to set up their own data center behind the firewall instead of relying on Flamenco Network's public data center. To that end, Flamenco Networks is also offering a packaged version with software installed on hardware.

Flamenco Networks prides itself on a no-programming API and insists that the learning curve is fairly low since the existing Web Services can operate unmodified (of course, the administrator does have to set up the appropriate parameters such as the IP address to properly initially configure the proxy). The platform does provide additional features, but Flamenco Networks has been careful to not release this functionality due to concern about diverging from the standards emerging from the W3C. As standards emerge (such as reliable HTTP messaging [HTTPR]), Flamenco plans to incorporate these standards directly into its offering.

▶ Factors for Selection

While the two firms are categorized as Web Services networks, we have seen that there are significant differences between the two. Given that building such an infrastructure is not trivial, firms that are serious about deploying and managing Web Services at an enterprise level should consider adopting one of these two solutions. In order to decide on one, consider the following questions and decide how important each factor is.

- Do the trading partners require significant routing and data transformation? If the answer is yes, then Grand Central is the more appropriate choice here since Flamenco Networks does not support this.

- Are bandwidth limitations and message sizes significant factors? This would be the case if the users connect via dialup as is commonly the case with a remote sales force or many small businesses. The Flamenco proxy provides additional functionality to overcome this through the use of streaming and compression and may be a more appropriate solution, especially if the parties need to exchange large documents. Moreover, the Grand Central network limits the size of messages to 4K, which may require documents to be restructured.

- How much IT expertise is available to modify the existing Web Services? Joining the Grand Central network requires that the Web Services be modified to fit the Grand Central API, whereas installing the Flamenco proxy does not require any modifications to the existing Web Services.

- Is a local installation of software allowed? The Flamenco proxy requires the use of a Java Virtual Machine (because it is written in Java), whereas the Grand Central solution is completely hosted beyond the firewall and, as such, does not require the installation of any new software. Keep in mind, though, that the Flamenco proxy does not need to be installed on the *same* machine as the machine executing the Web Services; the two machines simply have to be able to communicate with each other. The selection of this machine should not be treated lightly—while it is tempting to select a rarely used machine, this can lead to a potential security breach if the machine is not administered as carefully as rest of the network. Some organizations that require collaboration with external partners may not, as a matter of policy, allow installation of new software. Grand Central also requires a local installation in cases where the user needs the Grand Central software development kit (SDK) to make the outbound messages compliant with the Grand Central network protocol.

- Are there issues if messages are first routed to a third party? The Grand Central network requires that all outbound and incoming messages first be routed to Grand Central's data center. For some organizations, especially those that are implementing solutions behind the firewall, this may be viewed as an issue. The Flamenco proxy allows messages to be sent directly to each other, thus bypassing this issue. Additionally, some industries (such as health care firms, which have to comply with the Health Insurance Portability and Accountability Act of 1996 [HIPAA]) do not allow messages to be viewable (or altered) by a third party. Such a restriction is a challenge for Grand Central because the architecture requires that the body of the original

SOAP messages be modified before they can be routed to the Grand Central network.

- How much legacy integration support is needed by the trading parties? Grand Central provides more integration to third-party and legacy systems (ERP, etc.) because it operates more in an outsourced model. Flamenco Networks does not provide any support in this category.

The following two sections contain detailed conversations with the CEOs of Web Services network firms Grand Central Communications and Flamenco Networks; these may aid in the selection process as well.

▶ Interview: Flamenco Networks

Flamenco Networks is a start-up that provides a Web Services network through the use of the Flamenco proxy. In this interview, the topics discussed are parallels between the adoption of Web Services and relational databases, whether Web Services will replace or augment EAI, and the importance of standards.

Interviewee: David Spicer, CTO and CEO, Flamenco Networks

ALEX: *Please explain a little bit what Flamenco Networks does.*

DAVID: Sure. Flamenco Networks is a Web Services network that essentially enables business-class Web Services as opposed to non-business-class Web Services, which is what you get out of the box with the standards that exist today.

ALEX: *Web Services seem to promise many of the benefits that we heard a lot about, like lower integration costs and reusability. A lot of these benefits were touted by predecessor technologies such as CBD [component-based development], EAI [enterprise application integration], and application service providers. However, many would argue that these technologies never quite reached a critical mass to deliver on the promised benefits. Why do you think Web Services would succeed whereas these technologies did not? What do you think is different this time?*

DAVID: The primary difference is Web Services are based on internationally accepted standards, W3C standards. There have been other attempts to get applications to communicate, be it DCOM, CORBA, and Java RMI. None of them really succeeded, and that's because they weren't accepted as platform-independent standards. So there was always someone who disagreed or you couldn't get them to communicate with each other.

I actually believe that Web Services are now at the point where relational database technology was 25 years ago. When you think about relational database technology back then, the SQL [Structured Query Language] standard was just emerging. People like Larry Ellison [CEO of Oracle] built the first versions of those. Twenty-five years later, suddenly we have Web Services coming around. Again, it's based on a standard, and there are people now building to that standard. So Web Services are going to be a big deal, a deal that's going to last a long time.

ALEX: *You mentioned that one of the reasons Web Services will succeed is because of open standards. But if that's true, what's going to allow one particular vendor to win over another one? Wouldn't all of the vendors be offering vanilla implementations then?*

DAVID: Are you talking vendors of tools or vendors of platforms?

ALEX: *I'd be interested in your opinions on both.*

DAVID: Okay. We break the market up into three pieces. There's a tools component, a platform component, and a networking component. So a tools component would be someone like Borland; people like Microsoft would be both tools and platform. The network component is the newest one, and this is where Flamenco fits. Web Services networks have the ability to interconnect all these Web Services regardless of which tools produced the Web Service interfaces.

So can multiple people succeed? Absolutely. Again, I go back to relational databases. Multiple people did and are succeeding in that world. I think the same will occur in the Web Services world. For each of those segments, there will be two or more successful competitors.

ALEX: *One of the drawbacks in the past has been that, when a company actually needs [to] do something, it often can't wait for the standards to mature. Thus, the company will go out about 6 to 18 months ahead of the curve. Do you see that potentially happening with Web Services, where some of the standards will come after the fact while a lot of the pioneers blaze a lot of trails? And if so, what are some areas* *and maybe some of the things that your firm actually is working on right now?*

DAVID: Sure. I believe that will happen when people can't necessarily wait for the standards. So the basic standards that are out today include XML, SOAP, WSDL, and UDDI. Those standards get you the raw transmission capabilities. What they don't do is get you fault tolerance or reliable, secure, authenticated, and encrypted transmission, nor do they get you the management of Web Services, which is what Flamenco Networks is all about.

Over time, we envision that the standards will evolve to the point that they include the lower layers of our architecture, so there'll be an HTTPR, for example, that does reliable transmission, which is something we have embedded in our technology. We are anxious for that day, so we will just incorporate HTTPR when it comes along.

Our technology is such that no one has to develop to our API. We have no APIs—it's a *no-programming* interface. Specifically for that reason, we don't want to get ahead of the standards by proposing our own API, even though we do have an API to do dynamic discovery of services and things like that. We aren't releasing it at this point for that very reason. The standards are evolving. We don't want to go out ahead of time in areas that are not ready. If anything, we would like to help contribute to those standards.

ALEX: *Do you see Web Services completely replacing the EAI/B2B solutions or will the two of them coexist? What will become the role of application servers like, say, WebLogic and integration servers like webMethods?*

DAVID: I actually see both: in some cases replacement and in some cases cooperation. If someone has an installation of an EAI or a B2B vendor, all of those people [the tools vendors] are starting to expose their functionality as Web Services, which means using technology like Flamenco can reach out to smaller customers who can't afford those kinds of technologies. So in that case, it's cooperative. It's competitive for people who perhaps haven't begun with EAI today and are looking to solve some internal problems and are turning on to Web Services as a less expensive, more widely supported standards-based approach.

ALEX: *One of the supposed benefits that Web Services have over, say, EAI and the B2B solutions is reduced integration costs. But if there were a vendor that could actually provide an EAI or a B2B solution in* *a cost-effective manner, would that actually impair the adoption rate of Web Services? And for that matter, is it even possible for the EAI and the B2B vendors to lower the cost of the integration?*

DAVID: I guess it would be up to them to decide how low they could go. Independent of price, it goes back to the standards issue. The fact is that I can quickly take an existing piece of my application—be it a COM object or an EJB—and, using one of the commercial tools, generate a Web Service interface; it's very cost-effective to do that. Once I've exposed that function as a Web Service, I never have to do it again. So it doesn't matter who I'm going to integrate with. All I have to do is tell them I have a W3C standard Web Service interface, and that's all they need to know.

ALEX: *One of the other challenges right now of these solutions is, of course, not just the licensing fees, but the high cost of deployment, which usually translates to a big learning curve. Do you have any intuitive feel for what the cost of adoption for an organization would be if it were to adopt a Web Services paradigm as opposed to an EAI or a B2B paradigm?*

DAVID: The first component of that expense is the development of the service itself. And let's assume for the time being it's exposing some existing functionality as opposed to new functionality. Then they have the cost of actually defining a Web Service interface to that legacy application and developing the code that goes against that application on the receiving side.

Now, again, there are tools that will speed that up. So, if they happen to have interfaces already defined in COM or other technologies, they can generate Web Services very conveniently. That just leaves the big issue: the infrastructure cost of high reliability, fault tolerance, guaranteed transmission, encryption, authentication—all those things. And if they do this themselves, our studies show and in the literature we see that people are spending about 80% of the project cost doing that as opposed to developing the Web Service. And, of course, that's where Flamenco comes in.

We do all the hard parts—if you will, the heavy lifting—to enable Web Services, and we do it without requiring them to write any code at all. So I think it's the combination of Web Services and Web Services networks, of which Flamenco is one, that will win the day in terms of the cost-effective integration solutions.

ALEX: *It seems like the easy wins for Web Services are behind a firewall. What tipping point needs to occur for Web Services to be adopted on a mass scale beyond a firewall?*

DAVID: Well, in our experience over the last year, what we see is that very fact. People are employing Web Services technology behind the firewall, and I think it's for two reasons: One, it's a new technology; two, it involves decisions that they can make internally. They don't have to negotiate interfaces with anyone.

The second phase of that is exposing Web Services, also internally, to other divisions that perhaps they've acquired. So while, from a business perspective, it's internal, from a technological perspective, it has all the problems of external "through the firewall" problems.

The latter step we see is involving partners using Web Services. We think that's a harder problem to solve, only because you have to get agreements between the partners. The nice thing about Web Services is that companies can define their services internally and then choose later on to expose them externally. Using a network like ours, they can do that without writing any additional code. Essentially, just invite someone to get connected.

ALEX: *Let's take a typical corporation as an example. How would such a firm identify what processes are valuable to convert the Web Services? Should they try to convert some of these processes to a profit center? And if so, what challenges would such a firm face, given that most of them are usually structured from a departmental or inward-facing structure?*

DAVID: The first thing to do is just evaluate what interfaces you have today and which of those are not working the way you like them to work. That's what we see. When we talk to our large customers and prospects, they basically have a hairball that they created, [one] that has been created over the last 20 or 30 years, and they're looking for a way to start to integrate those capabilities. So these are target-rich environments for Web Services and certainly good candidates.

The next step would be developing new applications using Web Services technology. I see that coming on later. I think the initial payback is clearly doing integration that would have been done using more expensive proprietary integration tools, and instead it's generating Web Service interfaces. I believe that also means that there's a business for third parties to develop those Web Service interfaces. People who traditionally do integration work have a deep understanding of back-office systems, and they are ideal candidates for exposing functionality as Web Services.

As for turning a Web Service into a profit center, I believe there are a number of companies today who charge for information; an example would be credit reports. These would be natural Web Services profit centers. I'm sure there are other opportunities as well, but we see the initial use of the technology for internal integration and external partner integration.

ALEX: *One of the most promising places where Web Services can potentially provide significant value is actually supply-chain management. Can you provide a concrete example from your existing client, besides the obvious one which is to check inventory, an example that most publications have used?*

DAVID: In fact, we're working with one large company here in the Atlanta area that is doing that very one. It's checking inventory. So I wish I had something more colorful. But that does seem to be the first one people think of, and I think it's because it's the simplest one. Again, Web Services are new and people are just getting their toes in the water.

So what they're seeing is, if I take this inventory check and use it, I can develop it as a Web Service, and use it internally first because I've got these other systems that need that information.

I can then quickly turn around and expose that service externally to my partners. Then, after I've demonstrated what I want, I can move on to more elaborate services. I think subsequently there are a variety of obvious transactions, some of which are done in EDI today. While I don't see people necessarily throwing out EDI where they've already invested in that technology, I see doing new integration projects in Web Services. Now, for some companies, those new projects will be the things that you would have thought of doing in EDI before. So what's happened is that Web Services have basically lowered the bar, the cost bar to getting into those partner-to-partner communications like purchase orders, invoices, and all those traditional B2B transactions.

ALEX: *In one of your presentations, you used an analogy that a Web Service is a phone and that you're building a phone network. One of your competitors is actually using a railroad analogy. Can you com-*

pare and contrast the two different viewpoints and if there even are any major differences?

DAVID: Sure. What we see are essentially two different approaches here, both trying to solve the same problem, which is good. At least it says we're not the only one trying to solve this problem. Basically there's now a market segment that's been formed called Web Services networks. And what we see are two fundamentally different approaches: one is a centralized approach where transactions get sent to a central location. At that central location, you can do any transformations and then, if necessary, send the transaction along its way to the ultimate destination.

We have chosen a completely different path. We have chosen a peer-to-peer transmission model with a centralized management component. We're solving the same business problem with a different architecture. The difference is, of course, that the peer-to-peer model can scale to the size of the Internet. We'll do transformations at the edges as opposed to the middle.

We believe, based on our feedback, that people don't like sending their transactions through a central or a third-party node where they need to be decrypted before they can be processed with translations or transformations and then sent on their way. So, in a peer-to-peer sense, we do everything at the edges so nothing actually flies through a central node.

The other difference between the two architectures is that, in our case, we have a no-programming model, which is one reason we use a telephone-jack analogy. The telephone jack is actually a communication proxy that intercepts the Web Service and does all the business-class value-add with a peer proxy at the other end prior to hand[ing] it off to the ultimate Web Service, which also doesn't know that the proxy is there. So it's really a transparent network, very similar to the phone company.

An example would be the way the telephone network converts analog communications when I call someone on the telephone to digital at the edge and converts [it] back to analog as it's delivered to the receiver, transparent to either telephone.

ALEX: *Currently the UDDI directories are being controlled and, to a large degree, spearheaded by the technology vendors, including IBM,*

Microsoft, and others. Do you see directories for vertical industries formed by the market leaders of those industries in the future?

DAVID: I think it will be a big challenge, actually, just to adopt those standards for different verticals and adhere to the standards, such that they are accessible by people like Flamenco Networks. When someone registers using our network, they typically (or we believe they *will*) have already registered a lot of the information at the UDDI site. I do believe there will be vertical UDDI sites just like there are vertical ERP applications where people know a lot about a specific industry.

ALEX: *Are there other potential issues besides the technical ones that may slow down the adoption of Web Services—social issues, I mean?*

DAVID: The only thing I could see slowing things down is the learning-curve issue. Some companies have rapidly embraced Web Services, and there are people like Gartner [Group] pushing them along, not just *advising* them to adopt Web Services, but *imploring* them to adopt Web Services.

But even with that, there will be companies who, for whatever reason (capital, skill sets), aren't able to adopt Web Services. This means there's an opportunity for people who want to do Web Services consulting work or integration work, to fill that void.

So if there's an inhibitor, I think it's just going to be bandwidth: people to actually implement all the Web Services.

ALEX: *One of the things that, for example, slowed down the adoption—or actually very much impeded the adoption—of things like object-orient programming and component-based development, which some people see as kind of like the predecessor technologies to Web Services, was the concept of the NIH—Not Invented Here—syndrome. Do you see that as a potential social or business issue that can recur right here, or is there something about Web Services that is so compelling that the issue wouldn't be as big a problem as it was in the past?*

DAVID: What was the NIH issue? Can you give me an example?

ALEX: *Sure. One of the things that component-based development or OO [object-oriented technology] was trying [to] push was, instead of trying to do this yourself, a third-party can provide you either with that library or that component; that is, reuse existing stuff instead of building from scratch. And in a lot of organizations, especially in IT, the staff tends to have this attitude like: "Well, because it wasn't* *invented here* [NIH syndrome], *it can't be that good, so let's build it ourselves." I'm sure you've seen that in your experience.*

DAVID: Yes, I think to some extent, Web Services will suffer from the same thing, although, for people who want to do it themselves, using whatever toolkits exist, they can certainly expend as much effort as they like to expose functionality as Web Services. I think where Web Services are different—and I think the thing that inhibited a lot of the OO take-up—is the existence of standards.

There are so many choices, be it Java, C++, and different libraries that existed—even within those two camps—it made it very difficult for people to make choices and agree on OO interoperability. So again, I really believe it's the standardization effort. I go back to my relational database analogy that standardization is going to push Web Services over the top; too bad it's taken 25 years to achieve it.

ALEX: *A term that's been popularized with the concept of Web Services is the service-oriented architecture that advocates software development and enterprise development from a series of building blocks, essentially a palette of existing Web Services. This is very similar, again, to what component-based development did a number of years ago.*

CBD was used pretty much behind the firewall, inside the enterprise. Web Services, though, actually advocates integration on a larger level—interenterprise—which creates even more challenges. Given that there's no universal way to rate the quality of software offerings right now, how would this affect the creation and adoption of Web Services?

Is there a need for something equal to the software maturity model, which is popular in Europe but not popular in the United States? Is there an opportunity for an organization to actually certify some of these services? Or would that be established in a peer-to-peer fashion using a product like your Web Services network?

DAVID: I think that's the ideal, and eventually we'll get there. But again, what we're seeing is most of these ideas for Web Services architectures are being used behind the firewall first and in a rather practical way.

It's basically one-layer-deep access to a legacy system, which is something that is immediately useful. Again, I think people are very practical and, certainly these days, very cost oriented. They want to see value for every dollar spent. So the quickest way to do that is to get access to those legacy systems first.

I think the technology will mature to the point where people do invent more elaborate, sophisticated, and powerful service-oriented architectures with layers of services and using Web Services Flow Language [WSFL] and other technologies to provide process management between all these services.

The good news is, for those of us in hot pursuit of Web Services, there are plenty of good things to happen just behind the firewall in these relatively simple examples. As soon as you start going outside the firewall, you have lots of other issues about standardizing behaviors of services—doing things with reliable, secure, and authenticated transmission—which is, of course, what we provide.

But I actually believe, again, that people are going to be pragmatic and start behind the firewall and evolve outwardly. And someday I think we'll have the grand vision that everyone likes to think about, and that's a service-oriented architecture and new applications that employ it. I think that will mean, in some cases, developing applications from scratch to take advantage of it, very similar, I think, to what we saw in object-oriented systems, that you only get the ultimate value when you could actually develop the entire system as objects, as opposed to just an interface.

ALEX: *Let's focus on the business model for a moment. Is it really feasible for a Web Services producer to charge for usage on a transaction basis? Many firms, really, with the exception of eBay in the B2C space, have not had much success with this. Can you comment on why this would be the case?*

DAVID: I think the economic models will be the same for Web Services as they were for other B2B interactions, whether they're charged by transaction or by size of transaction. It really depends on the value of the information and what people are willing to pay.

Our model is to charge by connection, which is independent of the number of transactions and independent of the size of the transactions. I believe there is a usage [fee]-sensitive backlash that occurs when you try to charge for transactions. And I actually believe there are only a handful of services that can do it.

If you look at cellular telephone and other things that have gracefully come down to a flat-rate, predictable cost scheme, I think it just highlights the fact that there is this backlash against usage-sensitive charging, be it by the minute or by the drink or by the transaction.

ALEX: *Many of the application service providers are currently struggling and, according to analysts, will probably continue to struggle from a lack of customers for a variety of reasons. But, of course, Web Services have definitely caught the attention of the industry like few things before. Are ASPs and Web Services two completely different offerings, or are there lessons that ASPs can adopt from the Web Services adoption to improve their chances of success?*

DAVID: Well, when I think of ASPs, I think of people providing access to applications running on a hosted environment.

ALEX: *Correct.*

DAVID: I believe Web Services and ASPs are actually very compatible because, typically, people haven't outsourced *all* of their applications. So, if they're running an outsourced application at an ASP site that needs to communicate with another system running somewhere else, Web Services provide a networking capability that is an ideal way to integrate those systems.

So I've been asked this question before: is there competition between ASPs and Web Services? As hard as I try, I don't see any. I see synergy between the two because Web Services will encourage people to run hosted applications if they can get integration to their back-office systems that are not hosted or may be hosted at another ASP. Either they don't host everything or they need to talk to partners who have hosted somewhere else. So again, it all boils down to application-to-application integration, be it running on my machine or on a hosted machine. So I actually see ASPs and Web Services being quite compatible.

ALEX: *You kind of touched on this possibility a little bit earlier—the concept of composition and aggregation of Web Services. One of the touted benefits of Web Services is you can use something like the Web Services Flow Language and actually create higher level business processes from more primitive business processes.*

Do you think other technologies have to be in place before this can become a reality? Is it just an issue of time for it to reach critical mass and then people can actually start building this together? Or are there other more fundamental issues that have to be addressed?

DAVID: Again, I think it goes back to the learning curve. People are just now getting familiar with Web Services. They can comprehend exposing—call it one layer deep again—a given piece of back-office functionality with a Web Services wrapper or adapter that is implemented as a Web Service. Getting into Web Service Flow Language and essentially process automation that uses Web Services takes you to the next leap. We have some companies talking about using those concepts and have ideas for using WSFL, for example. But when I look at the examples they're actually pretty simple.

I believe WSFL will be very important as the standard matures. I think there's a certain set of people who are at the edge, maybe the leading edge, in wanting to look for applications for such technology. I believe the applications are there. I just think, given the learning curve and adoption curves we're on for technology in general, that the masses won't be doing that for a year or so.

ALEX: *One of the other technologies that surfaced a couple of years ago that is now getting a little bit more attention in the industry is the concept of the enterprise portal. The idea is that, by pulling disparate information from multiple data sources, an information worker can actually have all the relevant, timely information at his fingertips to do his job.*

Some people will say that the growth of the enterprise portal will partly be driven by the adoption of Web Services. I'd be curious about what your comment is on that and, also, are there other technologies that would also be driven by the adoption of Web Services?

DAVID: Sure. Portals—Internet portals—have been around for some time, and there are companies who sell platforms for doing that. They're a great idea, and today those typically have browser interfaces. Web Services can help with integration. So, when the portal needs to go off to some legacy application, there's a great use there for Web Services to retrieve that information and still have that browser interface.

But then if you take it one step further, that Web interface can actually be replaced by a Web Service itself. So you can imagine having a portal providing the high-level Web Services that it provides, and it invokes Web Services to pull all the information together, to provide the front-end Web Service. So again, this is just another case where Web Services are very fundamental. They're as fundamental as remote procedure calls, in my opinion. I think people will find it hard to think of an application that wouldn't benefit from Web Services in some way.

ALEX: *Let's explore that for a second. Let's take, for example, a company that has to do something fairly algorithm intensive, like, say, yield* *management. The company is actually responsible for writing mostly what one would commonly call number-crunching types of programs. Would those companies benefit less from Web Services than, say, a company that does lots of light transactions, more like a trading house?*

Can you contrast how those two firms would potentially adopt Web Services differently? Would the value proposition of Web Services be less compelling for one versus the other?

DAVID: Sure. I actually believe it's less dependent on the nature of the specific application than it is on the granularity. If you're doing a number-crunching application that [with] every iteration has to get a number from [a machine] or several numbers from other machines, then Web Services may not be a good fit for that model. The latency requirements of the application may require more tightly coupled communications than [is] possible with a Web Service over the Internet. On the other hand, you could also structure the application differently so that it is less granular and it gathers information from the source systems up front so that there is a Web Service that's retrieving those numbers: it's just being called less frequently. To summarize, I believe there will always be applications with requirements where Web Services probably are not a good fit. Just because you have a hammer doesn't make everything a nail.

ALEX: *You mentioned several times in our conversation that the obvious advantage of using Web Services is actually reducing the cost of integration. But for a company that wants to explore top-line growth, what are some factors they have to look at before they can actually use the internal business processes that are a source for potential top-line growth? Or are we too far away to explore that concept yet?*

DAVID: I believe some companies have already invested a considerable amount of human capital in understanding the power of Web Services for top-line growth. Several of our customers today have groups of people who are looking at revenue-generating applications in an exploratory sense. So they're getting up to speed on what Web Services can do very quickly.

Those are the ones I see exploiting Web Services and related technologies like WSFL to achieve top-line growth. They will be using Web Services strategically as opposed to tactically. I'm not sure how soon they'll be out, but it's pretty clear that the larger corporations that have the IT [expertise] and software intellectual horsepower will get there fairly soon, given the technology that's available to them through Web Services and now Web Services networks.

ALEX: *One of the companies, obviously, that everybody's heard of is eBay, and there's been a recent announcement where they actually are trying to, if you will, "Web Service enable" their core offering, which is essentially the auction capability to match buyers and sellers. Let's just take a brokerage house as an example—how would it use that same process to extend its reach and actually reach out to more customers using, say, a combination of toolkits and also, of course, your offering [Flamenco Networks]?*

DAVID: What was the example again?

ALEX: *eBay.*

DAVID: Okay. But as compared to a brokerage house?

ALEX: *Yes. I mean, eBay's already done it, so potentially e-Trade or Ameritrade or a similar firm, who has not announced anything like that offering yet, can do the same.*

DAVID: I think an interesting area to explore with Web Services is the notion of agents. Agent technology has been around for some time. The interesting thing about agents is they need to communicate, and, if you think about agent technology that communicates using Web Services, it's an interesting combination. So, I could have agents that do my trading for me. I could set buy or sell trades and essentially invoke Web Services that are hosted or exposed by the trading company and execute trades, look at my accounts, or do analysis on my accounts in an automated fashion. So I think there are plenty of opportunities for almost every industry to expose functionality like that. It's almost what they expose using a browser. It's a lot of the same information, only through a Web Services interface, to provide programmatic access to it as opposed to human access.

ALEX: *I'd be curious about what your predictions are on where Web Services will be in about one year and roughly in about five years. What has to happen? What do you think will happen? What are you basing some of your strategic plans on?*

DAVID: Sure. We actually believe Web Services are the most important thing to happen to (I'll call it) distributed business computing since the Internet itself. Again, I'll go back to a different technology, but I think Web Services are going to be the same kind of adoption curve as relational databases.

For a long time, people were happy with various storage mechanisms—initially files, then hierarchical databases. And then relational databases took off, and there were the naysayers who said, "Oh, that will never work," or "You won't have the performance," or whatever. I believe Web Services are now at that same point. And so a year from now, I suspect, we'll still be doing relatively simple but highly cost-justified back-office integration, 60, 70, 80% internal.

This is what I call the one-level-deep model where I'm getting real value very quickly. It's the "low-hanging fruit" thing. And then five years from now, I think there will be WSFL applications, agent technology and the whole notion of orchestration among Web Services being controlled by WSFL. It won't necessarily be widespread, but certainly the large companies who have the intellectual horsepower to do it will have made sophisticated Web Services available. So people who are less capable of implementing sophisticated Web Services development but still capable of invoking Web Services can avail themselves of this technology that's being provided by a partner and not really know what's going on behind the scenes. This hearkens back to the days of objects and the whole value of encapsulation and some of the things that manifest themselves in Web Services as they did in objects.

ALEX: *Well, I appreciate the time you've taken, Dave, to explain about some of your opinions and also some of the insights you have into the technology.*

▶ Interview: Grand Central Communications

Grand Central Communications is a start-up company that also offers a Web Services network but approaches the problem from a different angle. This interview covers the importance of a shared-costs infrastructure and the need for a third party when addressing nonrepudiation.

Interviewee: Craig Denato, CEO of Grand Central Communications

ALEX: *Can you please explain to our readers what Grand Central does.*

CRAIG: Grand Central is a Web Services network that enables business systems to reliably and securely interoperate between organizational boundaries. A good metaphor for Grand Central is the public switch network for telephones: Instead of enabling any two people [to] communicate, Grand Central enables any two applications to interact.

ALEX: *What layer of the Web Services model or architecture is your firm addressing?*

CRAIG: There is a large stack of agreements that need to be in place in order to have a true B2B conversation. Web Services standards really address only a small subset of these issues—the bottom part of this B2B stack—issues relating to data formats [XML] and communication protocol (SOAP). Everything beyond these standards needs to be put in place to ensure appropriate levels of security, reliability, and transactional integrity (i.e., correlation, compensation). Addressing these issues within a B2B context is especially difficult because you must coordinate a solution with your partners who are likely to be operating different B2B stacks.

There are two general ways to address this issue. The traditional B2B integration approach is to get everyone to use one stack: yours. If you use a certain schema, they have to use that same schema. If you decide to authenticate identity using VeriSign technology and a certain certificate authority, they have to use it as well.

Grand Central offers a new approach that embraces heterogeneity, allowing every partner to use their own B2B stack, with Grand Central mediating the differences between implementations. For example, you may decide to use a certificate authority to authenticate yourself, but your partners may have a different method of doing so. So, rather than forcing your partners to do it your way, you just set up a business rule in Grand Central that says, "I'll accept the following methods of authentication." After Grand Central authenticates their identity, it is validated against your authentication business rule.

We also do things like protocol and data format mediation. Just because you decide to deploy Web Services doesn't mean that all of your partners [will] do so. So we enable SOAP to interact with a Web site talking HTTP or an FTP server. We also can translate ASCII into XML and vice versa.

ALEX: *In a recent* InfoWorld *survey of 500 software managers, the respondents identified security as the biggest obstacle to Web Services adoption. How does your product help address that particular issue?*

CRAIG: When we talk about security, we mean four things: encryption, authentication, access control, and firewall vulnerability. Grand

Central's Web Services network not only provides support for each of these layers of security but, more important, we provide the mediation necessary to ensure interoperability between disparate security models.

As we previously discussed, Grand Central enables companies to establish business rules that allow partners to interact in a decentralized and heterogeneous environment. Authentication and authorization are two areas that can be deployed and managed through Grand Central. We support a variety of authentication mechanisms including username and password as well as VeriSign certificates.

Grand Central also provides rule-based access control. This allows you to decide which users have access to a service and which version they should map to, as well as functionality for things like availability windows. We also support the flip side of authorization, which is provisioning or granting new access to a service.

There is clearly a lot of activity in this area, and we're working closely with the major Web Services toolkits to ensure interoperability with their security models.

ALEX: *How are the policies actually created or managed?*

CRAIG: Policies are created via Web-based forms in Grand Central. In the long run, we also expect to integrate with tools that author and manage policies within an enterprise.

ALEX: *One of the classic problems of doing B2B integration is non-repudiation. How does your framework handle that particular issue?*

CRAIG: Grand Central provides both the sender and recipient with a common tracking slip. This allows either party to have full visibility into what's happened with the message.

ALEX: *So it's up to the individual partner to actually resolve the issue, but you provide the audit trail, correct?*

CRAIG: Exactly. We provide an independent audit trail similar to FedEx [Federal Express] that indicates when the message was sent and when it was received. This is a significant improvement over traditional integration technologies that require participants to do a lot of manual work resolving audit logs on both sides of the transaction.

ALEX: *Do you see Web Services completely replacing the EAI/B2B solutions or will they coexist? You mentioned the two firms earlier, TIBCO and webMethods. How do you see those companies in that* *space evolving? What about the roles of application servers, such as WebLogic, and also of integration servers?*

CRAIG: We don't see Web Services completely replacing these solutions. We actually see them providing a key role within an evolved Web Services architecture, that of the service broker.

To extend the phone system analogy that I used earlier, it is our belief that products like TIBCO and Vitria will act like PBXs [private branch exchanges] that monitor and manage internal service interactions, weaving them together into business processes. Just as PBXs connect into a public phone network, we believe that these platforms will plug into something like Grand Central's Web Services network.

In addition to being a platform for services, application servers such as WebLogic are also being used as service brokers. With traditional EAI vendors and application servers both attacking the service broker segment, we see this as the biggest area of contention in the Web Services world.

ALEX: *So far, Web Services—the few that have been implemented— are typically behind a firewall. What tipping point needs to occur in your opinion for Web Services to be adopted on a mass scale beyond a firewall?*

CRAIG: We firmly believe that, in order for Web Services to be adopted in mass scale beyond the firewall, you need to have two things; you need a shared infrastructure that will support a many-to-many world—FedEx, the public switched telephone network (PSTN), and VISA are all modern-day examples of shared infrastructures that enable a many-to-many collaborative world—and you need to have Web Services standards that allow business systems to interoperate with unprecedented flexibility and affordability. Alone, however, these two variables are not sufficient for most business-to-business interactions. Grand Central's Web Services network, which is built on top of the Internet, enables businesses to harness the power of Web services with the needed levels of security and reliability required for enterprise-class integration.

When you implement Web Services between firewalls you have a higher bar when addressing the issues that we brought up earlier around security and reliability. For example, username and password may be an acceptable internal authentication scheme, but it would not be suitable outside of the firewall. That said, I think you will see a lot of B2B Web Services deployments in conjunction with Web Services networks like Grand Central that address these deployment issues.

Moreover, I think B2B integration more naturally lends itself to a standards-based approach since it's inherently involved in deployments where you don't control what's on the other end. So you can't force your partners to always do it your way. With standards like SOAP and XML, you get around the problems with proprietary protocols and data formats. But, as we discussed, there are still a host of other issues that require you to use a Web Services network like Grand Central.

ALEX: *So would it be fair to say that the challenges are the same but it's just that it's easier to do a pilot behind a firewall because you can control all the various factors?*

CRAIG: Right. And I think you'll see clients first deploy a Web Service internally. Once they get comfortable with the internal deployment, they can then turn around and share it with selected partners. It's at this point that they need to deal with those issues that we talked about—security, authentication, provisioning, version control, etc. And if they use Grand Central, they can easily address these issues.

ALEX: *Can you describe the profile of a typical or an ideal client for your firm?*

CRAIG: It would be a firm that wants to exchange data, whether it be informational content or transactional content, with its partners, and typically in a server-to-server fashion. For example, they want to integrate their forecasting system with their partner's inventory system or their CRM system with their partner's purchasing system.

ALEX: *There was a recent study by AMR that's been quoted by some of the firms in the Web Services space. In that case study, the client saved 60% on the integration costs over traditional means. Have you noticed any similar gains or benefits using your platform and/or the Web Services architecture as opposed to, say, EAI or traditional B2B?*

CRAIG: Absolutely. When we work with customers, we are about one-twentieth the cost of a traditional software implementation.

ALEX: *So is cost the only factor? I would imagine that time to market is also important.*

CRAIG: No. In addition to being more affordable, ease of deployment and manageability are two other major advantages of using Grand Central's Web Services network for B2B integration. Traditionally B2B integration technologies tend to be very expensive, time intensive, and complex to manage, so only the biggest companies typically deploy, with their top four to five partners, for a limited range of interactions. With Grand Central you have something that can be effectively deployed by all sizes of companies, with all of their partners, for a very broad range of interactions.

I also think there is a strong return on assets story. At the end of the day, we can demonstrate that there is no need for an organization to implement and manage its own B2B integration network. We provide higher levels of service than they would implement on their own, and, because it's shared infrastructure, we can do so at a fraction of the cost.

ALEX: *Most of us understand the whole concept of how to write a traditional application from the ground up—I have an SDK and I write the application in .NET, J2EE, or whatever. Let's assume I have that application up and running. How would I actually take that and plug it into the Grand Central network?*

CRAIG: It's very simple and it's transparent. If your application can speak SOAP, you don't need to install any software or hardware or even open up any holes in your firewall. All you [have to] do is go to Grand Central's site and create a proxy for that service in our network. You then redirect users through that proxy. One metaphor that I use for people that are a little bit more technically minded is Akamai.

If I were Yahoo, I could have implemented my own caching network. I could have purchased software from Akamai, installed caching servers out on the Internet, and had every one of my customers download some sort of caching software into their browser. But that would have been very expensive and inefficient.

Instead, sites like Yahoo chose to use Akamai. They created a virtual proxy for their Web site in Akamai and redirected users through it. And these users don't even necessarily need to know that they're using Akamai. It just gets inserted into the conversation.

This is a very good metaphor for Grand Central. You create a virtual proxy in Grand Central and you redirect users through it. But instead [of] making Web pages faster, we enable B2B conversations to be more secure and reliable.

ALEX: *You mentioned the whole concept of the proxy and then there's also this issue of the Grand Central identity. Are they one and the same?*

CRAIG: Yes.

ALEX: *How does the Grand Central proxy help clients in provisioning new services and in maintaining existing ones?*

CRAIG: Customers wrap the proxy with business rules that enable them to effectively manage that interface. For example, rules can be used to support change management. All users access one logical proxy in Grand Central. Rules within the proxy then redirect those users to the appropriate version of the Web Service. To upgrade a user, you simply change their designation in your access control list. This process also supports provisioning. When you add a new user to your access control list, that user sees a listing for the service automatically pop up in their Grand Central directory.

ALEX: *What are some of the mechanisms you actually use to handle some of that mapping? Do you implement your own proprietary access control mechanism or do you leverage UDDI?*

CRAIG: We built our directory to be UDDI compliant. We've built functionality on top of it, however, to enable it to support issues surrounding access control and visibility. Most of our customers are looking to deploy Web Services to specific partners, not make them generally available. As such they want more control over who can access the Web Service and even who can see it.

ALEX: *Your product has a number of software development kits supporting multiple languages. In your opinion, are there any inherent advantages of writing Web Services from one language versus another?*

CRAIG: Our SDKs, which SOAP enable perl, Java, and COM applications, were implemented before there were good SOAP toolkits available. Today, we encourage developers to just use their favorite SOAP toolkit, which Grand Central will support out of the box.

ALEX: *A lot of companies have a lot of investments in legacy applications. How would they actually identify what processes they should convert to Web Services to share with outside partners? And, second, should they try to convert some of these processes to a profit center? And if so, what challenges would that pose?*

CRAIG: Web Services enable you to create a machine interface to an application such that you can broaden its ability to be consumed. Companies therefore need to find applications that would benefit from broadened consumption by other applications, and this could be by other internal applications or by your partners.

This is very similar to what happened with Web interfaces. Companies took applications and put Web interfaces in front of them so they could be more broadly consumed. Web Services simply extend this value proposition to make APIs more broadly consumable by other applications.

In terms of making it a profit center, I think that is a much higher bar that I wouldn't necessarily want to hold all Web Services efforts up to. I believe most Web Services efforts will be about providing a new way to consume something. And perhaps if I'm already paying for a service, I may be willing to pay to more efficiently consume via a Web Services interface. To this end, we enable the metering data that is tracked in Grand Central to be fed to billing systems.

ALEX: *So they can integrate directly through something like a Metratech* [an XML-based billing system] *or something like that.*

CRAIG: We haven't done that specifically yet, but it shouldn't be difficult. As I mentioned, all of the Web Services that we've seen deployed are to known partners and customers, and it's more about deepening the relationship than creating a new profit center.

ALEX: *Your technology uses a hub model to route messages. How would that scale as the number of client messages grow?*

CRAIG: This is probably a more detailed conversation than we can effectively cover in this interview. We have deployed a two-tiered architecture where there are a few data centers coordinating with a large number of lightweight POPs [points of presences]. We feel that this architecture will scale very effectively and while doing so allows us to maintain appropriate levels of security and reliability.

ALEX: *Can you go into a little more depth?*

CRAIG: Sure. By taking this approach we can ensure the integrity and reliability of messages but do so in a way that is extremely easy and flexible to deploy by our customers. All of our POPs, which manage the proxies that I was talking about earlier, are hosted in 24 x 7 network operation centers with fully redundant capabilities such that we can guarantee the security, reliability, and the integrity of the data. Because they are hosted they are incredibly easy to deploy in front of any Web Service. We can swing them in front of everything from an IBM mainframe to an Excel spreadsheet, providing these services with enterprise-class security and reliability without having to install any software.

ALEX: *How does your firm work with some of the existing authentication initiatives such as Microsoft Passport and the Liberty Alliance spearheaded by Sun?*

CRAIG: Well, those authentications are for user authentication. Mainly we deal with machine-to-machine communication so our focus is more on working with folks like VeriSign. To the extent that Passport and the Liberty Alliance extend their models to include machine authentication, we would certainly embrace them as part of our framework, but it doesn't appear that it will happen for quite some time.

ALEX: *Currently the UDDI directories are being controlled by the technology vendors, including IBM, Microsoft, and others. Do you see directories for vertical industries formed by the market leaders in those particular industries—say, for example, a Baby Bell creating a UDDI directory solely for the telecommunications industry?*

CRAIG: My stance is probably more radical than most on this issue. I think everyone's going to have a UDDI directory. You're going to use it to maintain your list of services that you regularly interact with. As such, I think UDDI will look increasingly more like LDAP than Yahoo. I also believe that there will be public directories that will emphasize discovery and, as you've suggested, I think they will map to specific vertical industries.

ALEX: *One of the technologies that's been around for a while but has gotten a lot more attention recently is enterprise portals. There are a lot of conversations around how that's probably going to be the first contact for most people with Web Services, even though the user is probably not even aware of it. Is that what you're seeing right now?*

CRAIG: Web Services are just architecture and as such can be applied to a variety of problems. This includes EIP, or enterprise information portals, as well as application development and integration.

Within the context of integration, you are using Web Services to tie applications together into business processes. Within the context of application development, you are tying components together to create applications. Within the context of EIP, you are tying modules into portals. As to whether the EIP use case is going to happen first, I really can't say.

ALEX: *You touched on this a little bit earlier about the metering for billing purposes. Is it really feasible for a Web Services producer to* *charge for usage on transaction basis? The only company that comes to mind that has been successful at this is actually eBay.*

CRAIG: I guess the analogy I would use is a Web site, where using the Web was just a different way of producing your interface. So if you're Dun & Bradstreet and you took credit card authorizations and you made it into a Web Service, could you charge for it? Sure. It's just a different distribution channel or packaging. If you charge currently for tariff calculations or tax calculations, if you put a Web Service interface in front of it, could you charge for it? Sure.

It's simply about allowing you to be more broadly consumed. So I think to the extent that people have existing service-level interfaces that they currently charge for, that's almost a no-brainer to create an opportunity for a billing interface.

ALEX: *There's been a recent announcement with SAP adopting the whole Web Services initiative, and I think it took a lot of people by surprise. Do you see other companies announcing that? And also what is the broad implication of a company taking an application that big and actually adding Web Services support? How does that differ than using ABAP [the traditional way of interfacing with SAP]?*

CRAIG: I think this is a huge opportunity for all independent software vendors [ISVs]. If you think about a company like SAP or PeopleSoft, they may have viewed their application in the past in terms of their GUI interface—their human interface—but really what they've created is an application that runs a business process or multiple business processes. And just as important as creating a human interface to that business process or business processes is creating a machine interface, especially since that enables it to interact with other business processes. And by more deeply integrating within an enterprise, it creates switching costs, which are very valuable to those vendors.

I think the big transition that I've seen in the last six months is that many ISVs assumed that Web Services were about delivering their software as a service. And I think people are starting to come around to the notion that it's not about that, although that is an interesting opportunity with services. The real opportunity lies in how to create a machine interface or a service interface, not just a human interface, to an application and [to] view the application more as the process itself, not just in terms of the human interface.

ALEX: *Do you want to make any prediction of where you see this technology going in the next year? What are some major initiatives or some major assumptions you make in making your strategic plans for the next year or the next five years?*

CRAIG: I think you're going to see by the end of [2002] Web Services being deployed by early adopters to do B2B integration and internal integration as well as for EIP-oriented deployments. Web Services are an interesting model for internal application development and code reuse, but there are a lot of issues around configuration and change management that I think have a long way to go before this notion of there being billions and billions of components in the network that can be dynamically assembled into applications. I previously worked at a company that marketed an application development platform for object-oriented components. I have a hard time imagining that having a standard protocol and data format solves a lot of the problems that you have with using external components, specifically issues around reliability and change management. If you used a component to build your application and a thousand other people used it, how does that component ever get upgraded? What happens if there's an Internet problem?

ALEX: *So you've lived through that as well.*

CRAIG: I've lived through that. And I used to be a real optimist about it and now I'm [a] cynic, but I still believe that it will eventually happen. I just think there are a lot of issues that people have to think through. It's not just about the protocol.

ALEX: *Thanks again, Craig.*

▶ Summary

To provide value-added services on the basic standards, Web Services networks provide features such as guaranteed messaging, provisioning, and versioning. The two providers include Flamenco Networks and Grand Central.

Flamenco Networks provides a hybrid model: a peer-to-peer model for sending messages and a hub and spoke for data gathering and reporting. Grand Central uses a central hub model and is targeting firms that can benefit from outsourcing business processes that involve multiple trading partners.

Web Services Architectural Patterns

A software architecture results from determining the business requirements and then making a series of decisions with trade-offs to meet these requirements. Many of these decisions involve identifying functionality in existing systems, determining the functionality gaps, and then producing a plan to address these gaps. An experienced architect rarely starts from scratch in making a decision. Instead, experience teaches the architect to look for recurring themes; such themes are called **patterns**.

The term **architectural patterns** describes decisions made by software architects; that is, they form a vocabulary in such a way that architects can communicate a series of decisions without having to explain each decision in isolation. A pattern should also point out the necessary preconditions for the pattern as well as the pros and cons of using the pattern.

A common architectural pattern, for example, delineates functionality so that the business logic is not dependent on the GUI. This allows the business logic to be reusable across a number of display mechanisms (desktop, wireless, etc.) without its having to be recompiled (recompiling creates vulnerability to potential bugs being introduced—a maintenance nightmare). In architecting Web Services systems, there are certain recurring themes, or architectural patterns.

Before we look at these architectural patterns, let's examine the differences between an architectural pattern and each of these: a design pattern, an architectural principle, a framework, and a software platform.

A **design pattern** (the term was popularized by the book, *Design Patterns: Elements of Reusable Software*) may affect how one or more classes are designed.[1] Two of the popular design patterns are **Abstract Factory** and **Composite**. An architectural pattern, on the other hand, is a higher level decision (and typically made earlier in the project than a design pattern) and involves the way in which systems should communicate with each other. Examples of Web Services architectural patterns are discussed in the next section.

- An **architectural principle** is a goal that an enterprise acknowledges or wishes to achieve, whereas an architectural pattern is a vocabulary built from recurring occurrences of a series of decisions. Software architects can use this vocabulary to meaningfully communicate architectural decisions, and designers can use it to communicate design decisions. An example of a principle might be "Plan for change and design for it." This does not boil down to any particular series of steps, but it is a goal the architect needs to pay specific attention to as the system is architected.

- A **framework** is an extensible set of classes that are commercially purchased or bundled with the language. Developers can use these classes to code systems. Two popular frameworks include the Standard Template Library (for C++) and the Swing framework (in Java). Frameworks are used exclusively with object-oriented languages (contrasted with libraries, which can be for both object-oriented and non-object-oriented languages). Frameworks and class libraries are also referred to as **application program interfaces** (**APIs**) because they both define the methods (or, for non-object-oriented languages, functions) that the developer must learn in order to be productive.

- A **software platform** is an environment on which a system can be built. A software platform is sometimes referred to as a soft-

---

1. *Design Patterns: Elements of Reusable Software*, [Erich Gamma et al., Addison-Wesley, 1995]. While design patterns are not used exclusively with object-oriented systems, the examples listed in the book use mostly object-oriented languages. For the sake of simplicity, this discussion on design patterns assumes object-oriented languages.

Chapter **7** | Web Services Architectural Patterns

ware stack because technologies are built on top of one another, forming a stack. Examples of a software platform include

- A series of frameworks such as J2EE, which defines an implementation language, a set of specifications, and a number of frameworks.
- An application server, which is yet another layer built on top of the J2EE platform. As an example, many enterprise software companies, such as Vignette and ATG, both of which provide personalization products, build their software products on top of the WebLogic application server.
- A database, such as Oracle.

Keep in mind that Web Services do not define any particular language, or even protocol, for that matter. Web Services architectural patterns revolve around loose coupling and interoperability—two of the main goals of Web Services. The architectural patterns are

- Native Web Services
- Web Services proxy
- Document-centric Web Services
- Orchestration Web Services

We will look at each of these patterns, listing the pros and cons of each at the end of its respective section.

▶ Native Web Services

In the case of the native Web Services architectural pattern, the existing functionality is directly exposed for outside clients. This pattern is useful for simple stateless services that provide read-only information, e.g., a stock quote or a weather report. Many of the existing IDEs and tools (Cape Studio from Cape Clear, for example) provide this service, taking an existing piece of functionality, such as a stateless EJB component, and then generating proxies with which to access the functionality. In this case, the incoming SOAP request is routed directly to a corresponding method in the EJB. Figure 7–1 illustrates this concept.

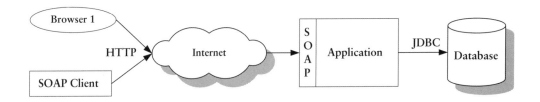

Figure 7-1   The native Web Services pattern.

Pros:

- Simple and automatically supported by many tools, even low-end ones

Cons:

- Requires direct exposure of classes, which can potentially create tight coupling issues

▶ Web Services Proxy

In cases where it is not desirable (or possible) to expose an existing piece of functionality directly, the **proxy** pattern is useful.[2] The proxy is an object that sits in front of the true recipient and forwards messages as necessary. This pattern is quite common and occurs in the case of stubs and skeletons in CORBA and RMI, as well as in other forms of middleware. In a sense, the proxy serves as the public interface for the real recipient, thus offering a form of decoupling. This would be used, for example, in situations where the destination is written in a language that does not offer SOAP bindings—the proxy communicates with the client in SOAP but with the recipient in some protocol other than SOAP. Figure 7-2 illustrates this concept.

---

2. Long-time readers of *Design Patterns: Elements of Reusable Software*, by the Gang of Four, would classify this as a design pattern. However, other works classify this as an architectural pattern.

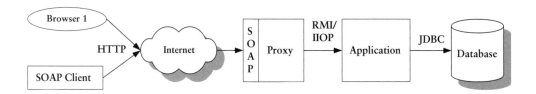

Figure 7-2 The proxy pattern.

Pros:

- Allows the reuse of existing systems without having to SOAP enable them
- Hides the implementation details of the real recipient from the public world, thus offering a looser form of coupling

Cons:

- Incurs an extra layer of indirection, which may cause performance issues

▶ Document-centric Web Services

As mentioned earlier, one of the characteristics of an enterprise Web Service is a business-level interface. This implies a document-centric form of communication, as opposed to an RPC-based communication. The document-centric approach is useful for reducing network traffic and is usually used with asynchronous systems.

Pros:

- Reduces coupling between the sender and the recipient
- Reduces the potential network traffic, thus potentially increasing throughput (not necessarily performance)

Cons:

- Requires significant investment in defining appropriate document format

▶ Orchestration Web Services

The orchestration Web Services pattern is useful for situations in which there is a workflow associated with the Web Service; in other words, the sequence in which the associated Web Services are invoked is important. Instead of building intelligence into each individual Web Service, the workflow is handled externally by an integration broker or an orchestration server, such as the one marketed by Collaxa. An orchestration server is similar to an integration broker except that an orchestration server has been natively designed to handle Web Services (Collaxa provides the concept of a Scenario Bean, which is the topic of Appendix C). Thus, the message may be transformed and/or routed, depending on the contents of the message. By externalizing the workflow outside of the Web Services (rather than having the Web Services directly call each other), each Web Service is more reusable and less fragile. Figure 7–3 illustrates this concept.

A variation on the orchestration pattern is an aggregator model, which takes rather primitive Web Services and builds them into more complex ones. Such organizations, called Web Services networks (and discussed in Chapter 6), may potentially provide additional value—billing, logging, etc.—that may or may not be on Web Services.

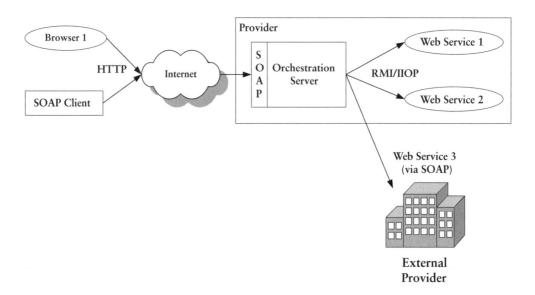

Figure 7–3   The orchestration pattern.

Pros:

- Allows for complex business scenarios through routing, transformations, and orchestration
- Provides reuse by externalizing the workflow

Cons:

- Can add significant complexity and costs to the solution

▶ Summary

Architects can use architectural patterns as a vocabulary for describing recurring themes when building solutions. Each architectural pattern includes pros and cons, and the software architect needs to be aware of these trade-offs before adopting a pattern.

A Plan for Adopting Web Services

As is always the case when adopting any new technology, companies should proceed cautiously when adopting Web Services. Fortunately, as we have shown, Web Services are not a completely new technology as much as extensions or refinements of existing technologies. Nevertheless, the most effective way to use Web Services is to identify the business objectives, take inventory of existing assets (skills, hardware, software, etc.), and then select a pilot project with which to launch the Web Service.

The following list of steps necessary for adopting Web Services is from the perspective of the Web Services provider because that role requires the most effort.

- Identify goals
- Select the pilot project
- Learn the standards
- Address gaps in the standards
- Re-evaluate the development process
- Organize the workflow
- Use existing infrastructure
- Publish the Web Services
- Manage the Web Services

- Pick the tools and vendor
- Build the budget and schedule

Each of these steps is discussed in detail in this chapter.

▶ Identify Goals

Web Services can offer many benefits:

- **Significantly lowering integration costs.** The case studies throughout this book have illustrated that some early adopters have seen significant savings for certain types of integration projects.
- **Opening new markets.** In many cases, certain markets are not accessible to a company because the adoption and support costs are too high. However, with reduced integration costs, markets that could not be profitably served before can now be reevaluated.
- **Reducing the skills shortage.** Traditional integration approaches (middleware, EAI, etc.) tend to require fairly esoteric skills (which, by definition, are rare and hence expensive), whereas Web Services offer the possibility of integration without needing such skills.

A firm may have one or more goals. For example, one firm may want to adopt Web Services to reduce the integration costs of an existing project, whereas another firm may want to use Web Services to penetrate an otherwise unprofitable market segment, e.g., the small business market.

▶ Select the Pilot Project

One of the key things Web Services offer is a better association between key business processes and technology. Therefore, before embarking on a pilot project, ideally the team should build a business process model and identify key business processes that would make the most use of Web Services. Pick two or three business processes that provide high value but are not overly complex; use these as the requirements for the pilot project. Those two or three business processes could easily translate into 20–30 low-level method invocations.

Remember that the public interface for the business processes should be coarse grained (i.e., at the business level) rather than granular (at the method level). This translates into a lower learning curve for the Web Services client, regardless of whether the client is internal staff or an external trading partner.

Learn the Standards

Given how fast the standards evolve (even faster than most other segments of the high-tech industry), the team should stay current on the core standards (XML, SOAP, UDDI, WSDL). Just as important, the team needs to determine how well the selected platform (see the "Pick the tools and vendor" section) implements these major standards. Unfortunately, given the embryonic stage of this market, the team may not be able to determine the platform's support (or lack thereof) of these standards until the pilot project is completed.

Note that the team should also be aware of industry-specific XML standards. For example, in the HR industry, there is the HRXML Consortium, which is defining the HRXML standard for sharing HR-related information. Likewise, in the financial industry, an emerging standard is RIXML (Research Information Exchange Markup Language), designed for sharing research information among buy-side and sell-side firms.

Address Gaps in the Standards

As discussed throughout this book, the core standards do not define the necessary infrastructure required to build and deploy many types of enterprise Web Services. Missing standards include security, transaction control, guaranteed messaging, and workflow. However, these standards may not be completely necessary, depending on the nature of the project.

Let's look at one example. The IT team at the investment bank Putnam Lovell Securities (see the case study in Appendix B) used Web Services (in conjunction with a Web Services network, Grand Central) to publish personalized financial data for its customers by integrating two key applications (both hosted by third-party vendors outside of the firm's firewall). Previously, this business process was performed manually, which was time consuming and prone to errors. However, since the financial information is read only by the customers, the lack of a transaction standard did not affect the success of the first iteration of the project. The firm still met its goals of improved customer service and saved a significant amount of manpower. In addition, the CTO estimated that using traditional middleware would not have been feasible (or cost effective) since the applications did not reside in-house.

The team should also determine whether initiatives such as ebXML would be helpful in addressing some of the gaps. For example, ebXML provides a predefined catalog of business processes—this can potentially provide a jump start on many projects. (For more information on ebXML, see Appendix A.)

▶ Re-Evaluate the Development Process

For many teams, the ability to expose and share business processes with the outside world may be uncharted territory and can potentially affect how systems are developed. Undertaking the task of publishing the processes to outsiders requires involvement from the business analysts because the interface to these business processes tends to be coarse—i.e., to have fewer operations—than would be the case if the system were exposed using traditional middleware. Nevertheless, deciding which of those operations—even though fewer in number—should be made public is not a trivial matter.

For these reasons, the team should perform an explicit business modeling step—a step normally missing in most organizations during the development process—to identify how these business processes can best be shared, invoked, and maintained as they are deployed. To learn more about this step, see the Pantechnik International case study in Appendix B.

▶ Organize the Workflow

Once the business process modeling is accomplished, there is a possibility that the identified business processes require the use of external published processes. Remember that one of the advantages of using Web Services is composition—the ability to create higher level business processes from more elementary ones. This then requires orchestrating with external providers to define additional parameters such as these:

- What is the expected data format that the two parties need to exchange?
- What happens if the primitive Web Service fails?

Of course, this should all be handled so that it is transparent to the external Web Services consumer. Consider a lender who requires the financial history and potentially the driving history of the loan applicant before approving a loan. In this case, the lender is probably using two external services—one for the financial history and the other for the driving record—to determine the creditworthiness of the loan applicant since neither of these services is in the lender's core competence.

This workflow can be handled by the underlying application logic or it can be externalized through an orchestration server, such as the one provided by Collaxa's Orchestration Server.

▶ Use Existing Infrastructure

Again, Web Services are not about a total rebuilding of a company's entire IT infrastructure; they instead provide a way to facilitate communications between systems. As such, an organization should maximize existing infrastructure wherever possible. This includes skills, hardware, and software.

Skills

From a skills perspective, Web Services require that the developers be familiar with XML, SOAP, UDDI, and WSDL at the minimum. This is not as daunting as it sounds: Many of the tools can help generate the code necessary to register the Web Service into the repository and the WSDL necessary to invoke the Web Service. XML is a fairly easy language—or, more specifically, metalanguage—to learn, although designing the appropriate XML schemas (for maximum reuse and maintainability) for the documents is not trivial. Remember that the majority of the Web Services' functionality resides in some system behind the firewall; therefore, the skills necessary to develop or extend that application may be scarcer or more critical than those needed to register and invoke the Web Service.

Consider a firm that wants to expose to a limited set of trading partners three key business processes of an application that is executing on a mainframe. This requires three steps:

1. Defining the interface in WSDL
2. Publishing it to a UDDI registry (public, protected, or private)
3. Defining the document structure to pass information into and out of the mainframe application (via SOAP).

In this case, the scarcer resources may be the developers who understand the mainframe (and the associated business processes) rather than the people who are necessary to produce the WSDL and SOAP documents.

Hardware

The additional parsing of (potentially large) XML documents can affect the need for additional hardware, but it will not be an order of magnitude greater. However, network latency should be taken into consideration, depending on whether the system is built using an asynchronous or synchronous architecture. For an asynchronous system, the initial passing of the document may be noticeable depending on the size of the XML document. For a synchronous system, the network latency may be noticeable if there is a sufficiently high number of round-trip invocations. To address the issue of passing large documents (which can result in time-outs depending on the network connection), see the next section.

Software

The majority of existing vendors—including application server vendors (BEA Systems, IBM, etc.) and middleware/integration broker vendors (Iona, webMethods, Vitria, etc.)—are adding Web Services support to their product offerings. This usually means that the product can parse incoming SOAP requests and return the results in a SOAP-compliant envelope. Other vendors (e.g., Cape Clear and Shinka Technologies) are providing toolkits that can take existing functionality (such as Java EJBs) and expose the desired functionality as SOAP calls.

However, as mentioned in the previous section, there are other issues that may need to be considered. For example, a firm would like to provide corporate data to a remote sales staff. By the nature of its work, this group can connect using only dial-up connections. Thus, the challenge of passing potentially large XML documents is not trivial. In this case, consider adopting a software solution such as Flamenco Networks[1] (more specifically, the proxy that is installed on the local machine) which provides streaming of XML documents.

If guaranteed messaging is required, consider investing in a messaging software infrastructure such as Sonic Software's SonicXQ or IBM's MQSeries. Remember that network performance *behind* a firewall is considerably more reliable than performance *beyond* the firewall; hence the potential need for a messaging infrastructure.

▶ Publish the Web Services

Of course, in order for the Web Services to be useful, they need to be published to a registry. For our pilot project, the decision then becomes whether the registry should be private or protected. For most pilot projects, the decision will be private.

---

1. It may seem odd to list a network under software, but Flamenco's product is not a physical hardware network. Instead, with this product, the firm installs a small proxy on the local and remote machines, resulting in a peer-to-peer network.

The next challenge is how to notify the appropriate parties of the existence of the Web Service. This can happen in a proactive mode (notifying the consumer through multiple means such as fax, email,[2] or phone) or reactive mode (the consumer needs to contact the Web Service[s] providers). Of course, unless the Web Service is completely intended for mass consumption, there should be an authentication and an authorization step.

Manage the Web Services

Once the Web Service has been published and used, the next issue that has to be resolved is how to manage it. Many business processes are associated with an SLA (service-level agreement) that defines acceptable parameters for the execution and management of the Web Service (a common metric is the uptime of the application). Since there are no existing Web Services standards for defining the management of Web Services, the provider needs to add custom functionality to report this information back to the consumers, should they ask about it.

Another option is to buy (or rent) this functionality in the form of a Web Services network (two examples, Grand Central Communications and Flamenco Networks, are profiled in Chapter 6). At minimum, these products provide data collection and reporting features that can report the success of processed messages; this can be correlated to the uptime of the back-end systems handling the Web Services.

Pick the Tools and Vendor

In selecting the tools and vendor, the team should focus first on the business objectives. Is the intent to reduce integration costs for an existing project, or is it something else? Taking integration cost reduction as an objective, the team then needs to answer questions such as what development languages/tools are currently being used and do they provide the necessary features. Again, as mentioned earlier, many

2. An advantage of using email is that a link can be embedded in the email. The notified party merely needs to click on the link to activate the Web Service.

Chapter **8** | A Plan for Adopting Web Services

(but not all) vendors have pledged or have already delivered support for Web Services.

Most of the examples provided in this book have focused on the J2EE platform (where Java is the predominant development language) and Microsoft's .NET (which supports over 20 languages, but the languages of choice are VB.NET and C#), but there are SOAP libraries (a prerequisite for adopting Web Services) for perl and other languages as well.

Again, Web Services do not provide any processing functionality per se, so the choice of selecting the tools and platform should be considered with multiple factors in mind—e.g., the cost of training on those languages,[3] the availability of already trained staff (internally or externally), the existing investment, licensing costs,[4] support options, deployment costs, and finan-cial stability of the vendors.[5]

▶ Build the Budget and Schedule

Once the business objectives have been determined, the scope has been defined, and the tools have been selected, a preliminary budget and schedule should be built. While it is always advisable to build in a considerable amount of padding when estimating the level of effort needed for working with new technologies, an interesting contrast here is that these figures may be less than originally envisioned. Early adopters have quoted significant cost savings due to lower licensing costs and ease of integration. For more information on these case studies, see Appendix B.

As a caveat, most of the case studies included in this book are from early adopters who are quite proficient technically; they already understood many of the underlying principles behind Web Services (including a service-oriented architecture, *n*-tier architectures, pros and cons of synchronous and asynchronous architectures, and pros and cons of

---

3. For example, many analysts are claiming that there may be a large defection of VB programmers from the Microsoft world because of the large learning curve in learning VB.NET due to many changes in it.
4. Note that open-source alternatives such as open-source application servers (JBoss, etc.) exist for many of these tools. In addition, there are efforts to port a portion of the .NET platform to open-source technologies as well.
5. Since this is such an embryonic market, many of the vendors that exist today may not be around in 18 to 24 months.

stateful and stateless servers). Thus, the figures quoted need to be balanced when building a budget and schedule for a team that is currently doing mainframe development or client-server development. Developers who are adept in these two broad environments require a longer learning curve because they have to learn other aforementioned issues in order to deploy Web Services effectively.

▶ Summary

Adopting Web Services requires planning and identifying gaps in the existing standards. Many of these gaps can be addressed through third-party products such as Web Services networks or through industry initiatives such as ebXML. Fortunately, the skills necessary to develop Web Services already exist in many firms because they are an extension of many existing technologies, including application servers and XML.

One thing that organizations need to determine is how best to manage the entire life cycle. Developing Web Services is often more straightforward than trying to manage them after they have been deployed. Again, products such as Web Services networks can help address this issue as well.

Emerging Trend: Software as a Service

While much has been written about **Software as a Service (SAAS)** and Web Services, there is still much confusion. Although the two terms are related, they are not necessarily synonymous. The premise behind SAAS is that software can be ordered, delivered, upgraded, and supported as a utility similar to voicemail or electricity. One key that differentiates an SAAS firm from a traditional software firm is that the revenue is recurring. This model has gotten more attention lately because major firms such as Microsoft, Computer Associates, and Oracle are moving toward this revenue recognition model.

Web Services, on the other hand, use an integration approach along with related technologies. An SAAS firm may or may not be using Web Services to provide the service to the customer.

This chapter looks at some of the characteristics of an SAAS solution as well as some factors that have to be considered before adopting such a solution. It concludes with an interview with an SAAS pioneer, Employease.

▶ Value Proposition

SAAS affects the way an application is accessed (operational issues), the way an application is installed (deployment issues), and the way an application is billed (the revenue model). On one hand, many would argue that an SAAS firm is simply another way of saying ASP (application service provider). For our purposes, we define an SAAS application as one that is billed on a recurring basis and that was built from the ground up to run natively on the Internet. Contrast this with a typical ASP, which starts with a large ERP application (a monolithic application) and then requires the client to have either a high bandwidth connection or a local installation of the Citrix Winframe application just to execute the application. Obviously this severely limits the accessibility of the application as well as the deployment costs. In addition, the challenge for the ASP is that each customer needs an instance of the application (thus requiring an instance of the database as well), which means that signing on new customers does not bring the economy of scale as expected.

The main proposed benefits of an SAAS application are

- **Considerably less up-front investment.** Unlike a traditional enterprise software sale requiring a large initial capital outlay, an SAAS application is billed on a recurring basis (usually monthly) and, as such, requires a payment spread over time. See the following section for different examples of how SAAS firms bill clients.
- **No hidden costs.** In many cases, the true cost of a solution is not the price of the software (and hardware) but the level of effort required to install and potentially customize the software. In most cases, the cost of customization can be 3 to 20 times that of the purchase price. Also note that, for most applications, the majority of the **total cost of ownership** (**TCO**) occurs after the application is in production. This is sometimes known as the **iceberg factor** because the hidden risk is much more than the visible risk.
- **Shorter launch time.** To adopt a solution through an SAAS firm typically requires provisioning the service, and in many cases this can be accomplished in a few days to a few weeks. Contrast this with building an in-house solution which can take months of development time.

- **No in-house development expertise needed.** For many firms, the scarcest resource is the availability of properly trained developers. By adopting a solution offered by an SAAS firm, this scarcity is no longer an issue.

- **Definable operational parameters.** Since most SAAS firms have to support a large customer base in order to be profitable, they are heavily financially motivated to deliver quality software backed with an SLA to measure operational reliability.

- **Automatic upgrades.** Again, most SAAS firms invest in adding new features to attract new customers; existing customers can benefit from these newly added features.

- **Access to business domain expertise.** In many cases, SAAS firms offer business expertise bundled into the application being offered. For this reason, SAAS firms are often called **business service providers (BSPs)**. Some examples of successful BSPs and what they do: Employease (profiled below) focuses on delivering an eHR solution; Fidesic focuses on delivering an electronic invoicing and payment system; eBuilder provides a service to help reduce design and construction times; ClickLogistics provides logistics-outsourced services. All of these firms have captured their expertise in their respective domains in the software offering, and subscribers can benefit from this domain expertise.

SAAS firms often get the undeserved reputation of being a good solution for small and medium-sized businesses. However, many large firms often decide that IT is not in their core competence and, in such cases, an SAAS offering may be the way to go.

As with everything, making a decision involves making a series of trade-offs. In selecting an SAAS vendor, keep the following points in mind:

- It is highly unlikely that any software service will offer 100% of the functionality desired by a client. In this particular case, the 80/20 rule may need to be applied; that is, get 80% of the functionality for 20% of the cost. The remaining 20% of functionality often requires massive customization and many times is not possible due to the fact that these firms focus on keeping their implementation as generalized as possible to minimize additional development and maintenance costs.

- The SAAS firm's financial viability should be taken into account because many SAAS firms have seriously underestimated the capital requirements needed to provide an acceptable level of service and the customer acquisition costs.

Revenue Models

Another key characteristic of an SAAS firm is the billing model. Most firms in this category do not charge a lump sum for the initial purchase. Instead they charge on a per-user (or per-beneficiary) basis, a transactional basis, or a connection basis. The SAAS firm then bills its clients on a monthly basis.

An example of a firm that charges by the beneficiary is Employease. Employease provides an electronic human resource (eHR) solution, in which the target user is the HR administrator, but all employees are the actual beneficiaries of the system. The next section is an interview with the cofounder of Employease, a pioneer in the SAAS market and a market leader in the eHR business.

Interview: Employease, an SAAS Pioneer

Employease was founded in 1996 and produces the Employease Network System for HR administrators to administer benefits and related tasks. In this interview, the firm shares how it has used Web Services, the importance of XML vertical standards, and the role of ebXML.

Interviewee: John Alberg, cofounder and VP of engineering of Employease

ALEX: *Please explain what Employease is and your role at the organization.*

JOHN: Employease builds, sells, and operates a hosted Human Resource and Benefits Management Application. It was built from the ground up for the Internet. The rationale is that we can deliver this type of solution much more economically to large companies and make this type of capability, i.e., complex business applications, accessible to smaller companies by delivering it in this way.

I am a founder of Employease and have been in charge of technology for it since its inception in 1996. My role has included both writing the software originally and, more recently, directing the engineering group and the strategic direction technology for the company.

ALEX: *Your organization was probably the first organization to promote the concept of Software as a Service. What motivated you to go down that path when everybody else was doing client-server?*

JOHN: Employease was actually started in the heyday of client-server. In 1996 you had PeopleSoft and SAP, and they were making a fortune off the client-server model. When we started Employease, I was working for a company called Booz Allen Hamilton [and] worked on a lot of large technology infrastructure projects. The project of mine that was most influential in our thinking was for the Department of Justice. It was an automated booking station that allowed law enforcement professionals to take a suspect's fingerprints, take their picture, enter charges and demographic information, and then combine all that multimedia through a client-server application. The information was synchronized through the client-server interface to a centralized national repository of booking records.

At the same time, the Internet was appearing on the horizon. Netscape was about to go public, and Amazon was still a business plan. But I was very aware of the Internet and using the Mosaic browser in my work and thought, "Wouldn't it be an interesting thing to connect browser to a database?" It's a pretty well-understood concept now, but it was fairly novel at the time.

And so, while brainstorming with a friend, we thought, "Okay, what is the area of corporate America that could most benefit from having an Internet browser directly connected to a database?" Human resources seemed like an obvious area for this technology. We thought that based on a number of experiences. To give you one, my office mate had recently been married [while I was working at Booz Allen], and he spent the entire day on the phone with the human resource department trying to figure out how to get his spouse into his benefit plans. So, not only was he a billable consultant, spending his day trying to figure this out, but it was wasting the HR person's time too. And I thought, "Wouldn't this all be more efficient and cost effective if you could go on to the Internet and enroll in these benefit plans?"

Now, our decision to actually implement what is now called Software as a Service stemmed from a couple of things. One, it seemed like it was a pretty economic approach, as we were a start-up company and didn't have a lot of resources. Building an application, managing multiple versions, printing CDs, and sending those out to customers seemed like a pretty daunting task. One likes to think that we had some grand vision of Software as a Service in 1996, but we didn't. We were actually just looking for the most effective and economic way to deliver our vision, which was taking database applications and delivering them to people through a Web browser. And the most effective way that we could see to do that was in a hosted environment.

ALEX: *Your platform supports multiple customers on the same instance. How did you account for this scalability?*

JOHN: Well, there are a couple of things. We actually find that, if you have one instance, the system's going to be more scalable because you're not going to have to manage a separate system for each customer. Therefore, if you do an upgrade, you have to upgrade one system. If you do any sort of maintenance, you're doing it to one system. We have over a thousand customers and, if we had to manage a thousand separate instances of the application, it would be a nightmare.

The same is true if you had a thousand separate instances and your customers have very specific customization requests. You'd be tempted to actually change the code. Managing a thousand different code bases and a thousand different databases is not, in my opinion, an economic way to scale a business. And I actually think that's the failure of the ASP model—that they went out there thinking they could take a client-server application and economically host separate instances for each customer.

In the end, what you end up doing is putting so many resources on the management of each individual installation that it is difficult to realize any profit margin from the business. The only way you can be really successful in a Software-as-a-Service world is if you have a single instance of the application and you have all of your customers accessing it.

One of the terms or phrases we've coined here (on how to build a profitable operation) is you need to ensure that the **complexity** of your operation doesn't increase with the number of customers.

If the complexity of that operation increases with the number of cus-tomers, your costs are going to increase with the number of customers. If your costs increase with the number of customers, again, you can't lead a profitable business. So the way that we've looked at it is: we build one system; its *complexity* never changes, but its *capacity* does. So, as we add new customers, we add more servers to the system, but the complexity doesn't increase. And in the end what you get is a very scalable system.

ALEX: *Can you comment a little on how you actually do capacity planning and also how do you account for the various loads of the number of concurrent users since, as an Internet-based application, you don't know how many people are going to be using the system on a given time?*

JOHN: Well, yes and no. I mean, we are able to accurately measure how many users are on the system, and we know how many customers are in implementation. So we can predict pretty easily 30, 60 days out what the utilization of the system is going to be.

But for a company like Employease, it's all about peak usage. There are certain times of year when people do a lot of benefit transactions, and that's in the fall when companies are enrolling in benefit plans [with] a first of the year effective date. So what we attempt to do is plan for that peak and estimate how many open enrollments there are going to be during the course of September and October, and we'll make sure we have the system in place to handle that.

To us, that means we set the maximum system utilization at 50% of our capacity. If utilization ever goes over 50% of our capacity, we add more servers. And the way that we've architected the system—through an application tier that has many servers—allows us to scale by adding servers.

It's as opposed to the more traditional scaling model where you have a single machine (with multiple CPUs) that handles all of the transac-tions and maybe a fail-over machine for redundancy.

I think what we've seen within the last five years on the Internet is that people are looking not toward bigger machines with more CPUs but [toward] lower profile machines with one CPU and a network-attached storage device, and then stacking those servers to handle the load.

By doing so, you scale with the network as opposed to scaling with the number of CPUs. And that seems to be much more efficient; performance scales linearly by adding servers to a load-balanced application tier. I think we've proven over and over again that adding CPUs to a single server doesn't scale linearly.

ALEX: *The Employease Network System is actually integrated to other business partners for additional value as well. Can you elaborate on an example of how the integration happens on a technical and on a business level?*

JOHN: Yes. In human resources, payroll, and benefits, it's very important to be able to connect to other systems. And we understood that right out of the gate—that in order for this to be successful, at a minimum, we'd need to be able to communicate payroll information from the Employease Network into payroll systems.

So we invested quite a bit of energy and resources into building something we call Employease Connect, a product which allows us to easily integrate the Employease Network into other disparate systems. This was a challenging problem because, unlike in the client-server world where all the systems were in the four walls of the company and they're all on private networks, we're having to transfer data between or integrate systems that may be 3,000 miles apart and behind very secure firewalls.

So we create an export capability where you can set up jobs on some frequency such as daily or weekly or monthly. You can export those jobs in any format to the third-party vendor or third-party system. In addition we developed a programmable interface that allows one of our customer service engineers to build an export to an arbitrary specification. And it's a plug-in architecture, so, once a plug-in is created, we can drop it into the production environment without bringing down the system or doing a major release. We can drop it into the system so that customers can start receiving their export at whatever frequency they want.

ALEX: *Can you comment on the level of effort it takes to integrate a new partner and also the level of effort it takes to provision a new customer?*

JOHN: Implementations are done between 30 and 60 days. The important thing here is that we measure implementations in weeks rather than months. First, an implementation typically involves loading the Employease database and setting up the business rules. The second part of the implementation is building connections to the one, two, or three other systems that the customer wants to connect with. A connection may take a week to build, but typically the connection-building [time] is not in the actual time to code it. It's in getting the specification and testing it, debugging it, and making sure that it works properly in the production environment.

Usually we can crank out a connection pretty quickly, especially if it's a system we've already built to. We categorize our connections into two groups. One is productized connections (which are connections that we do over and over again, such as connecting to a major payroll system) or unproductized [custom-built] connections. And we charge separately for the different types of connections.

ALEX: *How are you taking advantage of XML on your system, and what XML standards are important to you as an organization? You mentioned ebXML and HRXML in a previous presentation. Can you elaborate on how those standards help or how you take advantage of them?*

JOHN: Well, ebXML gives us a business layer. XML is very broad in its range and its specifications. ebXML gives us a way to do a business transaction layer in a way that it's generally accepted. There still probably needs to be more convergence on how these wrappers and business layers work. But for the most part, we choose an existing standard rather than building something proprietary. We adopted ebXML.

We're also a member of the HRXML Consortium, and this is where our involvement and enthusiasm for XML is pretty high. We're one of the charter members of the Consortium. HRXML is a group of companies who are particularly interested in using XML in the area of human resources, payroll, and benefits. They have gotten together to set standards in a way that HR and benefit-related information are communicated.

Right now we will communicate data to a customer or a third party in any format they choose. But it's expensive for them because they have to hire us to build that connection for them. What we would like to have customers adopt on a larger scale is to transmit data in standard HRXML and XML formats. When we do that, turning on a connection for a customer is literally the flick of a switch. By using that kind of prepublished standard, we could bring the cost of integration down for our customers by a large margin. And so that's the main reason we've adopted it [HRXML].

We also feel that it's worthwhile for all of the vendors—whether it's PeopleSoft or Employease, Aetna or U.S. Health Care—to adopt a similar standard. That's why getting involved with the HRXML Consortium has been very important to us. To summarize, we do exports for our customers in any format that they want, and we've been doing that since inception. With the advent of XML, we saw an opportunity to start setting standards for how information is exported and, therefore, reduce the costs for our customers. And that's where we've put a lot of our emphasis in the last year.

ALEX: *So would it be fair to say that, with HRXML, one of the key benefits that it provides is to find a standard structure which companies can agree on so they don't have to define their own proprietary data formats?*

JOHN: Yes.

ALEX: *Can you elaborate on the cost structure, of, say, for a customer to adopt your product versus, say, trying to do the same functionality in-house? Is cost saving the biggest factor, or is it time to market? Or are there other benefits? If there are savings, can you elaborate on what is the savings over an annual basis? On a monthly basis?*

JOHN: I'll articulate this the way that we articulate it to a prospect. When you're looking at a license-based product versus a Software-as-a-Service offering, you typically only see the tip of the iceberg in terms of cost. For initial costs, you're looking at $100,000–$200,000 license fee versus a monthly recurring fee of maybe $1,000 or $2,000 [for SAAS].

The reality is that the real costs associated with this decision are below the surface for client-server. In addition to paying the license fee, you're also going to have to get the software implemented. It's well understood that implementations can run three to five times the cost of the license fee. So, after you pay $200,000, you end up paying, for example, half a million in implementation fees.

Furthermore, with client-server, you need to hire individuals to manage, maintain the application, [and] upgrade the applications. A DBA [database administrator] can cost a company $85,000–$100,000 a year just to keep the system up and running. You need to invest in things like wide area networks [WANs], and you need to build out a data center.

With Software as a Service, the tip of the iceberg is the recurring monthly fee, but below the surface there's not much there. You have an implementation, but implementations, at least from what we've seen with Software as a Service, run much quicker than they do with traditional, complex, license-based client-server software.

In addition to the implementation, the only other resource you need is Internet access to use the application. All the other things such as building out the hardware, building the network, hiring DBAs are not a cost with a Software-as-a-Service model. So the result is that you can realize a tremendous cost savings. Employease has numerous customers that have gone on record and are claiming that they've saved something on the order of $600,000 a year from implementing and using the Employease Network over traditional client-server-based systems.

ALEX: *How is running the firm with a recurring revenue base different than running a firm with a more traditional structure where sales are built on a quarterly basis? Can you elaborate on how that affects some of your tactical and strategic decisions?*

JOHN: First, the issue of scalability is that much more important, because you're running an [24/7] operation. It goes back to my initial statement: you care about things like how scalable the software is. In the client-server world, you want scalable software because ultimately the customer will be happier if it scales better. With Software as a Service, if your system doesn't scale well, you go out of business. It's that simple. So obviously you spend a great deal of time thinking about the operational aspects of your business.

Beyond engineering, there are a lot of business things that have to be considered. For example, a dollar of recurring revenue is worth a lot more than a dollar of licensed-based revenue, and so investors think that's very attractive. It does, however, take longer to build a recurring revenue base than it does to build traditional license based because you're layering on small recurring fees as opposed to getting revenues in big gulps.

So for the software executive from the client-server world, that may be a little disappointing at first. But again, the investment community has shown again and again that having a recurring revenue base in the long run is highly rewarded, and entrepreneurs will be rewarded for their patience in building one.

ALEX: *You mentioned an advantage of your model is more streamlined upgrades where the customer simply doesn't have to have an operational staff in-house. But it would seem like there could potentially be a problem if you upgrade the entire network and the customer moves with the upgrade, even though they may want an earlier version. Has that ever been an issue? Additionally, are there any potential issues, in the future, if you have different XML schemas for the data migration?*

JOHN: Well, there are really two issues here. One is, when I think of the user of the Employease Network, I think of an HR administrator, typically a nontechnical person, and they use the product through a graphical user interface on a daily basis. Maybe they download a file and upload it into a payroll system. For the most part, they don't deal with data in the kind of traditional data analyst manipulation sense.

Typically, when they think of data integration, it is something that happens in the background. Data goes from the Employease Network directly to the payroll vendor or directly to the third party, such as an insurance company. The point I'm trying to make there is that that's very different than our integrations with third parties. So it's almost like you have two customers: one, which is the HR administrator who has upgrades and so forth to the product, and the other is the third-party vendors who we might have to upgrade the connections to their systems—two very separate products and entities, and, in fact, we call them separate things. One is the Employease Network and one is Employease Connect.

On the Employease Network side, it's interesting. Sometimes people say, "Well, isn't there an issue around automatically upgrading the product?" And my perspective is "Not at all." From our customers' perspective, it's nothing but benefits, and the way to understand that is to compare it to the client-server world. In the client-server world, when you had an upgrade to a product, it literally brought the customer—that end user, that HR administrator—their daily activity to a halt. And as a result, they didn't enjoy upgrades. They didn't look forward to them. They didn't look forward to the functionality. They had to get very involved. They might have had to help in the data manipulation and mapping.

A client-server upgrade is very painful. One of the biggest selling points of the Employease Network is the fact that the customer doesn't have to be involved in the upgrade. We do it [for the customer]. They literally go home, get a good night's sleep. When they come in on Monday, the upgrade has happened.

Now, people might say, "Well, what if the product has changed in such a way that we don't like it?" The answer is: We don't make wholesale changes to user interfaces as client-server companies have. They understood that the customer didn't have to upgrade. So they would make potentially more drastic changes.

When you're in the Software-as-a-Service world, you have a much more *evolutionary* development to your product rather than *revolutionary* developments. You bring in base hits instead of home runs. The result is that you add features incrementally and subtly so that it doesn't affect how the customer is using the product. We never take away any functionality from the customers. And any new features that you add have to be done in a very careful way so that it doesn't affect the daily activity of the customer.

I want to reiterate that this is a 100% benefit and zero negative impact on the customer. And in the future there'll be no other way to deliver software. I think it will be very clear that you do automatic upgrades. If a phone company changes how the back-end systems for voicemail work, they don't allow people to have different versions of voicemail systems out there. They just upgrade the whole thing in the background. As software transforms itself from these highly customized individual products—which I think is an immature model—to the type where an application is more like a utility, then people will start to get used to this concept and they won't even think about upgrades anymore. They'll think of it as improvement in service.

The other side of it is connecting to third parties. This is in the world of data management, data manipulation, and data transfer. It is a much more complex beast than the end-user interface. Upgrades to this capability have to be treated very differently. You don't automatically upgrade all connections. In fact, connections always have to be backward compatible because they depend or third-party systems depend on their output.

I think the way that you'll see this evolve is that, for every new feature that's added to the connection, you'll see a new revision of the connection, as opposed to replacing the old one. The reason is that there are these third-party systems that absolutely depend on the result set, and that third party can't always be expected to upgrade their system with upgrades to your system.

ALEX: *How are you using Web Services now and what, if any, benefits are you getting?*

JOHN: We have adopted a Web Services model for the Employease Network, and we see a lot of advantages to it. Let's start by thinking of it from a customer's perspective. Right now, the way that we've communicated data is primarily through exporting connections to customers and to third parties such as insurance companies and payroll companies. For those types of business transactions, that's okay because you don't really need to get that stuff reconciled in real time.

There are other business transactions where the Employease Network is a valuable resource as an authoritative source of employee information that could use the information in real time. Getting back to the authoritative source, the Employease Network is typically, within a company, the first place an employee record is put. The Employease Network, in a sense, owns that information for the company. So a lot of companies use the Employease Network as a way to extract this information. But they have systems that would like the information on a more real-time basis. They'd like to be able to pull the Employease Network for data such as employment verification: give me the details around whether this person's employed, what their salary is, and how long they've worked for the company, etc.

Being able to do things like post information about an individual on an intranet, not rely on a separate database for that information, and instead get that from the Employease Network in real time is seen as a very valuable thing to our customers. Just getting back to that, we thought the best approach would be a Web Services approach because we could leverage our existing infrastructure, sending back XHTML instead of HTML. And so it's something that we could easily step into, in terms of what our developers have been trained on.

That's why we adopted the Web Services model. In developing it, we are exposing as Web Services all of the transactions that can be performed through the GUI or Web site. As a result, you can kind of package on top of this API, this Web Services API, any type of application or functionality that you'd be interested in building that requires Employease Network transactions.

ALEX: *In wrapping up, the firm is almost six years old. Are there lessons that you've learned that you may want to share with the reader, potentially from a business perspective as an entrepreneur and also maybe even some technology lessons?*

JOHN: Well, the most important technology lesson from the Software-as-a-Service perspective is the one that I've already articulated, which is: Make sure your business scales really well. And the term scalability is misused a lot. Specifically, when I say that, it means you need to make sure that your operational complexity does not increase through the number of customers. It's fundamental to making and to building a successful Software-as-a-Service company from a technical perspective.

There are also other important technical things: Organizing your release structure is very important; making sure that you're very careful about how you add features into the product so that, when you do a release, it doesn't upset your customers; you haven't taken away any functionality or you haven't drastically transformed the user interface of something that they use on a daily basis.

You need to have great version control so that you can keep track of what's in production, what's in development, and what is in test. Again, we've found that in the Software-as-a-Service model, it's much more effective to do base hits in terms of product functionality than home runs. And what I mean by that is: Don't, as a development team, lock yourself in a room for a year and a half working on a project and then come out with release. Instead, take the customer requests and break them down into pieces. Work on one component at a time. Get feedback on the incremental release and let that drive the next release. So what we've moved to is an evolutionary product development as opposed to a revolutionary product development, and we find that that's very effective with our customers. We release product three times a year, major product upgrades. We do small upgrades, small feature enhancements on a more granular level, but the maor product upgrades happen three times a year, which is drastically different from what was being done in the client-server world, where they've moved to a 12- to 18-month cycle for product development.

On the business side and I already mentioned this but I'll reiterate it—it's that for those that are used to these high-gulp revenue, large influx of revenues through licensing fees, you've got to kind of re-attune yourself to how recurring revenue base grows. To the traditional software executive used to the client-server [revenue model], it might be disappointing. But, as I said, a dollar of recurring revenue is worth a lot more than a dollar of licensing revenue. The financial markets know that and reward businesses for building these models.

ALEX: *Thanks for your insights, John.*

▶ Summary

Software as a Service (SAAS) is a compelling alternative to the traditional enterprise software model; its advantages include a lower total cost of ownership and a faster time to market. Unlike the first-generation ASP, an SAAS firm provides additional value by including domain expertise along with the software offering. One of the pioneers in the SAAS sector is Employease, which provides a solution for the eHR industry.

Appendix

A

ebXML and Other XML Initiatives

Web Services and XML have a bewildering number of initiatives and standards, including many industry-specific ones such as RIXML (Research Information Exchange Markup Language). This appendix discusses some of the most important initiatives built around establishing and managing business processes (including ebXML and WSFL). These initiatives have not been officially adopted by the W3C, but there is enough critical mass behind them to warrant further discussion.

The appendix concludes with a discussion on two interoperability groups—the SOAPBuilders Group and the recently formed Web Services Interoperability Group. Finally, we look at the Liberty Alliance Project, a consortium established to handle identity on the Internet.

▶ ebXML

Technically speaking, ebXML is not a Web Services standard. Originally created in 1999 as a joint partnership between the **United Nations Centre for Trade Facilitation and Electronic Business (UN/CEFACT)** and the **Organization for the Advancement of Structured Information Standards (OASIS)**, ebXML is a global initiative of hundreds of members to define an XML-based standard that would accelerate electronic business, reduce deployment costs, and support global business needs. UN/CEFACT is an international body and is best known for its contribution to the EDI standards, including UN/EDIFACT. OASIS is a nonprofit consortium formed to promote open and collaborative development of interoperability standards such as XML and **SGML (Standard Generalized Markup Language)**, a predecessor to XML.

Unlike EDI, which has been criticized as being practical only for the largest organizations, ebXML intends to build on lessons learned from EDI deployment and deliver a set of specifications and technologies that businesses of all sizes can afford. Built in a modular fashion, ebXML allows companies to adopt it in a modular fashion, which in turn allows for incremental deployment to reduce coplexity and costs. The intent is that tool vendors will eventually produce tools that will be ebXML compliant, thereby facilitating the adoption of ebXML.

These organizations have made recent announcements around the support of ebXML:

- **Covisint**—a global digital marketplace that is funded by DaimlerChrysler, Ford Motor Company, and General Motors—has announced that it will adopt ebXML as its standard for conducting worldwide business. Since its inception in February 2000, Covisint has conducted billions of dollars of trade among its members.
- The **Open Travel Alliance (OTA)** is an initiative to develop standards for all sectors of the travel industry, such as airlines, car rental agencies, hotels, leisure suppliers, tour operators, and trade associations. OTA has announced an endorsement for ebXML in its latest specifications.

The next sections elaborate on ebXML, explaining its various parts. There is also a sample scenario on how companies can adopt ebXML to facilitate trading.

ebXML Basics

The ebXML architecture is composed of

- **Messaging.** ebXML uses SOAP as the protocol for message passing and extends it to support attachments, security, and reliable delivery.

- **Business process modeling.** ebXML provides features for modeling businesses beyond the usual message definitions. Through a **Business Process Specification Schema (BPSS)**, ebXML allows a company to model its workflow and describe all the activities in which it is prepared to engage with its partners. ebXML allows users to use the UN/CEFACT **Unified Modeling Methodology (UMM)** to model the business activities.[1] To facilitate its adoption, ebXML provides two additional features: preexisting templates that businesses can fill out to describe their workflow (instead of creating a BPSS from scratch) and a predefined catalog of common business processes (which companies can use as is or extend).

- **Trading partner profiles and agreements.** ebXML defines a **Collaboration Protocol Profile (CPP)**, a document or a series of documents that acts as an agreement between two parties. Among other things, a company's CPP defines its message exchange capabilities, the data formats (see core components below), and the supported industries of the organization. The intent is that companies can use this information to determine whether they have the capabilities to conduct business with each other (see the sample integration section next for an example of how two companies can use a CPP to determine whether they can conduct business).

- **Core components.** XML schemas that define the business formats for common data formats such as date, tax, and currencies,

---

1. The UMM is an implementation of **Unified Modeling Language (UML)** specifically for business modeling in an e-commerce setting. UML is currently endorsed by the **Object Management Group (OMG)**, a worldwide consortium of some of the largest companies in the world including Boeing and BellSouth. Historically, UML has been used mainly by business analysts and technical developers to produce requirements and technical deliverables (class diagrams, sequence diagrams, etc.) for building systems based on object-oriented technologies.

these core components are intended to be extended to support industry-specific variations.

- **Registries and repositories.** The ebXML repository contains information on how to initiate a relationship and conduct business with the registered businesses. A natural question to ask is: why is there another need for yet another repository format when UDDI already exists? The answer is that ebXML predates UDDI and contains functionality not currently found in the UDDI specifications. See the ebXML and Web Services section for the additional functionality found in an ebXML registry.

Sample ebXML Integration Scenario

In order to adopt ebXML, a firm generally goes through some or all of the phases listed in this section, depending on whether it is the client or the provider. In this example, let's assume that the provider is an insurance firm that wishes to provide commercial insurance to small businesses.

Provider Role

As a provider, the insurance firm would go through the following phases:

- **Design phase.** The firm must obtain the industry-relevant standards necessary to implement an ebXML-compliant system for the insurance firm's industry. This includes reviewing the business scenarios and business profiles in the ebXML repository and then either adopting existing ones or extending them.
- **Implementation phase.** The insurance firm then implements the systems necessary to support the functionality it wants to provide to its trading partners—in this case, small businesses. This can include writing a new system, buying packaged software, and/or integrating with an existing system.
- **Registration.** As a final step, the insurance firm then registers a CPP that organizations can search on. The CPP defines the communication protocols supported, security procedures, the role of the firm (provider or client), document structures, message reliability (e.g., number of retries, retry interval, duration of persistent message), and so on.

Client Role

A client (in this case, a small business) would go through the following phases:

- **Discovery phase.** The small business searches the ebXML registry based on the business processes that a company is registered to support (again, through the CPP).
- **Negotiation phase.** In this phase, both parties meet (most likely offline) to negotiate the terms. This produces a **Collaboration Protocol Agreement (CPA)**—a binding contract that is the actual implementation of the CPP. Think of the CPP as a template and the CPA as a specific occurrence of the template with terms that are specific to a given relationship.
- **Implementation phase.** The actual integration and exchange of ebXML messages can then be initiated.

Figure A-1 illustrates this sequence of events.

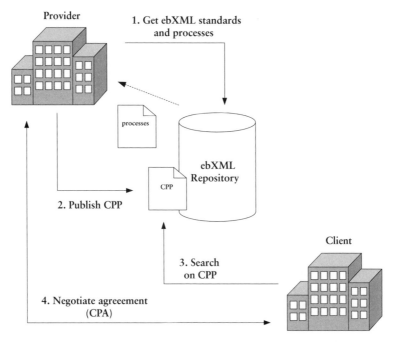

Figure A–1 Provider and client phases in an ebXML integration scenario.

ebXML and Web Services

In a sense, this sequence is very similar to how organizations can use UDDI to discover Web Services and WSDL to determine how to connect to each other. So how does ebXML fit with UDDI and other Web Services standards?

ebXML, in many ways, addresses issues that are still outstanding with the core Web Services standards. For example, whereas WSDL defines how to connect to a Web Service, a CPP defines additional things such as number of retries, security policies around the service, etc. In short, a CPP is a superset of a WSDL document.

To contrast, the UDDI registries list companies, the services they provide, and how to connect to these services; the ebXML registry, on the other hand, defines a mechanism for modeling business processes in a workflow (and a catalog of predefined business processes) so that companies can determine much more definitively whether or not they can conduct business. Likewise, ebXML defines constructs for handling negotiation (CPPs and CPAs), whereas the Web Services do not define these.

Overall, it is still not immediately clear how (and when) the ebXML initiative and the Web Services standards will converge.

▶ WSFL and Other Emerging Technologies

In most cases, a business process typically maps to more than one Web Service. A Web Service, in many cases, needs to be combined with other Web Services to provide real business value. Recognizing this need, IBM has released the **Web Services Flow Language** (**WSFL**), an XML grammar for the description of Web Services composition (i.e., chaining Web Services into a workflow). As of this writing, WSFL has not been adopted by the W3C, although there is industry recognition that such a standard is needed.

In order to adopt WSFL, a business would need to adopt these major steps:

- Determine which business process(es) they are trying to accomplish (restocking inventory, credit check, etc.).

- Identify the Web Services (along with their providers) and the business rules that control the sequencing of these activities. Note that WSFL does provide for **recursion**, which means that a Web Service can invoke itself.

- Establish the flow of information between each activity and the success/failure condition of each activity.

The result of these steps is a WSFL model (an XML document) that is essentially a workflow model. WSFL-compliant tools can then allow the user to visualize this model to facilitate editing and maintenance. As of this writing, there is only one WSFL-compliant product line on the market, the **eXtend and Composer** product line from SilverStream. For a more thorough discussion of how a tool would support WSFL along with some missing gaps in WSFL, see Appendix C.

WSFL is not the only workflow-related initiative on the market. Other initiatives include

- **XLANG.** From Microsoft, this XML grammar is currently supported only by the BizTalk Server product (also from Microsoft).

- **Business Process Modeling Language (BPML).** Produced by the Business Management Process Initiative, a nonprofit consortium of over 100 members (founding members include Cap Gemini Ernst and Young, Computer Sciences Corporation, BowStreet, and others), BMPL is (yet) another XML grammar for modeling business processes.

One of the most challenging issues to address when dealing with business processes is how to deal with long-lived transactions. Historically, most transaction standards (XA, etc.) assume that all the resources can be dictated by one central body and are tightly coupled. Transactions that involve Web Services span multiple companies, and the challenge is to determine how to manage loosely coupled transactions. The following two initiatives and companies are worth mentioning.

- **Business Transaction Protocol (BTP).** Pioneered by BEA Systems, BTP is an XML technology that can be layered on existing messaging technologies (SOAP, ebXML, etc.) to handle transactions in a Web Services context, which tends to be loosely coupled and long lived. BTP has been turned over to OASIS for standardization.

- **Orchestration Server.** The Orchestration Server—a J2EE technology that can be used in conjunction with popular application servers—by Collaxa is used to coordinate long-lived business transactions. For more on Collaxa and the challenges in managing such transactions, see Appendix C.

▶ Interoperability Groups

One of the recurring messages of Web Services is that interoperability is the key benefit. The fact that many of the vendors are actively focused on promoting interoperability and have formed groups to address this specific issue should be an encouraging sign for customers.

Two groups that are focused exclusively on this area are the Web Services Interoperability Group and the SOAPBuilders Group.

Web Services Interoperability Group (WS-I)

Formed in early 2002, WS-I members include major technology firms such as IBM, Microsoft, and BEA Systems. (As of this writing, a key player, Sun Microsystems, is not yet a member.) WS-I is focused on promoting interoperability at the implementation level and will offer a self-validated set of compliance tests to ensure that Web Services are using the existing Web Services standards (XML, SOAP, WSDL, and UDDI) in a manner that does not compromise interoperability. This organization intends to offer its support for other initiatives such as ebXML; authors of those initiatives can use WS-I's compliance tests to ensure their implementations' interoperability.

SOAPBuilders Group

This loosely coordinated group includes over 750 active members, who originally focused exclusively on testing SOAP implementations as the specifications matured. Since its inception, the group has hosted three interoperability test rounds. Sponsored by Iona and Microsoft, the latest round is testing WSDL, specifically, whether the tools can produce and consume WSDL documents under different scenarios.

▶ The Liberty Alliance Project

One of the biggest issues needing to be addressed along with the mass adoption of Web Services is the issue of identity tracking and identity ownership.[2] As we discussed in the chapter on Web Services platforms, Microsoft is promoting the use of Passport. Sun and other major organizations (including American Express, AOL Time Warner, General Motors, Sony Corporation, and too many others to list here) have launched the Liberty Alliance Project, a consortium whose main goal is to produce a standards-based, single sign-on identity solution that allows users to connect from multiple devices (cell phones, PCs, etc.) and conduct the next generation of e-commerce.

As of this writing, the Alliance has been formalized, but it has not produced any specifications or technologies. For a more thorough discussion on how a firm has utilized user identity to enhance the user experience, see the Talaris interview in Appendix C.

▶ Summary

The biggest challenge for many companies is not how to adopt a technology such as Web Services. The biggest challenge can be how to identify which partners to conduct business with and how to best do so. ebXML is a worldwide initiative that was formed to address this and other issues. ebXML uses SOAP to transport messages, but it has a complementary (and some may say conflicting) mechanism for implementing repositories.

WSFL and XLANG are both emerging technologies that are trying to address how to map Web Services to business processes. Unfortunately,

---

2. The Liberty Alliance Project is discussed here instead of in the J2EE chapter because technically it is not part of the J2EE specifications.

it is not immediately clear whether these two technologies will converge or continue to evolve separately.

To address issues around interoperability, two groups have formed independent of each other: the SOAPBuilders Group and the newly formed Web Services Interoperability Group. Both are trying to produce compliance tests to help firms determine whether their products can interoperate and conform to the standards (XML, SOAP, WSDL, and UDDI).

Finally, an outstanding issue is that of how to deal with identity. Microsoft has launched the Passport technology (which already has millions of users), whereas Sun and other major organizations have recently launched the Liberty Alliance Project.

B

Case Studies

Companies are using Web Services to gain competitive advantage, and this appendix includes detailed transcripts gathered from one-on-one sessions with key executives at these firms. The companies studied are drawn from multiple industries to demonstrate how Web Services can be used in different business scenarios. Even though the industries vary, the results are amazingly consistent. Each interviewee, without knowledge of the experiences of the others, is highly confident that there will be an eventual mass adoption of Web Services because the benefits are simply too compelling. These benefits include significantly reduced integration costs (savings of over $200,000 in licensing costs for a modest pilot project) and shorter time to market (weeks instead of months).

The case study companies tend to adopt technologies more aggressively than their competitors, usually to gain a competitive edge (Geoffrey Moore, well-known author of the best-selling textbook *Crossing the Chasm* would categorize these firms as the *early adopters* or the *visionaries*).[1] As such, they can offer some interesting insights and also provide some valuable lessons, not the least of which is how to get funding to undertake such an effort.

---

1. Moore, G., *Crossing the Chasm*, Revised Edition, HarperBusiness, New York, 1999.

▶ Lessons Learned from Case Studies

Certain activities stood out as being important in the interviews with the early Web Services adopters:

- **Clearly identify business objectives.** In the case of Putnam Lovell Securities, the intent was to integrate external systems to provide better customer service as well as to reduce distribution costs. In the case of Pantechnik International, the intent was to provide a platform through which customers can more easily integrate their own systems.

- **Be aware of the limitations of existing technologies.** Again, Web Services are not as mature as some of the other integration technologies such as integration brokers or classic middleware (CORBA, RMI, etc.). In the case of Putnam Lovell Securities, the firm is publishing read-only data to their customers and not relying on any transactions. The firm still experienced significant cost savings since this was formerly a time-consuming and error-prone manual process.

- **Deliver incrementally to allow standards to mature.** Since the functionality provided by the various vendors is still maturing, it is critically important to match the appropriate business objectives to the right tools. Likewise, instead of trying to deliver all of the functionality at once, identify the easy wins and achieve success (and, in return, build skills and project support) with the simpler processes. Many of these projects were delivered in weeks instead of months or years.

- **Use existing investments where possible.** These early adopters used their existing investments in skills and software to achieve quicker time to market. For example, Pantechnik International was already building its platform using a service-oriented architecture with COM, a pre-.NET technology. When .NET came along, Pantechnik migrated its existing code in the same language, resulting in a fairly smooth transition.

- **Outsource, when possible.** In all cases, the firms identified their core competence and outsourced the rest. In the case of Pantechnik Interational, it decided it was in the logistics business, not in the address validation business. Hence, the company has partnered with an outside firm to provide address validation rather than build the functionality internally. Likewise, Putnam Lovell did not build a data center, but instead used the network infrastructure of Grand Central.

- **Accept the fact that not all customers will adopt Web Services immediately.** As with any new technology, there can be a significant time period between the early adopters and the mainstream market (of course, this time period is difficult to predict and also highly dependent on the exact industry). Pantechnik International's previous product was a class library that a customer installed locally and then invoked in an application (making SOAP calls) to connect to Pantechnik's ePIX platform. The company has since released a native Web Services version to which clients can connect without having to use the library (this requires that the customers write their applications to make native SOAP calls). However, Pantechnik International is pragmatic and therefore is supporting both versions because it realizes that it will be years before all of its customers will migrate to a native Web Services environment.

Many of these lessons had to be learned the hard way by the early adopters of Web Services—through trial and error. If companies adopting Web Services now and in the future learn from these lessons, they will have a much easier time of it.

▶ Case Study: Reducing Integration Costs (Putnam Lovell Securities Incorporated)

Putnam Lovell Securities Incorporated is an investment bank based in San Francisco. As an investment bank, Putnam Lovell Securities serves major institutional investors. Before the use of Web Services, Putnam Lovell was manually constructing each email with information about possible investments to interested parties—a time-consuming and error-prone process.

At Putnam Lovell, the interests of each investor are stored in Sales-Force.com, a SAAS CRM [customer relationship management] solution; research information is provided by Blue Matrix, another SAAS firm. As its Web Services pilot project, Putnam Lovell decided to use Web Services to match the interests of each investor in SalesForce.com with the news provided by Blue Matrix (the firm also uses a Web Services network to distribute the results). Putnam Lovell estimates a savings of over $200,000 during this pilot project, and development time has been significantly reduced as well.

Whereas many analysts predict that Web Services will be used first to integrate applications behind the firewall, in this case, the integration between SalesForce.com and Blue Matrix occurred completely beyond the firewall—neither SalesForce.com nor Blue Matrix is hosted at Putnam Lovell's location.

Figure B–1 illustrates a partial architecture of the solution deployed at Putnam Lovell.

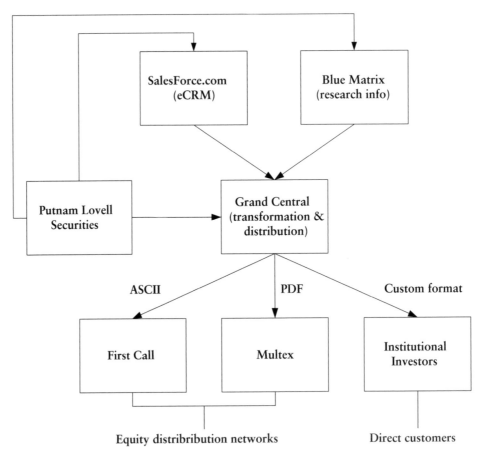

Figure B–1   Distributing research information at Putnam Lovell.

Interviewee: Rodric O'Connor, CTO, Putnam Lovell Securities

ALEX: *Please explain a little bit about what Putnam Lovell Securities Incorporated does and what your role in organization is.*

RODRIC: We're an investment bank specializing in the financial service industry. We have about 150 employees in four geographic locations. New York is our largest office, with about 80 employees. San Francisco is our corporate headquarters with about 50, and we have offices in L.A. and London. I am the CTO responsible for our global technology infrastructure and service. The Technology Group is responsible for desktop telecommunications and application infrastructure of the internal technology that the enterprise uses.

ALEX: *Please describe the process flow of the system at high level, including subsystems and major software technologies.*

RODRIC: We're currently using Grand Central as an application integration hub between the applications that we source via the Internet. Some of those applications are single-tenant ASPs; others are multi-tenant Web-based applications. We want to automate several business processes that span these applications.

ALEX: *You are referring to the SalesForce.com and the Blue Matrix applications?*

RODRIC: Yes. In addition there are a few other ones that we're in the process of building and integrating. The first process we automated using this technology was integration between our CRM and our content creation distribution system. Our CRM is SalesForce.com, and the equity research content system is provided by Blue Matrix. Both of these applications reside on the Internet. We have no servers and no infrastructure in-house, but we wanted to automate the process of distributing our research via email to clients. The client interests are recorded in our eCRM system, SalesForce.com. When a piece of content is ready to be distributed, Blue Matrix needs to get a list of people who are interested in that research and send out the email.

ALEX: *In this scenario, the analyst connects with the Blue Matrix system and requests research via the Web form. Blue Matrix then sends the results to third-party distributors. Who are your distributors?*

RODRIC: They are the traditional equity research distribution networks: First Call (a Thompson Company), Multex, Ibes, Bloomberg and Zacks. Traditionally, each one of those vendors wants the research in a proprietary format, with a separate vendor-specific method data file describing the research. Blue Matrix's core expertise is to automate that distribution point to the multiple distributors. What I am seeing is a move towards clients wanting research to be directly sent to them. They want to see it in their email inbox rather than having to go to the client-specific research aggregation tool to read the research.

ALEX: *I assume that not all the distributors are using XML yet?*

RODRIC: We are not contributing to them via XML. I believe that Multex has just introduced XML contribution. Each distributor has its own format. For example, First Call wants it in short-text format with a separate file describing the type of research in its own format. Multex can receive a PDF [portable document format], so it's at a richer content but with a different metadata description mechanism. What we are doing with the new business process is supplement the distribution to the third-party distributors with a direct channel to our clients.

ALEX: *So Step 2 is really not that relevant, given your focus.*

RODRIC: Well, Step 2 has two components. Blue Matrix sends documents to third-party distributors. When that happens, at the same time it [Blue Matrix] queries Grand Central for an XML list of clients and sends an email. The Web Services–based automation is a new distribution mechanism for the research.

ALEX: *And that's the one where you get information from Sales-Force.com to figure out who the clients are, and then Blue Matrix actually does it for you.*

RODRIC: Yes. That was the first business process that we automated. The second one was between the same two applications, but for a different function. Blue Matrix hosts our research library that is accessed by our clients via our public Web site. Our institutional clients are given username and password with which they can log in to our Web site. Once there they can view our research and equity metrics database. We maintain the permissions that indicate a client has access to that library in SalesForce. The new process is that, at least once an hour, Blue Matrix requests a list of clients who can access the research library. This allows employees to maintain their clients' permissions directly within our CRM. Within an hour clients can be provisioned or deprovisioned without any administrator intervention.

ALEX: *How did the users address the current business needs before this current implementation?*

RODRIC: We had a manual process for distributing research by email. Our production group would run a query in SalesForce.com. The query results would be imported and manipulated in an Excel file. Then they would create an email in the email client, download the content from Blue Matrix, attach it to the email, and cut and paste the distribution list from Excel into the bcc [blind carbon copy] field of the email.

The drawback of this was that it was time consuming. We were unable to scale the manual approach to allow the addition of more granular queries so we can track what type of research our clients are interested in and only send them research that they're interested in. We think that it is very important for the adoption of our research. If there's an institutional asset manager who's only interested in commercial banks, we just want to send them commercial banking research, and we could not move to granular targeting and continue to do it manually. It would be too time consuming. It would be a complex matrix to model an individual's interest. It includes a list of equities, a list of sector categories, and types of reports. Each is a variable that defines the interest. So the permutations can be very great. It would be a horrible task for somebody to spend all day running different queries and sending off different emails.

The value to our clients of the research is a function of how quickly we can deliver it to them. They base trades on this information. So, if they get it six hours late, then the market's already changed. It is a very time-critical distribution.

ALEX: *What are some business benefits that you are trying to achieve in using Web Services, and did you look at any other possible technologies?*

RODRIC: At the moment we're using it for what I think is probably the easiest return on investment and that's application integration. I have seen a lot of discussion indicating that the earliest uses will be within the firewall. I am in the interesting position in that I outsource the majority of my applications via the Internet, so they reside outside the firewall. If I had them inside the firewall, I would probably still use Web Services standards to integrate, but I'd probably have an integration engine inside my firewall. In my case, the applications are external. I don't have as much control at the underlying database level of the applications, so Web Services are the only way that I can integrate them. The only way the application vendors are going to be willing to give me access is via standard open APIs, i.e., SOAP and XML.

ALEX: *I see. So, given the fact that all your applications are Web-based, did you look at any other architectures?*

RODRIC: I could have purchased a Web Services–compliant hub and hosted it in-house and that would have cost me approximately $100,000 for software licensing and hardware. I would then have to pay consultants to implement as I do not have in-house developers. That would have been another $50,000 to $100,000. Therefore I would have to have a capital budget of close to $200,000 to consider owning the integration hub. But my philosophy is to outsource wherever possible, as I would rather have an external organization, whose expertise is in a particular application, support it, rather than to thinly spread my internal resource[s].

ALEX: *If I may summarize, your situation is actually better than many of the other early adopters because your applications are already outsourced. In many cases, the easy win seems to be behind the firewall, but in your case, the integration is beyond the firewall.*

RODRIC: I haven't got anything inside the firewall that I want to integrate. Maybe it would help if I tell you the next phases of integration. The next one that's coming up is probably between American Express credit card transactions (our employees' corporate credit card) and our Oracle 11i Web-based expense reporting system that's hosted at an ASP called Appshop. We use the Oracle Financials application for our general ledger and finance system. Appshop hosts and supports it for us as a single-tenant ASP environment. We own the software license; they own the hardware dedicated to our instance of the application. We are building the integration between American Express credit card and our Oracle application so that every night our employees' credit card transactions are prepopulating the Oracle expense report module.

ALEX: *The SalesForce.com integration with the Blue Matrix, I presume, is already in production?*

RODRIC: Yes it is—two business processes between two applications.

ALEX: *So, for the second one, was Blue Matrix hosting the client-accessible research?*

RODRIC: Yes, to automate client permission to our research library. The third will be American Express credit card transactions to hosted Oracle, and the fourth will be between Employease (our HR system) and SalesForce.com. Employee contact information will be synchronized between CRM and HR.

ALEX: *Is Employease actually doing the integration or are you doing that and turning [it] over to them?*

RODRIC: Employease is working with Grand Central on that.

ALEX: *So, those are the four major processes that you are in various stages of completion, then.*

RODRIC: Yes. Two are in production and two are in development.

ALEX: *What are some business benefits that you are trying to achieve using Grand Central? You've already mentioned the reduced integration costs and the lowered deployment cost.*

RODRIC: The primary business benefit has been to increase the value and reduce the cost of the distribution of our research. The cost reduction has a very concrete ROI. It is part of a strategy to migrate our research from print to electronic distribution. Our goal is to migrate 50% of our research distribution from printed material to electronic over a 12-month period. In the first quarter of 2001, we spent about $400,000 a quarter on print. So, if we achieve our goal, we should see a $200,000 [per] quarter saving. We believe we can achieve that goal because we can target the research to our clients and, therefore, they will be more likely [to] accept the electronic version. It will be quicker and focused to their requirements.

ALEX: *What other options did you look at besides Grand Central?*

RODRIC: We briefly talked to Crossworlds [acquired by IBM] and did some research into the Microsoft hub product. Grand Central was the only one we could find that was a Web-native service rather than an infrastructure that we'd have to buy.

ALEX: *I'm curious if you looked at any other Web Services networks.*

RODRIC: Like which ones?

ALEX: *Well, there's Flamenco Networks, Kenemea, etc.*

RODRIC: I've heard of them and I've done some research. When did Flamenco start their offering?

ALEX: *Depending on whether you're talking alpha or beta, roughly six months ago.*

RODRIC: We started talking to Grand Central early in 2001, about 12 months ago. At that time there did not seem to be a comparable product. One of the reasons we started talking to Grand Central was that they have a close relationship to SalesForce.com.

ALEX: *What specific problems does Grand Central address for you?*

RODRIC: Integration between our applications. It is the preferred way that I will integrate any of our nontrading applications.

ALEX: *You could obviously use Web Services without using Grand Central.*

RODRIC: Yes.

ALEX: *One of Grand Central's value propositions is that it offers a lot of value-added services on top of the bare, Web Services stack—things like authentication, transaction control, etc. Did you use those features of Grand Central?*

RODRIC: Some of them. It allows me to intermediate the security between my application providers, i.e., each vendor on the network only needs to know its authentication to the network. I control and manage the cross-connections between the vendor, hiding each vendor's specific authentication process from the other. I also use Grand Central as a central administration point that provides me with a single message status and reporting location.

ALEX: *So essentially they're giving you a slice of a data center which you otherwise would have to build yourself then?*

RODRIC: Yes, but they are offering more than a data center. They also provide an application layer, the messaging system to allow integration. I could do point-to-point integration using Web Services, but then I wouldn't be able to leverage the hub-and-spoke architecture. Every additional business process would be like starting from scratch. I prefer the hub-and-spoke architecture where I control the center. I get vendors to connect as spokes. My internal resource can manage the internal hub to provide centralized reporting on messages and events generated by all of our business processes.

ALEX: *So what you're leveraging is the hub-and-spoke architecture to reduce the upkeep of that architecture as well, and Grand Central also provides centralized reporting then?*

RODRIC: Exactly.

ALEX: *Are there any other features that you are taking advantage of?*

RODRIC: Well, as you mentioned, the fact that it's a service rather than an infrastructure that I have to own and support.

ALEX: *That's what they seem to promote to clients: the reduced time to market and lower total cost of ownership.*

RODRIC: I have a metric. If it's a multitenant Web-native application such as Grand Central or SalesForce.com, then I would expect to see 80% of the functionality versus having it in-house. I will not be able to customize or modify all aspects of it, and, if I wrote down a requirement list with 100 items on it, I would probably only get 80 of them, but it would probably be the top 80. The remaining 20 requirements would be nice to have but are not really necessary for the application to have value. In compensation for this I get the service for 20% of the cost. It's the 80-20 rule—80% of the functionality, 20% of the cost.

ALEX: *Did you have any performance concerns considering the real-time nature of your work?*

RODRIC: I do not use it for financial transactions. My data and process does not need to be real time. A delay of a few minutes is not an issue for me. [An] Asynchronous messaging system is adequate. I am not using it as a synchronous real-time network.

ALEX: *So it's more like a delayed transmission. As long as the latency is not too high, then it's acceptable.*

RODRIC: Yes. If the delay reached five minutes it would be a problem. But with our application, any delay has been caused by the end-point application serving up the result set rather than the network.

ALEX: *Currently there are two camps. One's saying that the reason Web Services are going to be so successful is because the technologies are very light and the protocols and the standards are very straightforward and simple, similar to HTML and HTTP. But, there's another camp whose main concern is that Web Services are lacking a lot of fundamental things, like transaction control and things like that. I'd be curious about what your viewpoint on that is. For example, let's just say, six months or nine months from now when Web Services are a little bit more mature, the issue is not going to be as black and white because at that point people are going to try and incorporate some of these features into the Web Services standards. At what point would you make the decision to use Web Services versus, say, more traditional middleware or B2B platforms, assuming you have applications behind a firewall? I realize you don't have such a scenario, but let's postulate.*

RODRIC: So in summary your question is, is it going to stay simple or is it going to bloat to meet all the requirements of every single possible usage?

ALEX: *Yes.*

RODRIC: I hope it remains simple at the lower layers of the protocol stack and enhancements will be added on top of the current standards to allow its use in other types of application—for example, transactional consistency. Perhaps some standards need to be defined to allow it to be implanted via a document workflow metaphor.

ALEX: *Or a Web Services network and Grand Central can address a lot of that for you.*

RODRIC: It could go either way. It could be driven by the applications, or it could be built into network. There have to be hooks in both the application and the network, and my preference is for these hooks to be built following standards. We have seen a little bit of this in some of the business processes we have implemented—for example, in the recovery from an error. We had to implement new logic in the application; i.e., the application that was feeding up information failed, and the only way we knew it was via a time-out in the application receiving the message. The data returned was incomplete; the middle section of its payload was missing, causing the XML to be malformed. The network was not aware that the message payload was incomplete, so it could not generate an error condition. To correctly identify this type of error, you would have to modify the requesting application to verify the result set with the supplying application, e.g., record count, byte count, or **checksum**. You have to design your applications around the asynchronous communication. It doesn't necessarily mean that the Grand Central network did not deliver the messages correctly; the issue was that message was formed incorrectly. There is application-specific logic that has to be built to ensure that the error and failure events are handled correctly.

ALEX: *Data integrity problems?*

RODRIC: Yes.

ALEX: *How many users are currently using the system and are happy with the results so far?*

RODRIC: Well, it's an application integration, so it's one application to another. So how do you count the users? The CRM [application] is used by all employees, so 150. The research content creation system is used by our equity research group—about 20 people—and the emails containing the content get sent out to between 700 and 1,000 people who do not know or care what technology was used to get them the information.

ALEX: *Which is actually the way it should be.*

RODRIC: Right.

ALEX: *What are some future plans for your system, and how does Grand Central fit into these plans, if at all?*

RODRIC: We have two more business processes in development, and, whenever any other business process comes up for potential for automation, Web Services via the Grand Central network will be our preferred mechanism.

ALEX: *What are some unforeseen technical challenges that you ran into? You mentioned one of them earlier already, for example—the document was malformed. Were there other things that you didn't anticipate?*

RODRIC: That's the only issue we have had since going into production.

ALEX: *So no really major problems so far?*

RODRIC: No.

ALEX: *So you would not have any reservations in recommending this form of integration to others?*

RODRIC: None at all. It's worked very well for us, and it was implemented very quickly, I think, due to using SOAP as a standard. It was relatively quick to implement because of its simplicity.

One issue I've had that I suspect has more to do with the state of the economy than anything else is related to the development of integration between American Express credit cards and our Oracle Financial application. At the moment it is running as a secure FTP client download from American Express. American Express delayed its plans to move towards an XML-based data feed. At the moment I believe it is on hold due to the downturn in the economy. So it is possible that the downturn in the economy has slowed some of my vendors' adoption of XML due to budget allocation.

ALEX: *Can you share, at least at a high level, the rough budget or scope of this? In man-weeks or in man-months?*

RODRIC: For which? For the whole business? For the whole application integration?

ALEX: *Let's just take the first one and maybe the second one, because they're both in production. Say from inception to your actual deployment.*

RODRIC: I did not do any of the development. The vendors, Grand Central, SalesForce, Blue Matrix, Appshop, and Employease are doing it for me. They consume resource that in some way is charged back to me. As an estimate I would say that the first business process took between 40 and 100 hours of development.

ALEX: *And I think most clients [would] be quite happy with that. Usually these types of projects run into thousands of hours.*

RODRIC: Yes.

ALEX: *From this experience, it seems to be possible to do quick, focused integration and get high payback.*

RODRIC: That is a good way of saying it. The first one—I'm talking about the SalesForce-to-Blue Matrix integration—it probably took 80 hours to build the first business process. The second business process probably took 10 hours because the applications were already plugged into the network. The second phase was mostly internal: Putnam Lovell created a different query in Grand Central (approximately two hours of Putnam Lovell time), and Blue Matrix had to build specific logic on their side, maybe another eight hours. So that's the interesting thing. Once you're already plugged into the network, the first one takes 80 hours, the second one takes 10 hours.

ALEX: *So you do get the payback very quickly.*

RODRIC: Yes.

ALEX: *Would you attribute the quick turnaround time to the fact that you are an early adopter, and therefore a marquee client for the vendors, or is it because of the fact that the technologies actually facilitate the integration to this level?*

RODRIC: Probably a combination of both. On the positive side, the developers involved are enthusiastic because this is interesting new technology and—as you said—as an early adopter and therefore a key customer, you do get high priority. Each vendor has different drivers that you need to understand and leverage. As everyone is enthusiastic and motivated, it is easy to get things done. The technology is also relatively straightforward. On the negative side, it is a new way of doing things for everybody. Therefore, there are the some issues of early adoption. I personally think that the benefits outweigh the risks.

I have a general technology strategy of being an early adopter. At Putnam Lovell we have to compete with much larger organizations that have much larger technology budgets. The only way we can compete at a technology level is to be more aggressive and take more calculated risks and hopefully get more return on the dollar.

ALEX: *Can you share some lessons learned from deploying the system, or is it too early?*

RODRIC: I think it's actually worked very well for us. One thing I'm still doing is to pay attention to the financial stability of the vendors. We are using the services of five different vendors. Given the current economic climate, I am concerned about their future viability. That is a risk that you have to manage. You manage it by ensuring frequent and open communication with their executive team to find out what their financial situation is. You always need to figure out what your contingency plan would be if a vendor ceases to provide your service.

ALEX: *So it seems like you're implicitly trying to maximize reuse wherever possible. And not at a code level, but this is very much an architecture, and also at an infrastructure level via the hub-and-spoke model through Grand Central.*

RODRIC: Exactly, you hit the nail on the head. In my first meeting with Grand Central, I stood up before they explained exactly what they did and drew a hub and spoke and indicated that I wanted to avoid the trap of building many point-to-point integrations.

ALEX: *And the other thing is it seems you're using technology where it makes sense because, as you mentioned earlier, you're not trying to force something. For example, Web Services, by its nature, is really asynchronous. So you're adopting all these automated business processes where it's not real time or synchronous in nature. You're not force-fitting solutions where it doesn't make sense. I think that there's a lot of confusion, in the sense that some people may see Web Services [as a] kind of panacea solution.*

RODRIC: Yes. I think what may happen is, for asynchronous applications, enterprises will use Web Services standards, but these companies will still have some synchronous infrastructure in place for specific tasks.

ALEX: *What is the significance of industry-specific standards—in your case, RIXML* [research information exchange markup language]?

RODRIC: I think the main benefit is for the consumers of content: it allows them to fragment equity research content into various components. It can then be aggregated with similar components from multiple creators to increase the palatability of the information. For example, an asset manager would be able to get a single daily email giving the headlines and rating changes of the equities that he is interested in derived from all the research providers that his firm has a relationship with. Without a standard, the cost of building each creator/consumer integration point would be prohibitive.

ALEX: *Is your system RIXML compliant? Is Putnam Lovell participating on the RIXML initiative?*

RODRIC: Yes, we can currently create RIXML versions of our morning notes. We have not yet seen any demand for this format. We do not participate directly, but are represented by our vendor, Blue Matrix. They provide us with our research content creation and distribution system as an ASP.

ALEX: *Thank you for your time, Rodric.*

▶ Case Study: Building a Marketplace with Web Services (Pantechnik International)

Pantechnik International is a European-based hub for the logistics industry. One of the main challenges in this industry is the large amount of coordination and information required between shippers, buyers, and carriers. Using a traditional model, an organization would provide custom solutions to connect to all of its business relationships. By acting as the central hub, Pantechnik gives its customers a mechanism to store their information and then authorize which other organizations should be able to view the relevant information.

One of the challenges Pantechnik faced was how best to create a business-level interface for its clients. This required multiple iterations; the firm credits its domain expertise for its success. Second, Pantechnik also recognized the fact that not all of their customers

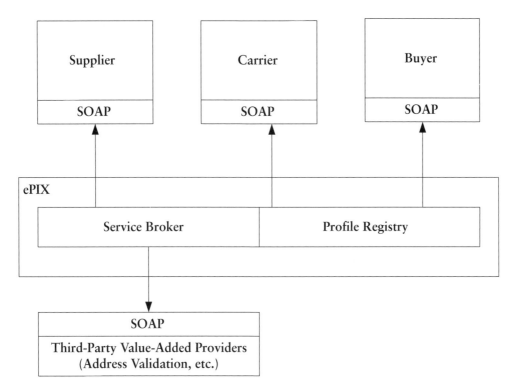

Figure B–2 The ePIX architecture.

would migrate to Web Services immediately and hence it had to provide a mechanism to support those customers until they are ready to adopt Web Services.

Figure B–2 illustrates the high-level architecture of **ePIX** (**Electronic Parcel Exchange**)—Pantechnik's solution.

Interviewee: Peter Nicholls, CEO, Pantechnik International

ALEX: *Please describe a little bit about what Pantechnik International does.*

PETER: We are a logistics information services company, so our customers are normally large distributors or third-party logistics providers working on behalf of large distributors. Examples would be—and these are not necessarily our customers, by the way—but examples would be companies in the high-tech business[es] such [as] Dell, Gateway, or Microsoft and basically, anybody that ships fairly large quantities of physical goods. Prior to coming over here [Belgium], I worked in the U.S. 15 years for a company where the solutions that we offered evolved quite a lot.

Fundamentally, when I came over here, my motivation was twofold. One was to work in a different market—a market that was more suited to the kind of services that we offer and where there was a possibility to achieve some greater margins—because in the U.S., for a number of reasons which don't necessarily pertain to what we're talking about, the margins had gone out of our business.

The second was that I wanted to transition away from being a software company that licensed packages into the capital expenditure budget of our customers. I wanted to move towards a service-based model. So I left the company in the U.S. July 1999 and spent about six months in design and early development work of the concept of a logistics information exchange platform that let my customers and their customers and the carriers that move the physical goods between them link their existing business systems together and exchange information with each other in a managed but content-neutral way.

There are some fairly revolutionary concepts in there, but at the end of the day, the business problem is not new. It's been there for a long time. It just maybe hasn't been solved particularly well. We did this ourselves based on the way we thought was the best way to go about delivering IT services. We didn't know about SOAP, .NET, or anything else. I actually developed a lot of the early coding concepts in Brazil, a long way away from Seattle and places like that.

It was about a year ago—in fact, I think it was just about exactly a year ago—that we were contacted by Microsoft in the U.K. who were putting together an initiative called the Web Services Initiative, and they had heard about what I was doing and said, "I think that what you're really doing is Web Services and you don't know it. If we come and talk to you about it, maybe you'd like to deploy them as Web Services on the .NET platform." And I said, "Come talk to me," and that's how we came together.

So that's the company. We're still very much in start-up mode, but we do have some live active customers and things are moving along.

ALEX: *Your original solution was to provide a class library which your customers can use to connect to your hub. What were some of the shortcomings of that original solution?*

PETER: Well, the reason for doing it was we really need to be pretty ubiquitous. You remember that when we first released that class library and made it available to customers and started working, there was no .NET. So, therefore, there wasn't even a SOAP toolkit. We wanted [it] to be very easy for people to integrate our services into Web pages, Excel spreadsheets, VB applications—call it what you will.

Essentially, the class library is a set of business objects and methods that proxy the services. On the client, when you're integrating a client's system or building an application that's going to consume these services, what you're making are simple Active X COM [Component Object Model] calls, which you can do from any existing Microsoft language platform, etc. Since it was all written in Java, we can also distribute Java classes for the UNIX folks. Now, a year and a half later, of course, there are SOAP toolkits everywhere, and pretty much every operating system platform has a development system whereby you can access services using SOAP. So it's not necessary to use our connector library anymore.

The drawback of using it is really quite simple: it's platform dependent. It's Microsoft. The upside is that—in addition to being very, very straightforward to use from languages like VB, C++, and scripting languages, and so on—there are quite a lot of additional methods, other than service proxies, in some of the business objects that make programming these objects a little bit easier.

And of course SOAP does not support that. You'd have to provide those methods across the wire and that's not always feasible.

ALEX: *You're saying that one of the advantages of using the Active X is that you can actually have more methods exposed?*

PETER: Well, take a business object, for example, an order. If you were to represent an order in SOAP, you basically devise an XML schema based around properties, right? You can expose properties of an order so you can set and get properties of an order, but you can't do much more than that. Let's say that I wanted to encapsulate within my order object some additional functionality of use to a programmer. For example, here's a good one: validation. For postal deliveries, in the address subject, can we have a method to determine, "Is this address within a certain postal code range?" So you give the address the postal code range and say, "Are you within it?" without having to laboriously go through and deal with all sorts of postal codes functionality.

So, the simple answer to that question is, "Well, make the methods in your Web Service." But you're looking at an awful lot of traffic across a network now as opposed to my services today, which are quite big, fat, and chunky with regard to their functionality.

ALEX: *Doesn't that basically come down to whether you're doing something that's at a coarse level or a granular level? Your service broker offers only a small number of public services. How did you identify these from the dozens of internal method calls that your library provides?*

PETER: Exactly. This is something that personally I have to say I'm quite proud of. It comes from a tremendous amount of experience in the domain that we work in as to exactly what are the services. If you make them too granular, then you make too many calls. If you make them too fat, then you find yourself working around the fact that, yes, this is the service I want, but it incorporates too much functionality and I can't break it apart and make it do exactly what I want.

So we actually spent a good deal of time designing the services, what they were to be, and then plugging the services into various scenarios to make sure we had the granularity correct before we ever started coding anything.

Once we got started, we found that there's a methodology to that and it can become more automated as far as, "Okay, I need this service. I think I can see right away how I need to deal with it." But actually, yeah, that was the first design. The first thing we did was design the services and test their usability by acting out scenarios, as it were.

ALEX: *How many services do you have?*

PETER: We have about 60 and all services are stateless. You make the request, you get the answer. The application server has probably forgotten about you so there's no persistence and there's no consistent connectivity of any kind. When we actually started, we were very, very conscious of programmability on the clients' side, and I'm going to run the risk of doing something I don't like to do, which is to talk about somebody else's services.

If you look at, for example, what FedEx and UPS offer on their Internet sites, they have some Web Services of sorts: tracking, asking for a pickup request, and sometimes wanting to actually execute a shipping transaction. The problem is that, in those cases, the services are far too broad.

What we wanted were services that you can easily program on the clients' side. At first we exposed each service as a separate Web Service—in other words, a separate URL. But what we found that did when you use, say, Visual Studio.Net to build an application, you ran into all sorts of problems because some of the business objects were shared between services.

For example, we've got a service that can rate a shipment, and the input to that service is a Shipment object. We've got another service that lets you publish a shipment onto the shared database, and the input of *that* is a shipment. The problem that you run into—if those are two separate *services*—is that, in your Visual Studio.Net Web reference, those are two separate *objects*. But they're *not* separate objects: it's the same object.

You can take a shipment and you can pass it into the right shipment function, get some results back, stuff the results into the shipment object, and then publish it. So what we decided to do was to group the services together as Web methods into three distinct—actually, one...two...three...four distinct—services now. We've just rebuilt them again.

That makes it a lot easier to actually go ahead and work with the services. Now what we have is: each Web Service contains 15 or 20 Web methods. But realistically speaking, each Web method is an independent service and the decision to bundle the services—bundle the methods into a service as opposed to exposing all the services as separate URLs—was to do with the sharing of business objects and how particularly Visual Studio.Net treats them.

ALEX: *So basically, if I understand you correctly, you have roughly 60 or so business objects, but what you did is you actually grouped them so that they could be exposed as roughly four groups of services?*

PETER: I think it's actually now three URLs: system services, management services, and business services. They were broken up like that because, typically, the applications you write are to manage the system itself, like if you're an administrator. You have another application—which is a sort of management administrative application—so a user of the services can manage his profile and his configuration parameters.

The business services themselves then actually do the work. So we have three URLs, but within each URL there are quite a lot of methods.

It wasn't actually how I wanted to do that. I wanted each of them exposed at separate URLs, but it just wouldn't work. I don't know how IBM or Sun—how their development systems work at all. We'd have to just see that. To use the system services, you must be the system profile. You must connect as the system profile. Or let me back up and say, every time that you access any service, you must identify yourself by your profile name. There is a special profile called the system profile that can manage the system and establish client profiles.

So then when you access the management services, you do so as a client profile, and you are managing all aspects of your client profile. Having done that, a client profile can also access the business services which actually do the work of the logistics information work. So we use the term[s] **system profile** and **client profile**.

There's something in our architecture design that we support in our connector library approach, but, when we use SOAP, we work within SOAP. What we did with the connector library is that, when you send a business object across, it's wrapped in a request. A request has in it the name of who you are—well, let me say, the request has in it a list of transactions—collection of transactions—and a transaction is a collection of tasks.

The idea being that, if you wanted to do four things and [if] you wanted to execute four services in sequence, and [if] you didn't need to stop the process between one and the other, you could simply put those four tasks into a transaction and send them all across together and ask the server to do the work.

We never implemented that because—well, it's implemented in that it would work, but we haven't done anything useful with it because there comes the issue of how do you control under what conditions the output of one service becomes the input of another. That sounds to me like what you're talking about having to do with orchestration and we haven't really dealt with that.

ALEX: *Right. If you're interested, there is a firm, but it is on a J2EE platform. The organization is called Collaxa. You're now currently delivering the same offering through the Web Services on the .NET platform. Can you explain the benefits that your customers are seeing? Are there benefits that you're seeing?*

PETER: For the .NET platform?

ALEX: *Well, just through using Web Services in general.*

PETER: Oh, yeah. Well, let me preface this by saying this: Our customers don't know they're using Web Services. They know they're getting a business solution. They couldn't really care less whether it's Web Services or anything else. From my point of view, though, we're reducing the integration time by a factor of at least five. Our first project that we did was implemented in five weeks. I would be very surprised if anybody else could have done it in six months, and we think there are two reasons for this. One of the things about Web Services is this: To get them deployed and deployed correctly and get them working, you really do have to think about what is the business problem you're trying to solve. What is the most efficient way to start that process off, and what's the most efficient way to deal with the results?

So you're looking at very well rounded, very efficient business process plug-ins. Therefore, the process of integration becomes very, very straightforward. I think, with our connector library, we did some good stuff, actually, with regard to making it easy to program, easy to deal with. We're still looking at the .NET platform and Visual Studio.Net to make some decisions about—do we supply a C library to help with programming? I don't know yet. But, I mean, that's the best benefit we've got.

The other part is it's tremendously robust. Because the requests are synchronous, the server is easy to manage. It's totally managed by IIS [Internet Information Server]. We run on a Windows 2000 server, and we've just found that network usage has been efficient and straightforward. Customers like it. It never had a problem dealing with firewalls because it's all HTTP—very straightforward to deploy and very, very straightforward to integrate.

I did systems integration work for years with various client-server technologies. In fact, I have some patents in the area of client-server technology and its use in logistics. This is an order of magnitude more efficient from a business point of view.

ALEX: *Have you considered bundling your offering with other strategic partners? And if so, can you please give an example of such a partner? How would the combination be more valuable to your customers?*

PETER: Yes, absolutely. When Microsoft created the Web Services Initiative to Europe last year, they invited seven companies to join. Five companies eventually did join and deploy their services using Microsoft products and so on. Three of them were in Belgium. We think, therefore, this must make Belgium the Web Services capital of Europe, which is a strange thing.

But there's a company, funnily enough, just across the park from where we are that does address normalization verification and quite a lot of functions relating to address type information. They've been in business for quite a long time, and they originally sold big huge data CDs and so on. They've now moved towards Web Services.

Well, one of the huge problems that we get is very typically our customers' order management information is still on a mainframe. In order to get an address, you just have four lines you get to type in. That just doesn't work.

We're in the transportation business and, if we don't have quality address information, we can't do anything. So one of the things we're talking about with this particular company at the present time is to be able to incorporate their services with our platform so that a customer of ours making calls can see that they have an address. We look at the address and simply say we know this isn't good enough. We can't decide what's going on with it. Let's pass it on out to the Infobel guys and let's have them do their magic with it—because it's their specialty, that's what they do—and give us back something that we can use.

ALEX: *I see. So the customer will make a request to your Web Service and as far as the customer is concerned, it's still your service.*

PETER: Yes.

ALEX: *As they come in, one of the things you do is you would extract the address and then you'd forward it or essentially hand it off to this data normalization company. They could validate as best that they can, and then, if the thing is workable, then you would continue on transparently.*

PETER: Yeah, absolutely. I mean, the last thing in the world I want to do is start getting in the address validation business, because that's incredibly complicated in Europe. I mean, it's infinitely more so than it is in the U.S. for obvious reasons.

ALEX: *Yes. I've been there enough to understand that.*

PETER: Right. Well, roads don't go straight here, so certainly this is a whole big issue. Well, that's not our core—we don't deal with it—we don't know about that stuff. We know about transportation. So it would be a lot better that we just simply say, "Hmm, address validation, let's just go off to somebody else's server and let that happen."

We've done some prototyping on that, but we're now working with the customer where the issue has become extremely real. We actually have some meetings next week. We've got to get some address information, get it treated right, and get it normalized. They're called Infobel, and their Web address is *infobel.be*. Great little company. I really like them. I really like working with them, as well.

ALEX: *You're currently supporting both the existing technology, which is a class library, and also Web Services. When do you expect the majority, potentially over 50% of your customers, to be using the Web Service as opposed to, say, the class library?*

PETER: Good question. If one listens to Microsoft or IBM or Sun, I'm sure they'll be trying to tell me, "Oh, don't worry about it, Peter. This year for sure." I know my business that I'm in and my [time] domain is five years. At the end of last year we took a really close look at how we deployed them as Web Services—did some much more careful study of the programmability of the services and so on and rebundled them, moved some methods around, and came up with a structure that we really like. Then we went ahead and came up with a version 2 of the connector library with revised interfaces that mirrors it exactly.

And then we actually did a test of those in the U.S., and we did a little workshop a couple of weeks ago. We took some code that we had written in Visual Basic with the connector library and in Visual Studio. Took that same code over to Visual Studio.NET, made a Web reference to the Web Services interface, changed a couple of lines of code, and off it went just fine. The difference is next to none. So we feel, having gotten them synchronized, we're not going to make too big of an issue about it. If somebody's across the Internet, obviously I would recommend Web Services to anybody. But our customers so far are tending to want to host them on their intranet and this is largely because they're very large companies and they have very good intranets where security's already dealt with. That takes a burden off us as to having to deal with security.

ALEX: *As an early adopter, can you share any lessons or pitfalls you encountered?*

PETER: Phew, there should be some somewhere, shouldn't there?

ALEX: *Yeah. If there's none, that's actually a great sign.*

PETER: Well, I'm going to say there's not. I mean, we had a bit of a vision, I guess, about three years ago when I suddenly sort of started to think [things] through—from a purely business point of view, how can I (a) get to market quicker; (b) integrate with my customers quicker and easier [and], therefore, cheaper; and (c) produce really robust systems that run anywhere, run on a laptop, run client server, run on an intranet, run on the Internet. That's what I wanted to have. That was where I wanted the business to be.

Then we sat down and did what I thought was some very good work in deciding how to take the world of logistics transactions and make them into some services. Once we got past that, I mean, it was just a matter of getting on and doing it. We didn't find any technology issues [to] really ruin it at all. I can't think of any drawbacks other than, if anybody was to come to me and say, "Hey, I think I want to deploy my business functionality as Web Services. Where should I start?" I would hide all their IDEs and make them think about what their business is. "What do you want to do? How do you want your customers to see you? What do you want them to do?" Forget about the code because it's actually pretty easy.

ALEX: *So, in essence, they have to do some soul-searching and probably do some sort of business modeling exercise, then?*

PETER: Absolutely. We had four months of business modeling and service design work before one line of code was written. So I think it is not a straight port from a client-server application to Web Services. That is absolutely true. We kind of knew that instinctively. We didn't try to do that because we wanted to go forward to deploy services before we knew what Web Services and SOAP and everything else was. We knew that's what we wanted to do.

Now, if a company was sitting there today thinking—"Well, I've got this client-server application and everything's heading towards Web Services. I guess I better go that direction"—just putting a Web Services wrapper on your client-server API is probably going to get you into more trouble. I really think that is not a way to go. I mean, we didn't have to do it, but I could. In looking back, had we taken that approach, that would have been a mistake because there are all sorts of things that just don't hold true anymore.

ALEX: *I see. So I guess that lesson in itself is valuable: don't try to just "wrapper" an existing application like this because the benefits probably don't warrant the effort that's going to be put into it.*

PETER: Interestingly enough, I mentioned to you, with Microsoft's Web Services Initiative last year, that there were seven companies invited and five actually pulled it off. The two who didn't were trying to wrap their existing applications. I mean, it just didn't work.

ALEX: *Technologically or businesswise?*

PETER: I can't tell you. I don't know. I just know that, in our initial meeting, Microsoft said, "Well, how are you going to do this?" And I said, "Well, pretty much, we've already done it. We'll just use your technology instead of ours." Somebody else was saying, "Well, we've got the existing application but we've designed a set of services." And I'm thinking, "They're going to be okay." Then some of the other guys are saying, "Oh, we're just going to put some XML front end on to this." And I'm thinking, "You're probably going to have trouble," because things like state, persistence, and sessions—the things you can count on in a client-server environment where the client and the server are connected—exist, whereas, in a Web Services world, they just really don't.

ALEX: *Thanks for your input, Peter.*

Case Study: Building Private UDDI Repositories (Talaris Corporation)

As we discussed in Chapter 3, there are existing issues with the business registries operated by IBM and Microsoft, including lack of validation of incoming entries and the lack of a critical mass of service providers. Talaris, a start-up that has built a next-generation procurement platform for business services (airline flights, hotel reservations, etc.), provides some interesting insights into how to build large-scale repositories. In addition, the interviewee shares how the firm provides a migration plan for customers who are not quite Web Services compliant yet.

Interviewee: Roman Bukary, VP of Product Marketing and Strategy, Talaris Corporation

ALEX: *Please explain what Talaris does and your role at Talaris.*

ROMAN: Let me start with my role. I am the Vice-President of Product Marketing and Strategy for Talaris. Talaris is a company that, for the past two years, has been designing and building a solution that leverages Web Services technology to provide an enterprise-class product for the procurement of business services. Since I used the word "services" to describe our loosely coupled, Internet standards-based technology and the time-dependent business services our corporate clients utilize, I'd like to explain that a bit further.

We view Web Services as good underlying technology. The vision and the promise of "Write once, access anywhere" is the right strategy and the right evolution of software—from monolithic, mainframe-based code, to client-server topology, to object-oriented code that became portable, and ultimately to today's heterogeneous code with common formats, access, and invocation protocols. But the real challenge that we're solving for corporations is the development of next-generation procurement solutions for the scheduling and purchasing of business and personal services. These services are any time-dependent, nonphysical items in areas of business travel; office-related services such as teleconferencing; personal services; dining and entertainment related services; and personal services such as appointment scheduling. If a corporate user requires an offsite conference room somewhere in the city of New York, the user can "ask" Talaris to execute this request on his or her behalf. What we've built is a procurement engine that deals with [potentially] thousands of suppliers, multiple access points, and protocols to each supplier ranging from XML via SOAP all the way to structured email or just simple IVR [interactive voice response]. We make all of this happen in the context of corporate policy and corporate rules and by knowing the user's individual preferences and requirements. To make it all possible, we chose Web Services technology as the architecture and XML as the data interchange format to power our enterprise application.

ALEX: *How does the Talaris product take advantage of Web Services?*

ROMAN: One of the most exciting things that has recently happened in the development community is the recognition that software should be able to access other applications, services, or solutions using existing protocols such as HTTP or HTTPs and then be able to do so, whether these applications are inside or outside the corporate firewall. This is the promise of Web Services, and Talaris has built a solution that leverages and employs those standards. For example, all of our content is managed using XML payloads, and we have implementations with some of our suppliers' SOAP connection. Most of our service suppliers are listed in our own UDDI directory.

This flexibility of Web Services and the promise of "Write once, access everywhere" is a great start, but the industry has a long way to go to make these standards robust enough to handle real business transactions. To overcome some of today's limitations, Talaris has generalized and augmented Web Services technologies with our value-added code to build a fully featured transactional system to deal with thousands of users and suppliers.

ALEX: *Did you look at any other way of integrating these disparate data sources?*

ROMAN: Absolutely. The reason we chose to employ Web Services but still write custom code to complete our solution is that, although Web Services have garnered a lot of attention and some suppliers and corporations have began experimenting with Web Services, lots of companies are still looking and evaluating them. Talaris took a pragmatic approach and said, "We're going to build this transactional platform for procurement, but we want to provide an immediate value to our corporate users on the front end and to suppliers on the back end." That really means that, while we will employ Web Services for our product and in our architecture, we're not going to force our customer or our partners to adopt Web Services. We're not going to force them to build out SOAP adapters. What we will do is try to speak to them in the *language* or the protocol of the highest level of technical sophistication that they are currently comfortable with. We have a field engineering organization that goes out there and works with suppliers to try to get them to move higher up, if you will, on the technology stack. We work with them on building out XML schemas, but we also have capabilities in the product to "speak" Java-based APIs, proprietary APIs, screen scraping, structured email, and a wide range of other data access or data integration formats so that, to the user, the overall service procurement process is seamless regardless of the technology we use on the back end.

Our goal ultimately is to get everyone to transact using Web Services, but, for the time being, we are prepared to "speak" all sorts of languages and all sorts of data interchange formats, ranging from XML to HTML screen scraping, to proprietary API in order to show immediate business value. As the adoption of Web Services increases in the corporate world and in the service supplier communities, we'll need to think less and less about access protocols and boundary conditions and much more about process modeling and optimization.

ALEX: *What were some of the challenges that you found working with Web Services given how early they are in the adoption cycle?*

ROMAN: As you know, Alex, the standards are still evolving, but, because we really are an application company that leverages Web Services as opposed to a tools company, we are not quite as dependent on the adoption of those standards. We look at the trends and we employ the best technologies we can, but we let the tool and middleware vendors worry about the standard's changes from Version 1.1.1.1 to Version 1.1.1.1.a. Seriously though, the biggest challenge is that there's been a lot of misunderstanding in the market of what Web Services are and what they can deliver. Some people look at them as the magical cure-all, others as the dreaded thing that's coming that's still totally undefined. Part of our job has been to go out and talk to our client corporations, our business customers, our suppliers, and say, "Look, number one, Web Services are not that scary. You've been really doing this kind of stuff for the last 10 to 20 years. It used to be called EDI, then it became EAI, then it became B2Bi, and now it's called Web Services." The alphabet soup has been changing, the protocols have been improving, custom coding requirements are decreasing, but the underlying idea of interfacing has been pretty consistent.

Number two, Talaris continues to talk about Web Services not as a cool technology but as a valuable business infrastructure, and all of a sudden the conversation shifts from protocols to business uses and ways to lower costs and improve service procurement efficiencies. We always say, "We provide a business implementation of Web Services. Forget tools, forget middleware, forget plumbing—let me show you what this really accomplishes in your environment." Such an approach gives great comfort to both corporations and, again, to the suppliers who say, "Oh, I know why you're doing this, I know how you're doing this. You're right; it's not that foreign. Okay, I know how we can get involved." It's like the old joke about how do you eat an elephant: the punch line is that of course you eat an elephant one bite at a time.

ALEX: *Please explain a business scenario of how Talaris integrates with a portal or the various things that a person uses in their day-to-day business activities.*

ROMAN: Let me break this question into two parts. First is the issue of the portal; the second is the issue of what a business user would use day-to-day. On the portal side, that's a simpler issue to address. Lots of corporations have deployed portals: some are homegrown; some come from commercial vendors such as BowStreet, Plumtree, Epicentric, SAP Portals, PeopleSoft, and any number of others. What a portal is designed to do is give users a single aggregated jump-off point to all sorts of resources and do so while managing basic role-based permissions and individual preferences. The resources a user may access from a portal could range from an analytic dashboard that is being fed SAP data to a news ticker tracking a particular customer with data feeds coming from external news sources.

Talaris looks at a portal as having great attributes that we want to leverage. One, of course, is that it "knows" who you are. So when you log into your corporate portal, you've already provided your identity and it knows your title, what department you're part of, what some of the role-based permissions and individual access levels are. We are using SSO [single sign-on] functionality from the portal to our application, thereby eliminating the requirement for users to reauthenticate themselves. It's also a very simple way for us to ensure that only authorized users access the Talaris application. If you were outside the corporate firewall, you would first log into the corporation, access the corporate portal, and then from there you would come into Talaris. We know that everyone originating from a portal is a trusted user. That's number one.

We also use portals to provide feedback to the user alerting them to such things as service request status information, notification of calendar updates, service changes, and corporate policy compliance metrics. Instead of us having to reinvent the wheel, what we really do is we leverage portal capabilities. Using their APIs and a combination of their technologies and ours, we provide windows or *portlets* where Talaris pushes a subset of our business logic to the portal as a Web Service enabling users to ask, "Hey, Talaris, did you get me that flight that I needed to meet with Customer X?" Talaris' component of the portal would acknowledge the request, reply, and graphically show that the work has been completed and would then provide the user with service-specific itinerary, schedule, price, location, etc. A user may want to know if the application has scheduled and provisioned a teleconferencing line to conduct a conference call between two partners. Talaris would update the portlet and, in a very compact form without invoking the entire application, would provide feedback in effect saying, "Yep, I got that conference call set up, it's all set for

11:30 in the morning; here are the people who will participate, and here are the details for the dial-in. How else can we be of assistance?" We leverage profile data and single sign-on capabilities from the portal into Talaris, and then we use the portal and its features as a way of providing real-time feedback to the user on the activities that we're doing as a transactional application.

Now, your second part of the question has to do with what do we do or what capabilities do we have to support these cross-devices or multiaccess point interfaces that the user may access during the day. We have spent a great deal of time understanding the specific service requirements of our business users across multiple service verticals. Because we've built out the underlying XML schemas for our services and our GUI is a very thin, device-portable front end, for us it's actually quite easy to provide users with access from a browser or a voice portal or a PDA, whether that's a Palm Pilot PDA or a PocketPC, or from any of the other touch points, such as a WAP phone or a RIM BlackBerry. The reason we can provide this access is that, because our UI is very thin, we don't need a heavy client, we don't need any plug-ins, and all of our business logic resides on the network, not on the physical device. The service requests that users define are in XML format, so that's very portable. As a result of our architecture, we do not require any rewrites to our application in order to avail it to the user regardless of the access point they might choose. We've had users access our application on RIM's BlackBerry devices, on Palm OS PDAs, on PocketPC devices, on WAP phones, and, of course, via Web browsers.

We try to make sure that we have built a very portable application and, to support that mission, we maintain persistent identity. That means that if I log in from a WAP phone, the Talaris application *knows* who I am and it knows my preferences and the corporate policies under which I operate. The Talaris application has, for example, users' billing options and their approved credit cards on file. The application knows exactly who I am, not because the Web browser or my phone remembers my credit cards or my notification options but because my profile—my identity—is maintained away from the user by the Talaris application.

No matter how I access the application—no matter whether I'm using my laptop or your cell phone—my access is pervasive and my information is portable and always accessible. Pervasive access, persistent identity, coupled with an always-on, user-centric application for service procurement—that's the value of a Web Services–based architecture, and that is exactly what we've built.

ALEX: *In one of your presentations you defined a term, "intelligent Web Service." Please elaborate on what that is as opposed to a regular Web Service.*

ROMAN: Web Services are really a logical and very intelligent evolution from their EDI ancestor. From hard-coded point-to-point connections in EDI, which began the definition of access protocols and data interchange, to EAI, to B2Bi, and then using a number of alphabet-soup technologies, to Web Services. Web Services are all about applications talking to one another over the Internet using standard protocols and data definitions.

Talaris recognizes that Web Services are an important technology, but, to make the stuff truly intelligent, truly user-centric, we have to couple the portability of a Web Service with [the] user's identity and historical data. Microsoft's Passport, Sun's Liberty Alliance, or AOL's Magic Carpet all deal with the issue of identity management in either monolithic or federated models. Talaris integrated identity management with Web Services with pervasive access and with the memory of who I am, what I've done, what I like, and what I dislike. Now that I have a full profile—a full mapping of Alex or some other user—and I know who these people are and what you've done in the past, now I can start to become an intelligent proxy working on your behalf.

As an example, let's look at an employee working for Company X. The corporation has certain attributes in their users' profiles, plus a list of approved suppliers, negotiated rates, etc. This company has deployed American Express Card as their corporate credit card that employees must use. With these variables set, Talaris can start to procure services for the employees of this company using only American Express, using only approved suppliers with negotiated rates, but [Talaris] identifies those end-user options that the company has chosen to leave undefined or unregulated.

For example, an employee at Corporation X has to take a business flight to get to a meeting. The corporate employer has approved vendors and negotiated rates for the service. The employee has an option to stay over a Saturday night and thereby decrease the fare basis on the airplane ticket. Talaris can easily find the cheapest fare with a Saturday night stay, but the intelligence and the benefits of identity management become readily apparent when Talaris asks the user whether it should purchase tickets to a hockey game since the application *sees* the itinerary, *knows* the user's preferences, and can communicate with suppliers who can provide appropriate sporting events tickets.

ALEX: *A lot of what you brought up requires many basic building blocks such as single sign-on and also issues of personalization. How do you address some of these challenges? Were they built in-house as proprietary technologies or are you leveraging existing packages?*

ROMAN: You're exactly right, Alex. We have always, from day one, made sure that NIH—Not Invented Here—was not part of our vocabulary. We are constantly evaluating our solution and our technologies; we look at the value that we provide and we ask ourselves, our advisors, and our partners if this [is] something that we need to build ourselves because we understand the nuances of service procurement better than anyone else or if there are commercially proven technologies that we should be using. In the case of, for example, identity management, there are great commercial technologies out there—everything from LDAP to Active Directory servers to, of course, the initiatives that I've talked about earlier: Magic Carpet, Passport, and Liberty Alliance. Our goal is not to try and come up with some other standard or to try and compete with these established companies in areas of identity management. These companies are doing great work, and they are building industry consensus around identity management. Our goal is to leverage those technologies wherever possible to deliver significant additional value to our end users.

What the technical team at Talaris has had to do was build an application that looks at you as a user—I'll use you again, Alex, as an example—it really looks at you as a user and says, "Oh, it's Alex and he is using Passport." How do we know this? Well, we know because, when you access Talaris, there are APIs that Microsoft is releasing that allow us to detect Passport and say, "Oh, yes, Alex is a known user." If you've made a decision to use Passport, all that Talaris needs to do is leverage that identity system and transact based on that information. Because in this example, if you're a Passport user, I know your name. Because you're a Passport user, I know other elements of your personally identifiable identification (PII). The application has access to those personal attributes you've chosen to expose. How much I know about you is a function of what your employer pushes into an LDAP or

Active Directory servers, or, in the case of an individual consumer, it's a function of how much information you wish to reveal about yourself.

You asked about single sign-on. Unfortunately, today there is no agreed-upon, third-party, single sign-on protocol or API. We had to really work with some of our partners and the major portal players to figure out what the touch points should be. In the case of identity management, we are absolutely going to leverage someone else's work because they've done it; they've thought through the issues and have had commercial or consumer success. Microsoft claims 160 million Passport users, and I'm not going to try to reinvent the wheel. The same principles apply across the entire Talaris solution stack. We always look and say, "What's our specialty? What third-party technology or standard can we leverage that will provide users with a better experience? Once we identify key technologies, we do a basic build-versus-buy evaluation. Build versus buy is a tactical decision; the strategic decision is to make sure NIH is not part of our approach.

ALEX: *Who decides what suppliers are added to the repository, you or your customers?*

ROMAN: We've built out a network of over 120,000 service suppliers across multiple service categories, but it is the customers who decide if we have enough suppliers and if we have the right kinds of suppliers. Talaris has a team of business development professionals who establish strategic partnerships with all sorts of players ranging from telco [telecommunications] providers to conference room providers to golf reservation providers to ticketing agents to travel agents to rental car companies. If you choose any user-centric service vertical, I'm sure we've either mapped it out to understand business processes, or we've already established strategic relationships. Our goal is to build a massive, transactional ecosystem of service suppliers. How we expose them to the corporate users is really a question of what do our corporate customers require. One company may say, "I need my users to access Service X from your network." If Talaris already has a relationship with Service X, then we simply say, "Done. Here it is and it's already been enabled." If we do not, then we would go out there and we would establish a relationship on behalf of our customer with Service X.

In cases where we've identified a strategically important alliance that allows us to provide business-critical services—for example, external conference room reservations (and I'm using this just as an example)—in that case we will look at the top 3, 4, 5, 10 suppliers in that space and we will establish strategic relationships with them, map the processes, and define transactional XML schemas, but we will wait for our customers to say, "Yes, I need this right now." If the customer doesn't say that, then we will put it in our product road map for a future release. It is the customers that define their business pain points, and we do whatever is required to make sure that the customer is delighted and finds great value in our solution. We have strategic directions and strategic alliances that we are always developing, but ultimately our technology, our IP [intellectual property], and our alliances are all done to solve business issues for our customers.

ALEX: *A big concern for many adopters of Web Services is the lack of security features or the lack of security standards. How do you address these concerns for your customers?*

ROMAN: That, I think, is a very valid concern. What we have are Web Services APIs as a somewhat platform-independent means for communicating across suppliers and across the corporate firewall. But the current Web Services protocols do not provide security standards, for example, as part of a SOAP definition. So we use SSL for all communications associated with any requests or any communication between users, the application, and supplier. We make sure that the data on both ends is encrypted and partitioned so that there is no way to say, "I've just cracked this code, so now I have access to all this information." We leverage specific technologies that our customers have validated on so that, when we deploy at one account versus another account, we conduct security audits as part of our deployment. For example, we ask our users, "Where do you maintain your employee information? Do you maintain an Active Directory? Do you maintain it on LDAP server? Do you maintain it as part of your HR system?" We support and frequently exceed our customers' securities standards and procedures, and our security infrastructure is designed to comply with their toughest requirements. We're working on making sure that every interface—every channel of communication from users to the Talaris application and from our application to our service suppliers—is secure and reliable and that data is never exposed and never maintained in open, unencrypted format. An individual's privacy and security are a paramount concern for us, and we make sure that that is never jeopardized. As a team, we work very closely, making sure that our engineers work side by side with our operations people to make sure that both the code and the infrastructure support our corporate security and reliability objectives. We work with our advisory board to make sure that the best practices that they have learned are leveraged by our application.

ALEX: *How do the UDDI specifications and public repositories fit into your vision and architecture, if at all?*

ROMAN: I think UDDI, or ebXML for that matter, offers the right vision and direction. The problem of UDDI or even of ebXML is the problem of yellow pages. Just because Bob's Auto Repair has a full-page ad in your local yellow pages does not necessarily mean that Bob is the most qualified person to work on your car. What would you do in an everyday situation that has nothing to do with Web Services? You would look at the full-page ad in the yellow pages for Bob's Auto, and then you would turn to your friend, your colleague, or your next-door neighbor and, in an attempt to validate identity and the vendor's claims, you'd ask them about Bob's Auto. They might say, "Oh, yeah, absolutely. I had great experience with Bob's Auto Repair." You would take such anecdotal data and you would establish a certain amount of assumed trust, but you would probably also want to know if they were a member of the Better Business Bureau. The point is that as a consumer you would validate the advertised information you discovered in the yellow pages' listing.

The problem today is that UDDI does not have any sort of body or standards committee that determines if you're authorized to advertise the services you've listed in a UDDI schema or that you really are who you represent yourself to be. Our bet is that, for the foreseeable future, UDDI will be adopted really as private directories behind corporate firewalls or within an environment such as Talaris where we establish service definitions, WSDL markups, and enforce SLA [Service Level Agreement] compliance.

We've really built out a private UDDI directory of over 120,000 service suppliers inside our firewall where we have taken on the responsibility of knowing who the supplier is, how they process requests, what the XML schema on the back end is. We understand how we invoke the communication with the supplier. And if we tried to "speak" SOAP to a supplier and it fails for whatever reason—the server is down, for example—we know that our backup condition is to try to speak a Java API to the supplier. If that fails, then we know to speak proprietary API or attempt some other format of communication.

So our bet is that UDDI is the right foundation, but a public UDDI directory is still a long way off.

ALEX: *Your framework provides many features that are currently missing from the standards, one of the most important being guaranteed delivery. Can you elaborate a little bit on how that was implemented?*

ROMAN: Some of the stuff is our proprietary IP [intellectual property], so I will need to be brief in those areas. Quite a bit is just recognition on our part and, I think, on the part of your readers that SOAP implementations of Web Services standards are not quite complete yet. Two of the most important issues are lack of security standards and the robustness of messaging. We have built this underlying technology inside our product that, number one, takes care of the security of the transmission, spanning everything from encryption to making sure that we're looking at PKI [public key initiative] where appropriate and really making certain that the data is secure both in our environment, in transit, and in our partners' environment.

The second part that's missing in the current Web Services standards is the robustness of a transmission—the things we take for granted within any transactional system or an RDBMS [relational database management system] such as two-phased commit or support for non-repudiation. Web Services today are very much of a fire-and-forget model that is missing basic features you would assume your local ATM [cash machine] supports. This transactional support is not part of the current Web Services standards. Talaris has implemented—in our architecture, in our workflows, and in our code—ways of compensating for that. Quite a bit of our solution is our own proprietary IP, but, yes, these two major deficiencies that you've highlighted are the two biggest challenges we've had to deal with. We've had to not only build this out, but also build it in a very scalable, robust, and portable manner.

ALEX: *You touched on this a little bit earlier, but I just want to explore this a little further. How do the various identity initiatives such as Liberty Alliance and Passport affect you, if at all?*

ROMAN: User identity management as we've discussed is a very important component of our overall solution. We have ways inside of our application to leverage everything from third-party identity management implementations, such as Liberty or Passport or Magic Carpet, to internal corporate identity resources, such as packaged applications' relational tables, LDAP, or Active Directory. We leverage all these things for the same purpose. The more we know about you, the less we have to ask, number one. But number two, the more we know about you, the more we know whether you are permitted to, for example, take advantage of SSO and gain access to a specific service. If you are listed on a corporation's LDAP server and you are given permission to corporate resources, well, then, I don't have to ask you and I don't have to ask corporate administrators, "Does this corporate employee have permission to this service?" If the LDAP server lists your desk phone and your corporate email and your title and the full proper spelling of your first name and your last name, well, then, the application doesn't have to ask you that. The Talaris application can start to be more intelligent and more efficient when it creates your accounts and when it manages corporate accounts, whether a new employee has joined the organization or another employee has moved on.

ALEX: *What are some missing features in SOAP, WSDL, and UDDI that would have made your job easier in building the Talaris product?*

ROMAN: In the case of SOAP, we're of course looking for the day when SOAP standards start to include security as part of the SOAP definition. We're also looking for SOAP to start to support a transactional environment with basic nonrepudiation capabilities. We've talked about the missing features that would address nonrepudiation and two-phase commits in SOAP standards.

In the case of UDDI, well, the issue with UDDI is not so much the issue of a standard or the definition, although there have been arguments made pro and con that ebXML is a more extensive and a more expandable standard. But the real issue with ebXML, or UDDI for that matter, is, in fact, the absence of some sort of a third-party certification body that would do the administration and validation, that would say to UDDI-listed services, "You have complied to industry standards and you've reached an appropriate level of certification." Some equivalent to a trustee needs to be established to deal with privacy and identity and the associated processes for the UDDI-listed service providers. Those are the two or three things that would help us: security, reliability, and identity certification of service providers since on the Web you really don't know who you might be dealing with regardless of what they might represent.

When you and I as individuals transact on the Web, I don't know if you're Alex in Midwest as you claim to be or if you really are Alex from California working for my competitor. You don't know if I'm an individual or if I'm actually a group of people. The standards on the Web and in Web Services haven't quite caught up to the point where we can establish with certainty service suppliers' identities, and we'd love to see these technologies and processes emerge.

ALEX: *Many of the features which you've had to build, such as transaction integrity and guaranteed delivery, are currently being offered by a newly emerging sector called the Web Services networks. Do you see Talaris partnering with these firms to leverage their technologies?*

ROMAN: Which firms would you list as providers of this middleware layer?

ALEX: *Grand Central, Flamenco Networks, Kenamea, Killdara.*

ROMAN: For example, we've looked at Kenamea and we've said, "This is good technology and perhaps we should partner with them to incorporate technologies they've perfected." The challenge for anybody publishing a Web Service and then exposing it in some sort of a networked environment is a logical evolution of what happened in the early days of Java when people started writing the first bits of code and exposing those snippets for anyone else to use: it was a good way to experiment with Java and understand its capabilities, but over time business-critical Java code had to be written using professional methodologies, certified, and QA'ed [quality assured].

I'm right back to where I started with authentication. Unless I really know and trust you, why would I ever trust a snippet of code that you've given me? Unless I really know and have authenticated you and have certified you in some way, why would I ever employ your unregistered Web Service? You may describe a perfectly valid Web Service that performs a useful function, but, embedded within that Web Service module there could be a malicious component that I'm not seeing or didn't catch, or didn't look at. So I think there's value to the Web Services networks as infrastructure providers. I think that they're pushing technology in the right direction, and I think that over time we will leverage their tools.

But the real value that we provide to our users is that, until certification and standards become uniform, we've built a proprietary UDDI directory. We are building out a proprietary Web Services network that we'd love to expand over time and expose publicly to permit any service supplier to be included. Gartner Group just created a category they call Web Services brokering, and they listed Talaris as a representative application provider. I could imagine using some of those infrastructure providers' technologies in the future, but those technologies would need to prove themselves out. What I really would love to use are some of the tools that they themselves are using for managing, testing, and validating Web Services. That, I think, would be very useful technology for us to employ. As much as they continue to push the envelope in middleware development, I think that's a win for them, for us, and ultimately for our customers.

ALEX: *Where do you see Web Services heading in the next 12 to 18 months and potentially also the next, say, 3 to 5 years? Or what needs to happen is probably a better question.*

ROMAN: My belief is that companies such as Talaris that talk about the business use of Web Services and establish Web Services SLAs between customers and their suppliers are showing corporations what can really be done with this newly emerging technology. In parallel, some companies, on their own, will explore Web Services technologies for the sake of basic technology initially inside their firewalls. As corporate users gain experience, they will begin using Web Services to interact with their suppliers. It doesn't necessarily mean on the manufacturing floor only, but companies will deal with suppliers using Web Services in areas where they can get their toes wet, but not put their corporations at risk. I think that, as companies such as Talaris provide real business value using Web Services and industry standards mature to address urgent issues of two-phase commits, nonrepudiation, security, robustness, and scalability, then corporate America will start to broaden its adoption of Web Services.

No one today in corporate America, or anywhere for that matter, says, "I'm going to play with cool, unproven technology simply for the fun of it." Corporations frequently use applications that leverage advanced technologies, but there has to be a significant ROI or business value. Corporate users have become very disciplined, requiring substantial ROI and short payback periods. Web Services is a very powerful technology that will revolutionize how business is conducted and how software applications interact.

ALEX: *Thanks for your time and insights, Roman.*

Perspectives of Web Services Vendors

Web Services are evolving so quickly that it is almost impossible to predict where they are headed. This appendix attempts to provide you with a 360-degree view through detailed one-on-one interviews with the executives at many of the leading Web Services vendors.

▶ Interview: SilverStream Software, an Early Adopter of WSFL

SilverStream Software was an early entrant into the Web Services space and made a decision to incorporate Web Services technology into all of its products early on. The result is SilverStream eXtend, a visual integrated services environment (ISE) for building complex service-oriented applications. At press time, SilverStream offers the only commercially available implementation of WSFL.

Interviewee: Steve Benfield, CTO of SilverStream Software

ALEX: *Please explain a little bit about what SilverStream does and your role with the firm.*

STEVE: What we've always done at SilverStream is—our one founding principle—is to help make software development easier, especially Web development. And so we started about five and a half years by delivering an application server with associated tools that made it easy to build a very dynamic Web site. That was back in the time when putting a Web page through database was considered cutting edge. We also bundled that capability with the app server, so it was all in one package. You could get up and running very quickly. We have evolved since then, as application development has evolved, to now provide the tools, the runtime services, and various engines to help support today's fairly complicated application development requirements.

Our major product line is called SilverStream eXtend. That's the family name. Within SilverStream eXtend we have a product called Composer, which is for XML integration of legacy systems and business process management. We also have a product called Director, which is for the front-end building piece, where I can consume services and data and crank out very complex sites fairly quickly with a variety of front ends, whether they're wireless devices, whether they're browsers, or 3-tier client-server devices. We have a development environment called Workbench, which ties all this together into one cohesive whole, and we also have a J2EE application server. One of the big differences that we have today from when we started was that everything that we built at SilverStream is now based on standards. When we started there were really no standards; Java 1.0 wasn't even formalized yet when we started the R&D on the products. At this point, everything we have is 100% J2EE [and] runs on a variety of application servers; over the past year and a half we've done a lot of work in the Web Services standards, as well. So that's what SilverStream does.

What I do as CTO is help ensure that the products that we create have a market, and that the markets understand our products. I also translate between R&D, between sales and marketing, in between our customers and the market in general—to make sure R&D is accountable for what they're building. I also keep my eye out for trends to influence what we wind up actually building. I call [my role] CTO—Chief *Talking* Officer or Chief *Travel* Officer.

ALEX: *Your product is one of the first in the market to support emerging standards, specifically the Web Services Flow Language, or WSFL. What are some benefits to the customer in having WSFL support in a product?*

STEVE: Well, it's based on the standard so we're not saving things in a proprietary format. Over time, as more tools come out to support WSFL, then customers will have a variety of tools that they can use to manipulate WSFL or interact with other systems. WSFL, to us—and one of the reasons we chose it—is a way of describing business process flows that is intuitive, very flexible, and 100% Web Services ready. WSFL is built on top of the Web Services standards, so it fits very well with our Web Services direction. We also like the fact that all of the external interfaces to a process flow are described using XML. The traditional workflow architectures tend to present some sort of API for hooking up external application functions. We do everything through XML so the integration of logic from many different business systems is very fast. In the end, what customers get is fairly great flexibility with standard support for the things that they're looking at doing now.

Just to give you an example, in a traditional workflow model, if I have an action and then I have a variety of other actions that could happen after that, I choose a link type such as maybe an AND link or an XOR [exclusive or] link, and if I then have to modify that diagram later and my workflow changes, it can be quite painful to make that change. By having our environment based on WSFL, it's actually relatively easy to make that change. I can add a new link at any time without affecting the other links. Each link is independently evaluated for whether that link is going to be true or not. And so it offers quite a bit of flexibility in the user experience, and the things that [users] can do.

ALEX: *Since WSFL is an emerging standard, what were some of the challenges you, as a firm, encountered when working with it?*

STEVE: Well, the problem with standards is, if there is a standard, then you can follow it but, if there's not a standard, you have to make one up. You run the risk of choosing something that's not going to be the standard, and so it actually goes to another question, and that is, "What are the things that we have to do over and above WSFL?" You can call them weaknesses in WSFL, or you can call them areas that just haven't been addressed yet. We worked with IBM [the authors of the WSFL specifications] on our implementation, basically going back and forth and digging deep into the specs and talking about areas of weaknesses. I would say that we really didn't have problems working with emerging specs, just that the spec itself wasn't fully complete.

So a couple of things: WSFL doesn't have anything for what is called endpoint processing, so things like how to specify time-outs and retries—such as "Try this thing five times until it fails, and then you go do this."—you can do that in WSFL, but you would have to then actually write all those actions manually, so it's a lot of coding. Since WSFL doesn't have anything to specify that, that's one of the things that we decided to add to our implementation. That way our customers don't have to write those timing-type things manually.

WSFL also has limited specifications for in-process execution. Essentially, everything is assumed to be a SOAP binding to Web Services, but there are times where you'd rather call that service locally, inside the engine. Let's say you want to call an EJB or something like that. [Either] you can reduce the latency of a SOAP call, or you still have it as a pure Web Service, so we added that capability to the product.

Additionally, there's an area of B2B integration that WSFL doesn't support very well. WSFL has something called a **process ID**—but if you're going to do B2B and you're going to do an interaction between two businesses, then you need additional IDs to get to a certain workflow item—and so we added something called a **correlation ID** to do that. If I'm running a process and it's intended for a certain type of worker, I can give it a correlation ID and then, when somebody goes to pick up that process—let's say a human being—then I can make their queue go pick up anything with a correlation ID of, let's say, 100. If I have the correlation ID of 100, then it's intended for that person, so it's kind of a level deeper than process ID.

ALEX: *So is correlation ID, then, a particular task inside a larger activity?*

STEVE: Yes, or it's a type of task. It depends on how our users actually use it. If you have a correlation ID that you need for every task, then it's potentially the same as a process ID, really. If you set your correlation IDs at a higher level, you can then group your tasks. It's stuff needed to do some sort of approval. Well, there's no human or no machine way of doing that approval. It's a human workflow. And so I've got a task waiting with a correlation ID of 100. Well, that means you need to write a program that will go query the business process engine looking for things with an ID of 100, present it to the user, the user does their work, and then we send it up, print it on the pipe. It's a way of addressing processes to individuals or to groups.

ALEX: *Can correlation IDs be nested?*

STEVE: Well, you could, depending on how they're assigned. One of the features of WSFL is that you can have recursive calls. But at any certain point, you're only going to have one correlation ID to a given task. You're not going to have multiple correlation IDs [mapped] to one individual task—it's a one-to-one relationship.

ALEX: *Do you intend on supporting BPML* [business process modeling language] *in future releases?*

STEVE: We're not committed to that right now. It's an open question. The thing about workflow right now is that it's starting to get a lot of attention, and we expect to see movement in the standards. There's talk of WSFL and XLANG coming together, depending on how the market moves. So the good thing is that we gear ours toward the information analysts, or business developers, versus the hardcore Java developers. One of the benefits of this is, when you're working with our Designer [tool], you don't really know that you're doing WSFL. So, if we have to change the underlying representation of how we store information about the workflow and how the engine processes it, we'll be able to, and we ought to be able to do it without much impact on what the user actually is doing. That's one of the benefits we get by abstracting the underlying implementation in the design environment.

ALEX: *Your product's really aimed at information architects or business analysts rather than developers. What features besides being more user-friendly do you think are more important to business analysts than to developers? Are there specific tools that business-oriented personnel would look for that developers may not care as much about?*

STEVE: Let's define "developer," right? Composer itself is not designed and specifically geared toward your hardcore J2EE developer. They're going to be more comfortable in an environment where they're going to be coding more and they have full control over everything that gets written. A business developer—somebody whose essential task is just to crank out business applications—wants something that's going to abstract that. So they're willing to give up a little flexibility in the underlying implementation for speedy development, whereas people that tend to be more systems-oriented programmers—very, very hardcore J2EE programmers—don't want anything interfering in what they can do, and they're willing to sacrifice the development environment for that. They essentially have two competing kinds of goals and ways of looking at the world.

Now, having said that, our designers for Composer are very much geared toward the business developer: very intuitive to use, high use of graphics, a lot of drag and drop. But at any point, somebody can go look and manipulate with the underlying XML that defines WSFL or the integration points that we have in Composer. So we try to be a balance between the two. The business developer can get maybe 80 to 85% of what they want done through drag and drop and point and click, maybe another 10% done through scripting—Composer uses JavaScript as its scripting language—and then 5% of the work can be done via Java, and so you get a Java developer in to build those lower level things. What that allows you to do is be very productive [with little coding], but at the point where you need to drop down and do something fairly specific, or extremely complex, you've got the hooks in to do it.

One of the features of the business process management piece of Composer is animation, and this actually sets us apart from most products on the market. This is another thing that is of use for a business developer: you can go in and actually create a workflow without specifying any of the underlying implementation. Somebody can work with it and then define their XML structures, and you can then go build Web Services or map to Web Services to actually fill in the actual action yourself. It's very much a top-down type of approach.

Likewise, if you already have all your services, then you can add services directly to the model and go from there. You have some flexibility in how you actually design your business process. Once you've got a process in place, in the Designer [tool], you can visually step through the entire process and watch all the XML that's going back and forth. You can watch the decisions that are being made. If your Web Service was built in Composer—let's say it's a CICS interaction that you've got—Composer will actually step into that service. You can see inside the service to see what's going on. Obviously, if it's not one of our Web Services, then you can't because it's just a public interface.

You can then step through the entire process. If you've got these things in production and you've got a process that's either going crazy or is raising an error, we've got consoles and logs that are all HTML based, where I can go look at that individual process and I can look at the data associated with that process. I can then take that data and go put it into my animation environment and I can step through and actually determine why this thing is going bad. When it comes to maintaining these business processes in a production environment, we've got a really nice way of pinpointing problems, so they can be solved fairly quickly.

What people are used to doing with business process products is they build their business process, which is a mixture of some graphing but also a lot of coding, and then when there's a problem during execution they essentially have to go hunt it down manually. They have to follow the process flow through code. We give them an opportunity to actually run this thing, simulate the environment and see what's going on. It's a nice feature that people get pretty excited about when they see it.

ALEX: *Let's assume that I already designed a workflow in another tool, which can generate a WSFL-compliant model. Could I then import that model into your tool, assuming that the WSFL standard gets robust enough?*

STEVE: Yes and that's one of the reasons for basing stuff on standards. Now, to say you could do that today, I'm not sure. If you wanted to use something like Rational Rose to use UML to define a WSFL-based model, and then bring that model into our environment to refine it and implement it, that's essentially why we decided to go with a standard like WSFL. Likewise, somebody could take the XML artifacts that we create and use another tool because they like the design tool a little better. Maybe it's got better documentation capabilities. That's absolutely the expected behavior that we hope to see: products offer this interoperability in the near future.

ALEX: *How are your customers currently visualizing their business processes? Are there standards and notations for workflow and orchestration beside the usual flowcharts and activity diagrams?*

STEVE: Yes, you have UML as a standard. For people that have workflow products today, most don't use UML. They use some other way of doing it—fairly proprietary ways—and that's how our customers have done it in the past. With Composer and our Business Process Manager, customers are actually able to now draw those workflows and then actually put stuff behind it. The area of business process modeling has gotten a lot of attention over the past few years, but what we've found, in the real world, is that most people just use it to draw, and that's it. So if somebody says, "Yeah, we use UML for this," they're using UML to define the process, but then they go hand code it all.

People will do a nice object model in UML and maybe generate some base code, but then they quickly deviate from the modeling tool and they're hand coding.

ALEX: *There's some justifiable performance consideration when working with asynchronous and XML-based systems. What are some optimization techniques that your products have implemented to address these bottlenecks, and have you found other bottlenecks, and, if so, how have you addressed them?*

STEVE: Well, if you're talking the business process engine, the overhead that you have of passing data around as XML is not really a huge issue. What you want with a business process engine is scalability. The fact that it may execute an individual process a tenth of a second later is probably not an issue in a traditional workflow. Traditional workflow processes tend to be fairly long-lived and complex, so the latency between the call from one service to the next is not the issue. It's "Can your system handle 3,000 concurrent processes?" That's what defines a heavy-duty business process engine.

Now, if you're talking about performance when using Web Services instead of going to a JDBC database, the marshalling overhead of Web Services could become a concern for certain types of application[s]. And dealing with wire protocols like HTTP is going to be slower because you've got more layers, and so—justifiably—people have brought that up as a concern. In addition, passing data around as XML in an uncompressed ASCII format definitely puts a lot more burden on your bandwidth than some binary way of passing data around will. Those are open issues in the Web Services realm. We think they'll be fixed over time either through hardware and more bandwidth, or through compression techniques and the ability to not necessarily pass the entire data set. It's going to come with experience.

Now, as far as specific optimizations and what we've done: one of the things that we do when we parse XML coming into our SOAP server is that we don't necessarily put it into an XML DOM as an intermediate state. What we do is, as the SOAP message is coming in, we actually get the data and populate it into an object. The client objects that we create with our SOAP toolkit actually populate instance variables of a Java object, and you don't have the XML DOM objects in their kind of intermediate state. This saves a little bit on memory coming in and on processing.

In addition, if the caller and the target service are actually running on the same machine, we actually don't go through the entire XML marshalling step. We do a fairly direct call. That assumes you're using our SOAP engine, so it is an issue. What it also says is that whether you build your application where all interaction with the back end is via Web Services, [the answer is] probably today, no. If you get better performance with EJB because you need to call this thing a thousand times a second, you'd be foolish to do it as a Web Service. But if you need to communicate between two different machines, two different divisions in your organization, or different operating systems and languages, then Web Services make a lot of sense.

ALEX: *What common characteristics have you seen of firms that have successfully adopted Web Services?*

STEVE: They don't jump in feet first and try to make the largest application. As much as we're in Web Services, and as much as Web Services have gotten hyped, the reality of Web Services is that most organizations are doing exploratory kind[s] of projects. They're doing proofs of concept, or they're doing departmental projects where they can kind of get their feet wet and see where the problems are, where the holes are, and not making the assumption that Web Services are going to solve all their problems and it's a magic bullet, because Web Services are pretty straightforward to understand.

But [when it comes to] the actual implementation, when you start getting between multiple providers and SOAP engines and things like that, you can run into trouble, and that's what the WS-I [Web Services Interoperability Organization] is all about, which is to ensure interoperability of services. Going slow is really our recommendation. Also, you can't build a Web Service out of a badly architected application because it's not going to perform well. You still need to apply your architectural rules to building Web Services application. Things need to be modular. It's standard stuff.

ALEX: *Do you have any predictions on where Web Services will be or have to be in 12 to 18 months, in 3 to 5 years? What are you basing some of your strategic plans on?*

STEVE: We're making the assumption that Web Services themselves will not be a competitive differentiator for any vendor in a year from now. This basically says every software vendor will have Web Service enabled—either their application, tools, or their engines. It may not be to the extent that everyone wants, but essentially, in the marketplace,

Web Services will essentially become a check box item—like CORBA was five years ago. Five years ago, somebody would say, "Does your IDE support CORBA?" You'd say, "Yes." They'd say, "Okay, great." At that time customers may have had plans for CORBA, but most never implemented them.

Web Services will become a check box. "Does your application have Web Services interfaces?" "Yes, it does." "Okay, good." Now, during the technical evaluation, you'll go deeper into the product[s] to see how well they actually implement them, but vendors in the marketplace will all have demonstrable Web Services support. I think definitely for the next year people will be working with Web Services internally, inside the organization. We're not going to see a lot of B2B uses of Web Services until certain standards are matured a little bit.

Three to five years, that's a hard prediction to make. But I think the predominant way of building new applications three to five years from now will be service based. People will have services in their applications. Orchestration will be a predominant way of actually building applications, so products like our Business Process Manager are obviously some of the initial steps in that area. There are more global issues, such as "Will Java be relevant in a Web Services world?" and things like that. We think the language that you build your applications in will certainly be important, and so we think Java and Microsoft still will be strong players, but interoperability will be there in three to five years.

Web Services will be much more mature, and we'll have consoles for watching the services run. An area of Web Services that has to be addressed over the next few years is how to build front ends to Web Services in a standard way. Now we have a standard way to communicate with data. We have a standard way for machines to talk to each other. But we don't have a standard way for defining front ends or interfaces, and there are a couple of proposed things going on in that area. You have XFORMS, you have WSUI [Web Services User Interface], and you've got WSRP [Web Services remote portlets]. Those will come to the fore over the next year or two. What I hope to see five years from now is people building applications in a very modular way, based on standards—and those standards will cover everything from the back end all the way to front-end development.

ALEX: *Thanks for your time, Steve.*

Interview: Collaxa and Web Services Orchestration

Web Services are the implementation of business processes and, in many cases, these business processes can be quite long lived. This interview provides the challenges that that have to be addressed when managing long-lived business processes including cancellation and versioning.

Interviewee: Doron Sherman, CTO of Collaxa

ALEX: *Please explain a little bit about what Collaxa does and your role at the firm.*

DORON: Collaxa is a start-up company founded by veterans of AOL, Netscape, and NetDynamics that came with extensive application server and enterprise integration experience to address what I would perceive to be one of the biggest challenges faced by IT organizations today. Collaxa is focusing on enabling solutions for delivering collaborative business applications based on a service-oriented architecture. These business applications span across the application development and the enterprise application integration domains.

In essence, the notion of a business application is changing, and Collaxa defines it with what we trademark as "The application is the orchestration." Collaxa's product is a Web Service Orchestration Server, which is built on top of standard J2EE infrastructure. The Collaxa Orchestration Server is primarily targeted at corporate developers skilled in Java. Collaxa takes a very complex problem and makes it simple, flexible, and easy to manage.

As for my role as CTO at Collaxa, it is to help direct a revolutionary product so it provides a compelling buy-versus-build value for IT decision makers while making it a highly usable and easy-to-learn solution for Java developers. One of the most critical challenges that I face in taking the CTO job is to drive adoption for a breakthrough and at the moment also a nonconsensus approach to authoring orchestration logic.

Collaxa's success, to a large extent, depends upon demonstrating that what we do is the right manner for solving the orchestration problem. Historically speaking, I actually faced a similar challenge before at NetDynamics when we created the first Java application server. At the time, the product category which is known as the application server, and, more specifically, the use of Java to author business logic on the server, was far from obvious or even an acceptable practice as it is today.

ALEX: *Please define the term orchestration as it's used, specifically in your Orchestration Server product.*

DORON: The basic IT challenge which is faced by organizations today is that businesses and people that work together need their applications and services to work together. The IT landscapes in most organizations are comprised of best-of-breed business systems and applications, which are implemented with a myriad of languages on multiple computing platforms. The existing solutions for enterprise integration are too costly, proprietary, and are primarily relevant in high-end cases, but never made it to mainstream implementations, which is restricting their utilization. This fact is driving the industry's move to Web Services, which holds the promise of enabling industry-standard interoperability.

When you make Web Services work, you're involved in a two-step process. First, you publish Web Services, and then you orchestrate them. Publishing Web Services means that you make the services available, while orchestrating means that you assemble and coordinate services into manageable business applications. Orchestration really becomes particularly complicated when one or more of the services that are used as building blocks for the application are asynchronous. In this scenario, orchestration of services entails handling of multiple asynchronous conversations with loosely coupled components over coarse-grained communication protocols. Handling these conversations invariably results in the need to address a number of interdependent challenges. These challenges include things like managing long-lived state and application context, supporting parallel activities and sophisticated join patterns, having to handle exceptions as well as events which are generated by both local as well as remote components, and dealing with business transactions and compensation mechanisms when failures occur. Last but not least, you have to deal with graceful upgrading and maintenance of application functionality, which is a complicated versioning problem.

In summary, orchestration includes a consistent set of requirements which most collaborative business applications that are built on a service-oriented architecture entail. The Orchestration Server was created out of the realization that this consistent set of infrastructure requirements should not be programmed as custom code by developers, but rather provided as standard-based server software. By utilizing the Web Service Orchestration Server, developers are free to focus on programming the orchestration logic of service-oriented collaborative applications as opposed to being burdened by building application infrastructure.

ALEX: *Two features that your product offers are parallel branching—which then subdivides into fixed branching and dynamic branching—and a nonlinear state management. Can you please define these terms and how they are useful?*

DORON: Sure. I think it's better depicted using an example. Let's take a loan procurement application as an example of a collaborative business application. In this application you have, as part of the orchestration, two external loan processors that can take anywhere from hours to even a few days to take a loan application and, through their own internal processing, in the end provide a loan offer. When coordinating parallel execution of conversations, you enable streamlining the processing of the business application as opposed to having to execute both processes sequentially, which would be a rather inefficient way of doing it.

There are two kinds of parallel branching mechanisms, as you mentioned—fixed and dynamic—and both of them are supported by the Collaxa solution. For example, a fixed branching example would be a travel reservation application where you have a fixed number of services such as getting a hotel room service, a rental car service, and an airline ticket reservation service.

As an example of the dynamic branching, we can take again the loan procurement application, where the number of service providers that process the loan application and provide loan offers in return is actually not known at design time, and hence the application should be able to handle a dynamic number of service providers at runtime when processing the loan.

As I mentioned, Collaxa addresses both the fixed and dynamic parallel branching, and we do that with the use of orchestration tags, which are embedded in Java code. One of the interesting aspects of parallel branching is the notion of sophisticated join patterns. For example, in the loan procurement application, you may have a rule that the customer is shown loan offers until he or she accepts one offer within a certain APR [annual percentage rate] range, and the processing should continue to enrollment at that point.

You also asked about nonlinear state. Nonlinear state is really interesting because it essentially involves the handling of events and exceptions which are intermixed with an otherwise linear execution logic. Being able to manage nonlinear state allows business logic, which is associated with handling of events and exceptions, to be specified anywhere in the application and making sure that it's always executed within the application context. Doing this is traditionally very difficult with EAI solutions, which are based on an event-driven architecture.

ALEX: *A key abstraction in your offering is the Scenario Bean. Please define the role and the benefits of Scenario Beans during development and also deployment.*

DORON: Basically, a Scenario Bean is a Java-based abstraction similar to a JSP, and it captures orchestration logic. Essentially, JSP [Java Server Page] for presentation logic is what a Scenario Bean is for orchestration logic. Scenario Beans, from an architectural standpoint of J2EE—we can say that it is a genetic evolution of a Session Bean. It adds the ability to define a logical contract on orchestration behavior, which is separate from the physical binding. Each statement in a Scenario Bean can represent a long-lived conversation.

What Collaxa did is we added five orchestration tags to Java in order to provide the Java developers with the ability to choreograph long-lived conversations. What Collaxa does also is instrument the Scenario Bean code to provide multiple capabilities to both Java developers, such as the ability to provide concurrent debugging. We also instrument it to provide business reporting for business users and provide the ability to do extensive monitoring for operational people.

In summary, a Scenario Bean is a self-managed component for which the orchestration container provides lots of automatic capabilities in the infrastructure layer without burdening the developer with dealing with those services.

ALEX: *As business scenarios get more complicated, the exceptions that can be raised likewise can get more complex. Does your product define additional exception handling on top of the standard SOAP faults?*

DORON: Well, SOAP faults basically let developers define exceptions and their associated data, but really the challenge is how you handle those exceptions, which is where Collaxa comes in. For example, in the loan procurement application, the loan processor service provider may raise an exception in the middle of a conversation with the collaborative application. Collaxa's Web Service Orchestration Server marshals the SOAP fault, which is communicated back to the collaborative application into a Java Exception object, and that Java Exception object is then handled inside the Scenario Bean using the standard Java try-catch construct.

This mechanism, which is rather straightforward in the synchronous world, is not trivial when such faults are encountered in the midst of asynchronous conversations. Scenario Beans provide a powerful mechanism to handle exceptions for both synchronous logic and within asynchronous conversations. Also, Collaxa has the ability to handle exceptions programmatically, and in addition enables straightforward involvement of a human operator through a user task when necessary. Again, let's take the example of the loan procurement application. During the qualification process for the loan applicant, an exception such as a bad credit rating, or customer-not-found exception can be raised, and, in that case, you would like to involve a human operator to manually make a decision or define the credit rating for the customer.

ALEX: *Your product provides the ability to handle long-lived transactions. How does your product handle canceling an in-process transaction?*

DORON: Well, the Collaxa Web Service Orchestration Server tracks all in-progress conversations throughout the execution of a scenario. What the Orchestration Server does is that it creates a list of all the conversations, all the activities, and all the tasks during the execution of those conversations. The Orchestration Server takes snapshots of the data every time a transactional node is encountered, such that it can go back and compensate with the original data when needed.

For example, imagine that we're in the midst of the loan procurement scenario and you have two open conversations with two external loan processors. If the user decides to cancel the loan application at this point, the Orchestration Server can propagate this cancellation event to all the in-progress conversations and throw an exception inside the scenario to enable the orchestration logic authored by the Java developers to execute custom cancellation logic code. As an example, cancellation of an airline ticket reservation may entail charging the customer an agreed-upon fee in addition to releasing the ticket.

ALEX: *What are some key issues that have to be addressed in dealing with versioning of business processes and the associated Scenario Beans?*

DORON: There are two problems associated with versioning of orchestration logic, such as in the case of long-lived business processes. The first problem is that the service providers change their implementation and they note it with a new version. This is known as an endpoint change. For example, a service provider provides a notification that the new version of the service is now available at a new location. In this case, the developer doesn't have to modify the Scenario Bean code, but only modify the deployment descriptor that captures the physical binding of the orchestration scenario to indicate a change in the endpoint. That was the first problem.

The second problem is caused by the developer changing the logic of the orchestration inside the Scenario Bean. In this case, the Collaxa Orchestration Server has the capability to run multiple versions of the Scenario Beans simultaneously and gracefully phase out existing instances of the old version while directing new instances to use the new version. Dealing with that type of problem is really important because, if we refer to the loan procurement application that I mentioned before, you may have 10,000 loan applicants that are in the midst of applying for a loan, and they may have still time to execute the orchestration logic and get phased out of the process. Meanwhile, you have many more loan applicants that are logging into the system and starting the loan procurement application, and those folks have to use the new version. So, as you can tell, the orchestration container has to have the ability to run multiple versions of the orchestration logic and gracefully phase in and phase out those instances.

ALEX: *There's some justifiable performance concern when working with asynchronous and XML-based systems. What are some optimization techniques that you have implemented to address these bottlenecks? Also, have you found other bottlenecks, and if so, how have you addressed them?*

DORON: First of all, the Collaxa Orchestration Server is based on standard J2EE infrastructure, so any incremental improvements provided by J2EE application servers for handling asynchronous or XML-based communication is directly reflected in the Collaxa solution. In general, the use of asynchronous communication increases the overall throughput and scalability of service-oriented applications, although developers normally need to take special care in designing these applications. With XML, we all know that on-the-wire communication overhead, in addition to the overhead of XML parsing, probably will always be slower than tightly coupled binary communications.

Collaxa, like other vendors, will directly benefit from continued improvements in XML parsing performance and related optimizations. Specifically, what Collaxa adds on top of that—we provide added-value capabilities in the form of caching, clustering, and persistence optimization. For caching, the obvious trade-off exists when architecting these types of applications—the trade-off exists between reliability, availability, and scalability. Caching is a common mechanism where different cache policies can be used to store data that changes infrequently, thereby minimizing traffic of data over the network, and that's an internal mechanism implemented by the orchestration container.

As for clustering, the orchestration container is designed to execute in a stateless fashion, which allows the addition of servers in a linear fashion to scale performance linearly to handle increasing load. For persistence optimization, asynchronous invocations always require persisting of the application context to guarantee that it can be recovered upon server crashes. The internal mechanism that is used by the orchestration container for persisting Scenario Bean instances include[s] things like partial loading of the context combined with lazy or on-demand loading of the scenario context during long-lived execution of the orchestration logic.

The Orchestration Server, by design, skipped a plain vanilla implementation using JDBC, and instead we provide a persistence mechanism, which is optimized for each relational database that is supported as persistence store for Collaxa.

To summarize, in terms of flexibility, Collaxa supports both Web Services for XML-based messaging, as well as JMS, where, for the latter, custom messages can be constructed for exchange with external components through a messaging provider. The Orchestration Server is making effective use of the allocated JMS connections to save on overhead, which is otherwise incurred while working with the exchanged messages. In this respect, we make the best of both the XML-based messaging world and asynchronous messaging world using JMS.

ALEX: *Do you have any recommendations on how companies should model and visualize their processes? Do you provide tools for visualizing the Scenario Beans during production? Also, are there standards* *and notations for workflow orchestrations, besides the usual flow-chart, that companies should adopt?*

DORON: At the moment, business analysts actually use a variety of different tools and methodologies for depicting business processes and communicating it to developers. Collaxa's main goal is to minimize the mental gymnastics needed and eliminate the communication break-down that often occurs between business analysts and the development team. Collaxa at the moment does not provide a tool for modeling and visualization, but we are looking at leading modeling and visualization tools and standards to enable that capability to streamline the creation and initialization of Scenario Beans. We think that UML activity diagrams and RAD process modeling practices should be widely adopted by business analysts to augment ad hoc practices.

Visualization of business processes happens actually at two different stages of the application life cycle. One stage is during design and brainstorming, when the model is being communicated to the development team, and the second stage is during business activity monitoring of the automated business processes. Collaxa supports the ability to convert UML activity diagrams into Scenario Beans that can be further customized by Java developers. Collaxa also, on the back end, provides a Flash application that enables effective visualization and monitoring of the resulting implementation. That Flash application is solving the communication breakdown problem that happens when the developers go off and continue migrating and modifying the application business logic without any effective means to communicate it back to the business analysts. That Flash application, which is part of the Collaxa solution, solves the problem.

ALEX: *You mentioned the Flash application actually animates the business processes. Can you elaborate a little bit [on] how that process happens and its benefits to a nontechnical person?*

DORON: Basically that Flash application is designed to address the communication breakdown problem that happens when developers go off and implement advanced versions or modify the application functionality without any effective means of communicating the state of the functionality back to business analysts at their own level of understanding since, as we know, business analysts usually do not read Java code.

The way Collaxa implements it is that we provide an annotation mechanism in the form of javadoc which is basically a standard way of commenting Java code inside Scenario Beans. Collaxa instruments these comments provided by Java developers and feed[s] that metadata back into the Flash application, which constitutes the portion of the Collaxa Orchestration Console. That Flash application then can take the metadata, which can also be added programmatically and [can] collect real-time statistics information that developers think is important for business users to view. The Flash application will then take all the data and animate it for business users to see what the application is actually doing at their own level of understanding.

ALEX: *Assume that I have gone through a business process modeling phase where I've identified key business processes. Is there a one-to-one mapping between business processes and the Scenario Beans?*

DORON: As I mentioned earlier, one of Collaxa's main design goals was to eliminate or drastically minimize the mental gymnastics that commonly take place when business analysts try to communicate the model of business processes to the implementation team. Since the orchestration container takes care of all the application infrastructure details and provides a powerful linearized abstraction to Java developers, we actually created a congruent model that allows straightforward translation from the business process as depicted using flowcharts or other similar means into the implementation of Scenario Beans done by Java developers.

If you look at real-world applications, visual models are generally inadequate for capturing all the different facets and nonlinear aspects of complex orchestration logic. In that respect, what Collaxa does is take the clarity of depictions of business processes and generate skeletons of Scenario Beans which then are augmented by Java code to capture the full range of complexities for implementing the application.

ALEX: *How does your product support ebXML and WSFL, and do you intend on adding support for business transaction protocol [BTP]?*

DORON: Collaxa Enterprise Edition provides support for advanced e-business protocols and standards. Today we support WSFL Scenario Beans and also part of the ebXML specification. The flexible design of the Orchestration Server allows rapid adoption of additional standard protocols such as XLANG and BPML and, as such, provides future-proof solutions as new standards emerge. We are constantly monitoring the evolution of transactional protocols such as BTP, which has the potential of ensuring consistent behavior among loosely coupled components involved in transactional scenarios.

BTP is attempting to bridge the world of XA (two-phase commit) transactions that are suitable for tightly coupled resources with the world of business transactions that are populated with loosely coupled services. Successful adoption of BTP is currently not guaranteed, but, if and when it does get adopted, Collaxa will provide for it a much simpler interface leveraging the power of the Scenario Bean abstraction.

ALEX: *Your product provides some functionality that is currently found in some of the Web Services networks such as Grand Central. Is your product complementary or competitive to their offering? If it is complementary, how would the two products interact and how would I go about using both products at once?*

DORON: Well, I'd say that, at a very high level, the difference between Grand Central and Collaxa is in the business model. Grand Central is a network where an organization can outsource their business processes or portions of their business processes to be handled outside the firewall. Traditionally, for a company like Grand Central to be able to scale its business, they would have to resort to repeatable processes that can be mass customized. And usually those would be kind of the low-hanging fruits, if you like—the simpler processes that would have to be implemented. But nevertheless, they provide a lot of value when they are able to do that.

Collaxa is an enterprise software vendor that can enable Grand Central to use the Collaxa solution for addressing more complicated business processes to serve more of their customers' needs. In general, because Grand Central is a complete business service, they have to provide a much larger gamut of services relative to what Collaxa provides. I see Collaxa and Grand Central [as] highly complementary in the short term and a great potential for synergy in the long term.

ALEX: *Do you have any predictions on where Web Services will be or have to be in 12 to 18 months and in 3 to 5 years? What are you basing some of your strategic plans on?*

DORON: [In my opinion] for whatever it's worth, Web Services are rapidly maturing from the initial vendor-hype stage into a mainstream design pattern which many IT organizations now actively experiment with. The vendors, on the other hand, which are lining up in both the Microsoft .NET and the J2EE camps, shift the conversation from the basic Web Services protocol stack (SOAP, WSDL, UDDI) into discussions about the issues that surround Web Services adoption—such as RAS [reliability, availability, scalability], topics like security, and, more recently, discussions about the actual application model that will emerge out of using the service-oriented architecture.

The leading platform vendors are adding Web Services support as a core part of the product application development, deployment, and management infrastructures. Possibly similar to the evolution of enabling technologies and user-facing Web applications, but likely in a faster pace, since the basic Web protocols such as HTTP; program languages such as Java, VB, [and] C#; and messaging formats such as XML are here already, Web Services will drive the emergence of a new class of applications which are based on a service-oriented architecture.

I personally expect that within 12 to 18 months we will see customers starting to implement integration solutions from an application development design perspective as opposed to using proprietary EAI solutions, which is currently the default choice. In the longer horizon, say three to five years from now, I'd expect Web Services to have a mature application development model which is well entrenched on top of the leading application infrastructure platforms, both on the J2EE and the .NET sides. At that time there should be a striving ISV [independent software vendors] industry leveraging these infrastructure platforms for delivering collaborative applications based on the service-oriented architecture within various vertical industries.

As a side effect, this will lower the boundary of attaining business integration solutions for smaller enterprises, not just for the Global 2000. Also what I would expect in a three- to five-year horizon is that there would be emerging businesses that would base their businesses on an outsourced Web Services business model.

ALEX: *Thanks for your time, Doron.*

▶ Interview: Iona Technologies, an Interoperability Veteran

Iona Technologies has been in the interoperability market for almost a dozen years and is a market leader in the CORBA market through their Orbix product line. In this interview, Iona's CEO discusses the likelihood of Web Services cannibalizing the CORBA market, the long-term movement toward open standards, and the way in which some of Iona's clients are adopting Web Services.

Interviewee: Barry Morris, CEO of Iona

BARRY: Let me just give you some general sort of commentary because I think that it's important to have some context for your questions. I firmly believe that the majority of the industry has failed to understand what this [Web Services] is really about. What we've got is a huge amount of hype and so on going on out there—people claiming everything from perpetual motion to world peace—and there's very little reality about it.

Yet there's something about this technology which I think is absolutely discontinuous, disruptive, even revolutionary. I think it's going [to] fundamentally change not just the way that we do computing, but it's going to be the enabler of the sort of next-generation digital society, and I have that very deep belief, but I think it's a very concrete belief. It's not about some sort of wild ideas of what might happen. And it's a concrete belief for the following reasons.

As you look at information systems of every description—and I'm including, of course, computer systems and databases and all that sort of stuff, but [I'm] also including the home appliances or sort of engine management systems or whatever, all of those systems right now—this issue of how they communicate with each other in a semantically intelligent way, the way the issue—what technical people would call the metadata issue—is unresolved at a standards level.

People understand how to solve it, but there hasn't been an acceptance of how to do so, and so there's nothing sort of revolutionary *technically* about this technology. What's revolutionary about it is the very broad adoption of these sets of standards, which are the three core standards and the others to follow, but the three core standards are enough for the moment. The very broad adoption of those standards enables the next layer up—the communication between different types of digital systems. That's something which we've actually been saying for the last 11 years. The company [Iona] has been profitable, based on some sort of service-oriented architectures that happen to be around with a different set of standards, but those standards are to some extent superficial.

The reality [of the industry] is [that] it's service-oriented architectures and it's standards-based service-oriented architectures. What you're going to see is that Web Services are going to start hitting reality in a number of phases. Unfortunately for the industry, people are talking about the last phase first. People are talking about that this [as though it] is the endpoint: the society that we *could* have—dynamic business webs and all sorts of things of that nature. But there are some phases before that, and there's going to be a phase which is maybe 18 months out, which is going to be driven by the Microsoft piece. There's going to be a phase, which is perhaps earlier than that, which is going to be where the sort of the ASP-type of software as a service bureau style stuff is going to start document-oriented services because it fits very naturally.

But the phase today is all about integration, and it's about integration because integration is one of the top three issues that's facing businesses today. It's an absolute P&L [profit and loss] leveraging issue. It's about how to improve your profits by managing costs and improving business velocity and things like that. Yet that integration problem, once it's a sort of many billion dollar problem out there, the kind of integration vendors that have been trying to address this problem have failed to get the kind of traction that you'd expect. There is no EAI or business intelligence company with three billion dollars in revenue, and there's no reason that there shouldn't be if you look at the economics of it. There's certainly the opportunity. There ought to be an Oracle-style gorilla in this space. The reason there isn't is because the approach has been wrong and the approach has been proprietary; it's been skills constrained; it's been something which has inherently what I call anti-integration technology—technology that's designed to lock people into a proprietary infrastructure rather than open things up so that everything can talk to everything.

Really, that's sort of the rub of this—that the end solution will look at lot more like the Web. It will have the characteristic that the Web has: you go out and you publish a Web page and anybody can get it. If you take that same concept and apply it to system assets, there's the database and application and a set of business processes or a transaction or whatever. You take those things and you essentially publish them for use by any arbitrary other system, obviously subject to security constraints that you impose. What you've got, then, is the potential for an explosive sort of collaboration between different computer systems rather than a kind of hard-wired, point-to-point kind of thing, which is essentially what's been going on in the context of these proprietary systems.

In addition, because it's standards based, you get around the skills constraint problem. For example, as Iona, I don't have to go out there and train thousands of people in my proprietary technology. Why? Because they already understand XML; they understand Web Services and so forth because there are standards. What you have there is the potential for a fundamental change in the economics of integration. If that happens, that's the disruptive change that we're talking about in this industry. It's the equivalent of the PC arriving on the hardware scene. The people initially that saw it arrive thought, "Well, let's add this to our mainframe franchise," or "Let's add this to our minicomputer franchise." They didn't realize it was something totally different and [that] it would spawn Intel and Microsoft and Dell and Compaq and Lotus and dozens of other companies that just simply didn't exist before that. And that's what we're saying.

Think of Web Services as a software architecture [in] the same [way] as the PC was a hardware architecture—it's a sort of industry standard software architecture that is good enough with sufficient support and that has such significant benefits that it (a) must succeed and (b) will change the industry. So that's really sort of the picture. It's not farther out we can talk about—plug and play of arbitrary consumer devices and things like that, that I think Web Services is going to enable—but today you can look at customers; we have announced customers. Nordstrom.com would be an example—actually, we're talking about them later today at the conference—they've used this integration and have proven exactly what I said. It's cheaper. It's faster. It requires less skills, and they're hugely happy with it. They could not have done the same thing using traditional integration technology. So the rubber is hitting the road today. I don't think Web Services is far out, and it's happening today, but it's happening in this integration space. The last comment that I'll make is that, when a disruptive technology appears, the behavior of incumbents—companies with significant other franchises—can often look like they're embracing it when, in fact, they're not because it's something which acts to undermine their franchise.

In your discussions with people in this industry, what you're going to find is a number of people that say, "We love that stuff, but..." and after the "but" there will be a list of bullet points. The "but" will be, "The standards aren't ready. It's far out there. It's not enterprise capable." There have been a whole bunch of things they're going to give you about it, not because those things are legitimate concerns, but because it's in their interests to push out the adoption of Web Services as far as they possibly can. Not least, of course, the people that believe in programming—a particular programming language everywhere, which obviously the application server community would be the most obvious examples. They, at the end of the day, have an interest, and it's a legitimate commercial interest, in putting Java everywhere, and it's not in their interest for Java application servers to be used for what they're good at, which is application execution. To the extent that you've got people trying to extend applications to other franchises to encompass the integration space, or people trying to extend application franchises to encompass integration space, and so on, you're going to find people that are essentially holding back the adoption of Web Services.

I'll make one last comment so that perhaps you can get at some of your questions. The reason that that's such a mistake is that it's something that Sun identified back in the '80s, and they came out at that stage and said, "The network is a computer." I'm not sure that their behavior is consistent with that today. Today they're sort of behaving as [if] the application server is the computer. Ironically, it's Microsoft that's saying, "The network is a computer," and it's Microsoft that's been pushing these standards. It's Microsoft that's essentially been taking what used to be known as the OSI [Open Systems Interconnect] stack—the kind of network and sort of protocol stack—up to the next layer and saying there is something about the transport layer. It's something which is called Web Services, and it has to do with this XML-based service-oriented architecture. So what you're seeing is that, if you believe the network is a computer, it's actually the Web Services camp that's really betting on that, and it's the other guys that are not. In that context, of the other vendors, it's really only Iona that is saying that, profoundly, Web Services is not something that you add on to the side of what we do. We don't say, "Here's our application server, and Web Services is a nice thing to have on the side."

What we are saying is the other way around: the design center is Web Services. The center of our architecture—the way we describe what we're doing—is about Web Services, and it's really only ourselves and Microsoft that are saying that. I'm going to be prepared to bet, in that context, that, if you came back in 20 or 25 years' time, you are going to find Web Services and Web Services derivative protocols running pervasively on this planet. There will probably be two or three new programming languages or programming paradigms in that timeframe. In other words, it's quite possible Java may not be the last programming language we ever invent. I *do* believe that Web Services or something very similar to it is going to be the service-oriented architecture and metadata framework for building distributed computing systems. That's *really* where we're coming from.

ALEX: *If the Web Services are about interoperability, can you explain what additional value features a product like XMLBus provides to the base Web Services standards?*

BARRY: The Web Services standards obviously refer to the three key standards: SOAP, WSDL, and UDDI. Those need to be implemented, and so a product like XMLBus implements those, and so that's the first thing that it does—it implements the base standards that are required to do this, and it does so in a way that's tested and proven to interoperate with…I think it's something around 15 or 20 other implementations that exist out there today.

Beyond that, what it does is that, obviously in the context of Web Services, there are three main things that you're needing to do: defining or creating Web Services in the first place, deploying Web Services, and consuming them in some way. So let me talk about those.

In terms of defining and creating Web Services, quite a lot of that can be done, if you understand the software entities that you're wanting to turn into Web Services. So, for example, XMLBus can take arbitrary software components, which might be EJBs or CORBA objects or something like that, and turn them into Web Services. And, across the board, on all sorts of different app servers and all sorts of different environments, we can do that. It helps you to do that. So there's a creation of Web Services piece of it. The standards say nothing about how you do that or why you do that or anything else. They just simply define WSDL.

The second piece of it is the deployment of Web Services, and the question there is: what sorts of environments do they run in? Again, if you think of the interests of various parties, people that happen to have an interest in application servers would love for Web Services to run in application servers, and a lot of them will. But then again, Microsoft customers would not be running them in a J2EE environment. They would [be] running in a completely different environment. On mainframes they'd be running yet a different environment, and so there's all these kinds of deployment issues. What XMLBus does is, it says, "That's okay. We can run it in an application server of your choice. We can run it standalone if that's what you want to do, or we can run it in a Microsoft environment or an IBM mainframe environment that's sort of, let's say, sensitive or sympathetic to the programming environment and sort of [the] execution environment of choice." So there's that whole deployment aspect of it.

The third piece of it, which is about consumption of Web Services—and of course, there are going to be various categories of this. Important ones include sort of peer-to-peer kinds of environments, which is one thing but very important to us is, in fact, business processes. That's one of the reasons that you expose assets. We talk about liberating assets. This is what service-oriented architectures do, is they liberate the system assets that you've got. For you to be able to take those and essentially string them together into business processes and workflows is something that we can do directly in the XMLBus product. XMLBus is the lowest end of our three Web Services products, but even in that product, you can do things like that.

ALEX: *On the issue of business processes: do you see companies needing to adopt some sort of workflow standard or some cooperation between the organization responsible for workflow and also the Web Services, so that that particular portion* [the workflow market] *doesn't get fragmented?*

BARRY: Let me say that it's inevitable it's going to happen, so, in a sense, it's an irrelevancy. It's going to happen that there are going to be standard definitions of workflows and they're going to be XML-based definitions, and there's going to be some standards that are set up around that. How crucial do I think it is? It's not constraining to Web Services or, indeed, to the use of business processes out there. So, I think it's important, but it's by far not one of the top 10 issues.

What I would say about it is that there is a lot of nonsense written about business processes. Business processes are extremely important to business people, but they tend to have a shorter life cycle than the assets that we're talking about. You may have a customer database that's 30 years old or something like. You're talking about the kinds of corporate systems assets that have longer life cycles than business processes. And so the key thing with business processes is that they're things which are iterated on—perhaps they have a 12-month life or something like that. Consequently, people that think about this integration problem purely in a top-down fashion can often create very fragile systems.

What's great about Web Services is that it allows you to think about the business problem in a top-down fashion. It allows you to solve the systems problem in a bottom-up fashion, which starts with the assets that are important to you.

ALEX: *You talked on this a little bit, and InfoWorld has also mentioned this in a couple of their surveys. Security's still a major concern for a lot of companies that actually want to deploy the Web Services. Can you elaborate a little bit on how your current three Web Services products help or enforce or implement the security aspects?*

BARRY: The security thing is, again, important, but it's not an immediate constraint for reasons I've sort of alluded to before. When you're talking about highly dynamic, consumer-oriented Web Services—that's to say that people go home to their home PC and they're going to try and hook up a sort of an airline reservation to a currency converter or something like that—you've got, essentially, anonymous users, or relatively anonymous users, that are needing to be authenticated and so forth. There's a standards-oriented security problem there which is different—subtly different—from the enterprise security problem, and there's a huge requirement for that to happen. There's a requirement for us to all agree on the authentication standards and the privacy standards and so forth.

That issue, which is an important issue, is not a constraint for internal integration or, indeed, even supply chain integration, where you've got much more control of both ends of the security strategy. Consequently, what you're going to see is all vendors in this space addressing this in ways which are sort of existing today, and so there are all sorts of security standards out there today. Our products implement a number of them. I'm including, of course, from the SSL stack upwards. What I would say is that I think a lot of this is going to be driven by the Microsoft GXA [Global XML Web Services Architecture] standards, and Iona is very clear about that—of all companies out there, I think, [we] have shown the most support for the notion that the Microsoft GXA standards are likely to be the dominant standards in security and other areas going forward.

ALEX: *On a related topic, can you comment only whether the mass adoption of XAML [Transaction Markup Language] would it be necessary for mass Web Services adoption, at least at the enterprise level?*

BARRY: Again, I don't think it's at all critical at this stage. I think it needs to happen. What you need to have from the transaction point of view is, in due course, you're going to need to have two-phase commit protocols implemented within XML and within the context of SOAP. But you don't need that today. Even just simple, straightforward, single-results transactions can be done today quite easily without the use of an XAML or any other kind of transaction standard.

ALEX: *Your firm has been into interoperability space for a long time—about 11 years—and I'm sure you're familiar with previous attempts at interoperability—committees or consortiums like OSF [Open Software Foundation, a consortium that included IBM, DEC, and other major firms]—from the late '80s. What do you think is different this time? As you mentioned, it's not a technology issue, but what is different about the landscape or some of the sociological factors?*

BARRY: That's the right question. It is absolutely not a technology issue. What this is about is standards: the value of standards is not in their sort of technical genius, but in their level of adoption—even to the extent that you see a lot of standards that today we wouldn't regard as particularly well designed, but nevertheless they continue. The serial RS232 standards, for example, are very widely used today. They're slow and ugly and so forth, but they work. The main point about them is that they're very widely adopted. Everyone understands them and does them in the same way.

The power of a standard is in its adoption, because of network effects, and the great thing about Web Services—even if you have no particular sort of sympathy for the design of the services, or don't particularly believe in service-oriented architectures or anything else—what you've got here is something which has got unprecedented support across the industry. I think the last time I saw the industry support a single standard to the extent that we've got people supporting Web Services was maybe ASCII or something like that. So the first thing is, you've got this very, very broad support.

The second is that the world's biggest software company, Microsoft, is going to put it into your company whether you want it or not. Web Services is going to happen, and you would have to actively try to prevent it from getting elsewhere in your organization if you didn't believe in it. So, there's no question in my mind that Web Services is going to happen. If you go back to the comment that this sort of ubiquity in support for standards is where its value lies, you have to say that we're talking about something here that is of a quite different order of magnitude from any of the previous things. And that would be my commentary.

Now, there are some further sort of more tactical comments I'd like to make. For example, one of the great lessons of our industry is that simplicity wins, and the beauty of Web Services is that it really is very, very simple. Now, you couldn't use it to do some of the things that we do with some of our other systems. You know, people use our software [the CORBA ORB, Orbix] to run national telephone networks in real time or to fly satellites or things like that. It will be some time before we're sort of using HTTP to do that, I think. But I think for the majority of business problems, the simplicity is a huge piece of value, and so I think that's clearly a driver for Web Services. I think those are the key items.

I think I mentioned that, in general, Web Services are inevitable. Now, I say that in an abstract sense. The multidecade trend of our industry is always towards standards, and you have proprietary software vendors trying to kind of pull back and grab a little bit of—sort of in a profit taking or some proprietary lock-in for a while, but eventually that proprietary lock-in gives way and you get some kind of "sort of" de facto or *du jour* standard emerges just because of sort of the economics of scale. It's inevitable that there will be a standard in this space. It's by far the biggest vacuum in the computing industry, and, if it wasn't something which Microsoft proposed, it would be something in two year's time somebody else proposed. It's inevitable, and I think now it's here, it will happen.

ALEX: *Many of the major consulting companies, some of whom are your partners, make their revenue base upon the large integration efforts; that is, the more complex the effort, the more revenue they generate. How would a reduced integration cost on some of these major projects affect the services industry?*

BARRY: The services industry—particularly when you go and look at the kind of the large consultancy companies—one of the things that they don't openly admit is that they've got an awful lot of work which is technical work, which is, literally, just how do I wire one machine to another machine—fairly grubby technical work when the value they're wanting to add, because it's the sort of high margin value, is business consultancy.

They would far rather be walking into a company and talking about the business processes that it takes to build a motor car or some form of steel bucket, or whatever it is that the company does, than spend all their time doing programming in Java and C++. Furthermore, not only is there a margin issue for them in doing that, but, it's very hard for those companies to really get the rocket scientists on board. Many of the best technical people and most experienced technical people are off doing other things elsewhere, because they're very valuable and expensive people. Even just this issue of the skills constraint that we were talking about before is something which is a big problem for those companies.

Where I think it takes them is in two directions. One is up the value stack to where they want to be, in terms of business-level consultancy, and the other is much more sort of customer service, maintenance, and those operational support kinds of directions, which a lot of them are in, in any case.

ALEX: *You mentioned how there are not enough rocket scientists in the world because a lot of these problems are too difficult, but if Web Services are going to be a disruptive change, then that has [an] implication on the educational system. How do you see this potentially affecting how people are trained as they come out of school, or even in the industry? How do you see their skills being retrofitted to address some of these new changes that are propagating throughout the industry as Web Services take off?*

BARRY: Well, let's go back to simplicity. I could ask the question: how did we change our educational system to get so many people building Web sites? Because there were many, many, many thousands of people worldwide that wouldn't call themselves programmers, but they were off building, writing HTML, and all this sort of stuff. In a sense, what we're talking about here is something more like that: The analogy is everyone becomes a programmer. What you're doing is, if you can dumb down the task of pulling Web Services together, if you can dumb that down enough, you get to an analogy with the phone system where we went from having kind of dedicated operators that were plugging little things into boards to the point where each one of us is an operator.

Each of us is kind of making our own connections and not needing somebody in between. So that's the one piece of it. On the back end of it, the beauty of it is—and this is one thing that I believe very deeply—that there is an inevitable sort of heterogeneity, if you want to call it that, about this industry. The training costs come in when you try to say, "Okay, everyone's a Java programmer, because that's the latest kind of programming language *du jour.*" Now we have to take all the guys that were skilled in PL/I and COBOL and C++ and C and whatever else, and FORTRAN and whatever, and teach them Java. Next year a new programming paradigm comes along and you need to teach them that. We actually have a very substantial customer that's got hundreds of PL/I programmers. They actually have indicated that the main reason they're not retraining them into Java is because they wouldn't be able to keep them, because they'd have to pay them too much to try to keep them.

So I suppose my comment to this is: the beauty of something which is focused around integration in this way is that people in the Microsoft world can carry on in the Microsoft world, and people in the J2EE world can carry on in that world, and people in the mainframe world can carry on in that world. People that are kind of SAP hackers or whatever, they can carry on doing their SAP stuff. None of them needs to get this kind of homogenous programming paradigm, because the integration paradigm takes care of that. So that would be my comment—no change. If anything, it's less stress because people won't feel that there's a need to go and retool themselves into new programming environments.

ALEX: *Picking up on an earlier thought that you had, when you mentioned that, when these disruptive changes happen in the industry, the established players, the incumbents, are the ones that sometimes can get caught flat-footed because they have too much vested interest in the current status quo. But would you consider Iona an incumbent? It seems like you have an application server product and you have a fair amount of investment in the middleware space as well. Wouldn't the mass adoption of Web Services erode the corporate market, which I'm assuming you're still deriving substantial revenues from?*

BARRY: They're kind of two different questions, so I'll try to deal with them both. The answer is no, obviously, in both cases. No and sort of no, is probably the way to put it. The answer, the underlying sort of concept of what Iona is about, is distributed computing. We understand large-scale distributed computing systems extremely well and, in particular, service-oriented architectures. Now, when you look at something like Web Services, in practice, it is a sort of a simplified set of concepts that are very, very similar to what we were doing in the early '90s. As you probably know, from a technical perspective, WSDL maps pretty closely conceptually onto what IDL [Interface Definition Language] does.

SOAP maps conceptually onto what IIOP [Interoperability ORB Protocol] does, and UDDI maps quite conceptually onto what Traders [part of the CORBA specifications] do and so on, so none of this is new to us. All of it, in fact, is relatively simple for us, because it's dumbing-down type of stuff. I suppose the comment that I'd make is that, from a go-to market strategy, our primary value to our customers is about that kind of architectural integration, that kind of high, large-scale, typically, integration of systems using service-oriented architectures. To those customers—and a customer base of over four and a half thousand, by the way—to them this is just good news. This is just the next phase of what they're trying to do.

Now, you asked a quite astute question: isn't this something which cannibalizes CORBA in some way? The answer is that they overlap, but there are things CORBA can do that nothing else can do. If you've got things that have got really high performance constraints, such as real-time constraints, or that are very highly distributed systems with security and whatever—all those sorts of enterprise reliability sorts of issues—there isn't any other way to build those systems, and that will, for the foreseeable future, remain that way.

However, it's a pretty big hammer to crack some much smaller nuts, and so there is certainly a proportion of historical CORBA users that were using CORBA to do things that you really didn't need the full power of CORBA to do, and that's okay. That part of the picture is a sort of an intersection between what Web Services and CORBA can do, and we're happy to deal with it whichever way our customers want to go. Then, of course, there's the other piece: there's a whole bunch of Web Services things that CORBA could technically do if everybody adopted CORBA, but, in fact, doesn't do because people haven't said, "All of our Web sites are going to support CORBA." We haven't got Microsoft out there saying, "We're going to run CORBA protocols on every network in the world." The things that Web Services will be able to do are things that CORBA can't do, and that's the standard sort of portfolio thing for us. We'll manage that quite happily.

ALEX: *Can you share with us how some of your customers, the early adopters, are using Web Services? You mentioned Nordstrom.com.*

BARRY: Right. The two customers that we've talked about are really Nordstrom.com and Boeing. I should give you some more details specifically about Nordstrom and then, as I say, you can actually attend that, if you want to. Nordstrom.com—the way to think about it—they determined that they wanted to do a holiday promotion, which was a gift card. That's the sort of thing you can buy for your grandmother or something, and then she can go and she can sort of go to either an in-store booth or she can go to the Internet, to the store itself, or whatever, and redeem it for some shoes or a hat or whatever she wants to get. That concept is what they wanted to implement. The problem with it is, although that sounds very easy from a business process point of view, the problem is that, in fact, you had to have a system where, if you buy one of those cards in the supermarket, somehow this transaction that happens, so that Nordstrom kind of gets remuneration or whatever. You have to have a mechanism so that that card can be connected to the Nordstrom systems from the in-store booth or from the Internet, or over the phone, or whatever. It also has to connect back into Nordstrom's own banking systems and all sorts of pieces to the puzzle.

Here's the tough bit: it had to be done very quickly, because they wanted to roll it out and actually get time to market it before the holiday season. So, they adopted the Web Services integration platform, the Iona product, and it was interesting that they managed to deliver it in a matter of weeks. It was very, very short on a delivery timescale and very, very easy and, again, no particularly specialist skills required to do so—all of the things which we were talking about as being the benefits of this technology. If you recall, I was saying: think of this a little bit like the Web site thing, the idea that you publish your Web page and anyone can get at it. That's what we called End to Anywhere.

If you look at our business cards and things, we talk about E to A [End to Anywhere], a notion of a service-oriented architecture. You define the service and anybody can get at it. That concept—Nordstrom kind of proved that in a sense the people that are programming on the Microsoft side, which are accessing the Web service, actually didn't have any Iona software at all on the machine. They were using Microsoft tools—Visual Studio.NET and all that. That's what we're talking about when we're saying there's a potential for this thing to explode in that Iona's not trying to own both ends of every connection, as every other integration vendor is.

We're saying, "It's okay. We'll stick to the standards, but we'll do them better than anybody. So that's what Nordstrom are doing and they're talking very broadly about how they want to drive this deeper into the organization to support their supply chains and so forth. So that's one piece. I should say that this is quite a common pattern—and we've actually seen this in the context of service-oriented architectures in general—that the customer subsequently turns around and says, "Well, wait a minute. We've got a big old mainframe sitting here which has now got a Web Service that allows us to do a transaction against it. We can come in and we can issue a purchase order on, whatever, a set of shoes or something." That is now a Web Service that's supported by the Nordstrom mainframe forever more, and the potential for reuse of that Web service, and all sorts of other pieces of their business is obviously something that's becoming visible to them. We've seen customers talking about 12 to 1 productivity improvements in that sort of context. So that may well be the first large corporation to have announced mission-critical deployment of Web Services–based integration for any company.

Boeing also announced late last year that their whole integration strategy was directed towards Web Services integration, and so we did a big transaction with them, which we announced with them late last year. Obviously, with Boeing it's much [more] general. This is a Fortune 50 company. To put their weight behind Web Services integration, and so it's not as specific exactly what they're doing, and those stories will come out in due course.

ALEX: *Your products support the existing standards and then they add a fair amount of additional value to it, and your comment about not trying to own both endpoints is very valid. But I wanted to get your opinion on the whole notion of the Web Services network, firms like Grand Central and Flamenco. How do you see a firm like Iona coexisting with that, and, also, how do you see them helping, if at all, the adoption of the Web Services as organizations try to adopt this switch of technologies?*

BARRY: I don't have any sort of particular sort of axe to grind in favor or against those guys. In fact, we're quite familiar with them. But the underlying concept that I think they're coming from is the notion of Web Services as infrastructure and I agree with that: it's back to "The network is the computer." You get back to the idea that, fundamentally, it's the next layer up from sort of TCP or something.

Now, the problem with it, for companies where that is their business model, is a different one. And, again, I have no axe to grind in any particular direction, but it seems fairly evident to me that, in the short term, the SOAP protocol is extremely important. In the long term,

WSDL is much more important. Why am I saying that? Well, if you go back to the historical precedents, we had a huge battle around transport protocols which was in between Novell and Microsoft. Microsoft took shots at them with LAN Manager a couple of times. You had IBM running SNA, you had Banyan and also some other people that tried different transport protocols.

Microsoft did something very clever which they've now done with Web Services, which is to say, "Well, if we can't own this, then we'll make sure no one can," and they adopted TCP. And, that, in many ways, was the turning point for Novell. Novell's whole kind of franchise, their whole lock-in, was around the network protocols. The moment the world sort of adopted TCP very broadly, which happened because Windows shipped a TCP stack—and which, in the end, drove the whole Internet revolution, you could argue—that thing that happened was, I think, was the first point which is what I'm saying now about a lot of the integration vendors and people: that they'll try and they're trying to have that Novell versus Microsoft battle.

What's going to happen is they're going to get blown away by the whole situation, the infrastructure coming up a layer. Now, what happened after that? Well, nobody really cares whether your TCP is running over Ethernet or Token Ring, if anyone remembers that, or anything. It could be running directly on smoke signals for anyone who cares.

Network protocols have this kind of dual benefit of being, on the one hand, extremely valuable, because they get locked in and never get changed. On the other hand, they become commoditized and ultimately can go away. What I feel about the whole sort of notion of .NET Web Services as infrastructure is that people need to be very careful. The long-term value, and I do mean long-term value, of Web Services is about the contract between the service provider and the service and that's the WSDL standard. I don't know if that gets an answer to your question, though.

ALEX: *What do you see beyond, let's say, the next 18 to 24 months? What are some major strategic milestones for your firm?*

BARRY: For the company, I really believe that we're well ahead on technology and, in a sense, that's not a surprise, because that's what Iona's always been very good at. We've got great technologies. We've got great technologists, and we've shipped the products and we've kind of bucked the trend with the industry when we came out and talked in early November about our strategy. We didn't come out and say, "We're going to ship something sometime." We said, "We have shipped it and here are some customers." As you may recall, not only that, but we had Microsoft on stage with us and a bunch of definitive system integrators and things. From a product point of view, clearly we're there. There will be tweaks and things that we need to do, but I think we've got the industry need. All of the mast ends are about adoption, and what you're going to see is that the company is very focused on developing go-to-market strategies with system integrators and partners.

We've got 250 ISVs [independent software vendors] out there. Those sorts of alliance strategies just get the momentum out there because the integration problem is there. It's a $10 to $15 billion opportunity today. The total of all of the integration companies together—you take all the EAI companies and everything together—it's maybe $2 or $3 billion of revenue. This is a totally unmined market, a huge opportunity. This integration challenge—there's nothing standing in our way other than [to] go to market, and a lot of that is, as I say, about alliances.

ALEX: *Thanks for your time, Barry.*

▶ Interview: Cape Clear—Simplifying Development

Cape Clear is a start-up company focused on simplifying Web Services development through its Cape Studio and Cape Connect products. In this interview, the firm's CTO discusses how to publish Web Services from existing assets and why SOAP proved to be more ubiquitous than XML/RPC [Extensible Markup Language/Remote Procedure Call].

Interviewee: Hugh Grant, CTO of Cape Clear

ALEX: *Can you please explain who Cape Clear is?*

HUGH: Okay. At Cape Clear, we're committed to Web Services. We think it's a technology that's got a potential to be really disruptive, but the real benefit is only going to be realized if it's brought to a wide audience, and so we're about ease of use. We look at the kind of real-world problems that people have to deal with [regarding] Web Services, and right now it's about integration—it's about trying to take your existing technology and expose it as Web Services so a wider audience can reach that over the Web, whether that's the corporate Web [intranet] or whether it's the actual Internet itself. So what we're about is making that [integration] seamless, basically providing tools that will automate the generation of WSDL files, mapping technologies—whatever you need to get your legacy systems onto the Web, the legacy systems in question being EJBs, CORBA components, or just plain Java classes.

In parallel with that kind of integration technology, we've been working on a product we call Cape Studio, which is our toolset for developing Web Service applications. One of the things people have to deal with here is mapping of incompatible XML formats. There are a lot of people out there who haven't used SOAP, who have used things like XML-RPC or FPML [Financial Products Markup Language], various financial formats, or whatever vertical format has been standardized for their industry. They'd like to use SOAP, and, since it's all XML, the natural thing to do is to use XSLT to do this mapping. However, XLST turns out to be quite hard to use in practice, so we've developed a set of graphical tools to enable people to generate these mappings automatically so people who aren't XML experts can actually sit down and work out how to map the data formats used in different parts of their organizations. We think that's key, really, to getting wider adoption, because there's a lot of stuff out there already that needs to be integrated if Web Services are to be successful.

ALEX: *Can you please describe the profile of your ideal customer?*

HUGH: Typically, our customers will already be users of some distributed object technology such as CORBA or EJB. We've got a growing number of customers who are really just Java users who have built existing Java systems and want to expose components of those as Web Services, so we're typically involved with people who aren't coming from a complete green-field environment. They're looking to integrate existing systems they have, or maybe systems from other vendors. So right now that's the kind of person we're dealing with. Looking forward into the future, we're very much looking to kind of build on our ease-of-use story and provide tools for less technical developers, to more of the business analysts or corporate developers who will be looking at tools around Web Service assembly and composition. That will take time to actually come about, because, clearly, until there are a lot of Web Services out there to assemble, there's a limited need for these tools. We believe strongly that Web Services will become pervasive, and this kind of Web Services design center is going to be key in the future.

ALEX: *Your tool includes an optimized SAX parser and an optimized SOAP parser, as well. Are there performance concerns which customers should be aware of with the standard SOAP or the SAX processor, then?*

HUGH: The thing that's going to affect anybody using SOAP or XML is really just the overhead of processing parsing, and, in the case of SOAP, because it's just based on XML schemas for its data types, it's going to depend on the complexity of your data. So my advice to people would be: when they're looking at designing the data for sending over SOAP, try to make it not too nested. If you can maybe do a transformation to convert from highly nested and complex internal type to the raw information you need on the Web, then that can actually improve your performance. But, in general, parsing technology and the XSLT processing technology is improving dramatically and very quickly. And so I don't think if there is an issue, it will be an issue for very long.

ALEX: *Your product uses a SAX parser, which cannot modify the XML documents. What happens if the user needs this functionality?*

HUGH: That's where we have an architecture which we call our interceptor architecture. It was just based on the standard interceptor pattern, which allows people to do two different types of modification. One is at an XML level, where they can run XSLT transformers automatically, and this is the most common form, because it's simpler; it's easier to integrate; it's easier to deploy. If you've got existing XML data formats you want to map into SOAP, or you want to modify a SOAP message and convert it from one form to another, you might as well just use XSLT. On the other hand, once we've parsed it, we have an internal representation in Java that people can plug into, so you can actually access the data types in a parsed form and, if you're doing something like taking that data and making a call, say, to an Oracle database, it makes more sense to do it that way. You don't have to get involved in XML parsing as well.

ALEX: *Earlier, you mentioned that your ideal customer is somebody who's already an adopter of technology like CORBA. Let's just assume that I'm already a customer of Iona, IBM, or BEA. What additional functionality do your products provide?*

HUGH: Well, it comes down to ease of use at the core. These other vendors, they're not pure SOAP or Web Service vendors. They're looking at providing a bridge from their technologies into the world of Web Services, and so they're more heavily API focused. So using their technology will typically involve writing some code—maybe writing some marshalling and unmarshalling classes. We're focused on just generating everything, so we use Java reflection to process whatever components you have (or maybe parsing CORBA IDL files), and we generate all the code and all the mapping for you. Our goal is that you don't need to have high-end developers doing this work. Developers just run their components through our tools and then generate everything they need to run as a Web Service.

ALEX: *Your products include two features: SOAPDirect and UDDIDirect. Can you elaborate on what features SOAPDirect provides?*

HUGH: Yeah. The goal of those tools was to provide developers with an ease-of-use library. We built a lot of our initial clients and demos using things like Apache SOAP and the IBM SOAP toolkits. We found that, while they're effective, they're quite complex. You need to be a pretty good developer to use these things to their fullest, and we thought that, "Hey, we've got all this mapping technology. Why don't we actually just roll that out as a client toolkit?" So the goal of SOAPDirect is that we want to recreate in Java what Microsoft has done with Visual Basic—basically, make it really trivial to write SOAP clients. So you don't need to know what types are being used. You can just pass arbitrary Java objects and the toolkit will work out on the fly what the correct mapping is from those types into SOAP. [The] Hello World [application] can run through a couple of hundred lines of code, if you're using something like Apache, and our goal is to have it down to 10 lines of code if you're using SOAPDirect. UDDIDirect does the same thing for UDDI. It's basically a specialization of our SOAPDirect API, with some ease-of-use wrappers around the UDDI specs, because UDDI is quite complex. Again, a lot of developers aren't going to be that technical. Web Services are going to be [deployed to] a much wider audience than your usual Java developer, and so we want to make it easy for those people to access the key services.

ALEX: *Your products currently work with stateless session beans, but let's assume I already have an application that has a combination of stateless session beans and stateful session beans along with entity beans. How would the migration work?*

HUGH: We've already had customers who have done this, and typically what they'll just do is use either a wrapper or a Factory pattern and basically create a level of indirection between their stateful code and the system. So you'll basically have a stateless session bean which looks up the factory or has a direct connection through to the back-end object or a component, and that works pretty well for people. We're kind of restricted to a stateless sort of model because of the way SOAP works, and people who will directly support stateful session beans or entity beans are doing it in proprietary ways, and you're not going to have interoperability at that level, so we believe it's better, in the Java domain, to just write a wrapper to give you that functionality.

ALEX: *You mentioned earlier that one of the key selling [points] of your products is the ease of use over the existing toolkit, and one of the technologies you mentioned was XML-RPC. Can you elaborate on why XML-RPC didn't catch on, whereas SOAP is so much more ubiquitous?*

HUGH: I really think it's down to the drive from the vendors. XML-RPC was something that has quite a following at an open-source level, but it was never really picked up on by any of the vendors. What's driving SOAP is the fact that you've got IBM, Sun, Oracle, and Microsoft for the first time on the same platform, saying, "We'll support this standard," and that's really the key thing: the value in SOAP is its ubiquity. The ease of use is really shared with any other XML approach, so what's driving SOAP is going to be Visual Studio.NET. It's going to be J2EE 1.4. It's going to be Oracle's SOAP support. That's what's really key there.

ALEX: *Are there actually any inherent technical limitations of XML-RPC that made it inferior to SOAP or made it too limiting, so that it didn't become ubiquitous like SOAP is becoming? What did it take for SOAP to come on the scene before a lot of the vendors decided to kind of standardize on it?*

HUGH: Probably the SOAP specs are more detailed and XML-RPC is maybe more lightweight and generic, and I think people probably just like the extra depth they find in the SOAP specifications and the fact that it's now being kind of filled out to include specifically how [XML] schemas work and different bindings, and in the future we'll see asynchronous support. I think really it's just that more work was put in, and in fact, it comes back to the vendors who invested more in developing the specification, whereas XML-RPC was the work of a couple of people, and very good work with a couple of people [in] the open-source community, but it just didn't have the commercial backing.

ALEX: *The Web Services model has several different pieces to it: creation, consumption, registration, and the last one is the deployment. Your product helps on the consumption and creation functionality and also to some degree the registration, but what deployment features does Cape Connect provide since the existing standards do not currently address this issue?*

HUGH: Well, the key thing for us comes back to ease of use, so we looked a lot at the way people are deploying Web Services, and they usually follow quite a complex model, maybe something like the EJB deployment descriptor model or whatever. We wanted to make it easier, so with Cape Connect it's really just dynamic, because everything we do is dynamic and based off [Java] reflection. If you want to deploy a Web Service you just have to register the WSDL file with Cape Connect, and then it knows how to do [the mapping]. That's really all there is, I mean. For us the goal is to make deployment as easy as development. It's just a push-button exercise. You point our tools at your components and then they're deployed. There's nothing extra you have to do. It's all about ease of use. Internally we'll be running on top of whatever platform you're using, be that a CORBA platform or a J2EE platform. Internally, things will be CORBA components or Beans or Java classes. But what we do is basically put a wrapper around that to insulate the user from all the details of how that's deployed, and we'd rather that we do the hard work so the user then gets to have a really simple experience to deploy Web Services.

ALEX: *Thanks for your time, Hugh.*

Product Review: XMLBus

[This appendix was written by Venkatranga Konda.]

XMLBus from Iona Technologies is a Java-based development environment for creating, publishing, monitoring, and managing Web Services. It is the entry-level version (XMLBus Edition) of their **End to Anywhere (E2A) Web Services Integration Platform**. Higher end editions include the **Collaborate Edition** and the **Partner Edition**.

Utilizing Web Services standards such as SOAP, XML, WSDL, and UDDI to achieve seamless integration between disparate applications written in .NET, CORBA, and J2EE, you can install XMLBus either as a standalone product or on leading application servers such as BEA WebLogic, Iona's Application Server, or IBM WebSphere.

We'll begin with an overview of the XMLBus platform, along with the components and tools it provides, and conclude with a short example on how to use XMLBus to take an existing application and then expose it as a Web Service.

▶ Overview

XMLBus provides an environment for creating Web Services from existing software assets (EJBs, Java classes, CORBA objects, etc.), managing Web Services, and also modeling Web Services.[1] XMLBus automatically generates a WSDL document and publishes it in a specified location so that clients can find it. This file can be registered with a UDDI registry so that clients can dynamically discover the service.

XMLBus uses the SOAP protocol to enable SOAP clients to access services in a platform-independent manner. It listens for a SOAP message from a client and validates this message against a schema described in the WSDL file for that service. Once this validation is complete, it will trigger a call to a method of the service as specified in the SOAP message. After the WSDL URL is called by the client and the corresponding SOAP message is validated by XMLBus, it is up to the XMLBus container to make sure it calls the correct method, whether it is in a plain Java class or an EJB (discussed in more detail in the next section).

▶ XMLBus Tools

XMLBus provides several tools to help create, deploy, maintain, and discover Web Services. This section covers the main features of each tool and what the tools are used for. In addition to the tools included here, XMLBus provides Java classes that can be used for administrative purposes such as deploying a service or adding a resource to an XMLBus Archive (XAR) file (see below for more information on the XAR file format).

Web Service Builder

The Web Service Builder provides a GUI to create and publish Web Services. Upon start-up it displays a list of projects on the left and the details of a selected project in the pane on the right. The wizard interface takes the user through a series of steps to create a Web Service. The main step of specifying an input file is done right at the beginning. A typical input file can be a simple Java class, an EJB, or even an XAR or a Java Archive (JAR) file.

---

1. The bundled edition of XMLBus is identical to the commercial version with the exception of the missing workflow engine. Thus, a discussion of the workflow engine is not included here.

The next screen provides an interface to choose the methods that should be exposed as Web Services. The resulting output file is always an XAR file. Using this file, XMLBus deploys the Web Service in the Web Services container (again, depending on the installation, this can be either an application server or XMLBus itself). Another useful feature is the ability to generate template code, which can then be fleshed out to complete the functionality.

Web Service Manager

Similar to the management consoles of other Web Services development environments, the Web Service Manager tool is used to manage the Web Services in XMLBus. The tool displays all the deployed Web Services and provides the means to enable, disable, or delete a Web Service. In addition to these features, it acts as a WSDL browser by allowing the user to view the WSDL file of a Web Service.

Test Client

This browser-based tool can be used to test a deployed Web Service. The interface accepts a URL of a deployed Web Service's WSDL file. To facilitate the testing of all the methods, the Test Client displays a list of methods of the Web Service, including the parameter types needed to invoke each method. The user can select a method from the list, enter test input values, and invoke the method. The results screen shows the return value of the method, the SOAP request, and response messages to and from the Web Service.

Message Spy

Message Spy provides a GUI to monitor SOAP messages between a client and a Web Service. Message Spy can listen on any port to monitor client activity. The listener port is registered while the client starts up. Once the listening port is registered and Message Spy is started, the user can monitor incoming and outgoing SOAP messages. In addition, the user can send custom SOAP messages to the Web Service.

UDDI Browser

The UDDI Browser is a browser-based tool that displays information about Web Services that are registered with a UDDI repository. This tool provides an interface for choosing a particular repository and accepts search keywords to search for registered businesses in a repository. Once a business is selected, the details of that business are displayed. These details include the registered services as well as the respective URL for each service.

The XAR File

Along the same concept of a WAR (Web Archive) file (a common format for deploying server-side Java applications), an XAR file contains all the files required to publish a Web Service.[2] This file is produced automatically by XMLBus during the registration of a Web Service and helps XMLBus manage Web Services. The XAR file also helps us keep track of the various files needed by grouping them in one archive.

An XAR file contains the following files:

- **WSDL file.** The file that describes the Web Services to a client.
- **Properties file.** The properties file is used by the XMLBus container to obtain information on how the Web Service was created.
- **SOAP configuration file.** This is used by the container to locate files such as EJBs that provide the functionality for the Web Service.
- **Java classes.** Non-EJB implementation classes that provide the implementation behind the Web Services operations listed in the WSDL file.
- **J2EE and CORBA support.** XMLBus comes with a built-in servlet engine so that it can run servlets and Java Server Pages as a standalone product. To expose EJB and CORBA implementations as Web Services, XMLBus needs to be configured to work with an application server. XMLBus supports integration with Weblogic, Websphere, and Iona Application Server. The integration process is fairly simple and is taken care of by the

---

2. At the moment, there is no standard file format for deploying Web Services in a Java environment.

setup process. All requests to a WSDL that belongs to an EJB will then be routed to the application server where the EJB is hosted.

▶ Publishing a Web Service

Now that we are more familiar with XMLBus, let's look at how easily an existing application can be published as a Web Service. For this example, let's take a simple Java class and assume that the preliminary work has been done concerning making sure that the class is appropriate for exposing it as a Web Service and deciding what methods to use when doing so. Figure D–1 illustrates the sequence of events that need to be followed to convert an existing application to a Web Service.

- Start the Web Services Builder and enter the names for the application and the XAR file for the new Web Service.

- Enter the Web Service name and the Java class that will be published as a Web Service.

- Choose the methods to expose the application as a Web Service and their SOAP encoding properties.

- Enter the WSDL filename so that it can be accessed; click **Finish.**

- This prompts the Builder to generate an XAR file and save it in the specified location ready to be deployed. The newly created Web Service should be displayed in the Projects pane of the Builder's main screen.

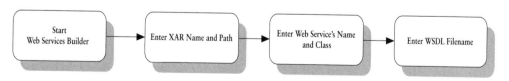

Figure D–1 Publishing a Web Service.

Deploying a Web Service

The Web Service can be deployed using the command line or the Web Service Builder. We will use the Builder for this deployment. Figure D–2 illustrates the steps necessary to deploy a Web Service.

- Select the application we just created from the Projects pane on the left of the Builder's main screen.
- To deploy this application, click **Deploy.**
- On the next screen, verify the service deployment URL and the path of the XAR file, both of which can be changed if desired.
- Click **Deploy** to deploy the Web Service.

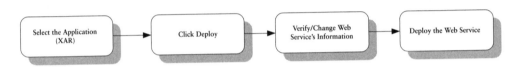

Figure D–2   Deploying a Web Service.

Conclusion

Overall, XMLBus provides a quick way for organizations to expose their services to new markets; at the same time, it helps them focus on their business process and service interface rather than worrying about how to create and deploy the service. The development and management tools provided by XMLBus help to quickly create, publish, monitor, and manage applications based on various platforms. XMLBus adheres to open standards; thus companies will not have to worry about any dependence on a proprietary application.

In choosing a platform, it is worthwhile to weigh other factors besides the features of a product. The vendor's reputation and viability should be taken into account. Unlike many other firms in the Web Services market, Iona is a veteran company in the interoperability sector, having worked with CORBA for many years. Iona has the expertise and financial resources to support this product for some time.

As a company's needs outgrow the XMLBus Edition, Iona also provides a smooth migration path through two other products in the E2A Web Services Integration Platform: the **Partner Edition** and **Collaborate Edition**.

Intended for small business enterprises (SMEs), the Partner Edition builds on XMLBus and provides additional features such as integration with desktop applications (Microsoft Excel, QuickBooks, etc.), data transformation services between multiple XML formats and EDI support. The Collaborate Edition is geared toward major enterprises and includes connectors to ERP systems (SAP, PeopleSoft, etc.) and support for key B2B standards such as RosettaNet and ebXML.

Glossary

API (Application Programming Interface) The public interface by which an application should interact with a class library or framework. Programming at an API level provides a level of portability.

application server A Java product that provides additional services on top of the J2EE standard including load balancing and database pooling. Popular application servers include BEA WebLogic and IBM WebSphere.

architectural pattern An informal vocabulary software architects use to describe recurring themes in software architectures.

ASP (Active Server Pages) A Microsoft technology that is used predominantly for building Web-based forms.

ASP (Application Service Provider) An earlier term for Software as a Service.

asynchronous An asynchronous system does not require the client to block and wait for a response (as is the case with a synchronous system) and provides loose coupling between the client and provider. An example of an asynchronous system is email.

B2B (Business to Business) Electronic commerce between businesses, usually focused on reducing operational costs.

B2C (Business to Consumer) Electronic commerce between a business and its consumers.

B2E (Business to Enterprise) Electronic commerce and operations between a business and its employees.

293

bind In a service-oriented architecture, the act of a requester invoking a set of operations offered by a provider. Binding happens after the find operation.

body The portion of the SOAP document that is marked by the Body element.

business-level interface An interface consisting of operations described more at a business level. Typically, such an interface contains fewer operations than would be the case with a low-level interface.

C# A new object-oriented language with features similar to Java that was introduced with .NET.

C++ A popular object-oriented language that is often used for systems programming and application development.

CBD (Component-Based Development) A software development approach that focuses on identifying components to maximize reuse. Many of the techniques in CBD are applicable in developing Web Services.

CLI (Common Language Interface) A feature in .NET that provides the support for an object to be defined in one language and extended in another.

client In a service-oriented architecture, the client is the one requesting the service. Synonyms include requester and sender.

CLR (Common Language Runtime) Programs written in the .NET environment are compiled to an intermediate language that works with the CLR environment to provide language portability.

coarse-grained interface. *See* business-level interface.

CORBA (Common Object Request Broker Architecture) A set of specifications from the Object Management Group that describes a set of services for providing distributed computing on systems running on different operating systems and languages. It is still arguably the most popular middleware platform in the industry.

CRM (Customer Relationship Management) Used holistically, CRM is a strategy and technology on how to best deal with customers. The term is used here to mean a software platform (such as a Siebel system or SalesForce.com) that provides support for that approach.

DCOM (Distributed Component Object Model) Microsoft's middleware platform for providing distributed computing: DCOM works only with Microsoft technologies. *See also* CORBA.

digital certificate A digital document issued by a trusted issuing authority such as Verisign.

digital signature The use of a public-key encryption mechanism to authenticate the identity of the sender and the contents of the message.

disruptive technology A technology that, with its adoption, has the potential to totally redefine the existing market.

distributed computing A term that broadly describes the act of splitting functionality to multiple machines rather than allocating it to a single (presumably larger) machine. *See also* CORBA, RMI, RPC, *and* Web Service.

DOM (Document Object Model) A platform and language-independent API for manipulating and updating documents. *See also* SAX.

DTD (Document Type Definition) An external document that enforces the constraints on the elements of an associated XML document. *See also* XML schema.

EAI (Enterprise Application Integration) An integration approach that is often used in a point-to-point fashion to integrate systems (a common example is moving information from a CRM system to an ERP system or vice versa). *See also* publish-subscribe integration.

ebXML A worldwide initiative to facilitate and increase the adoption of e-commerce. It includes a repository of predefined business processes that adopting firms can adopt as is or modify.

EDI (Electronic Data Interchange) A set of message standards and associated business processes for companies to use to exchange messages.

EJB (Enterprise Java Beans) The component model of the J2EE specifications, EJBs are used to house the business logic in a J2EE architecture.

element A building block of an XML document; it is identified by a start tag and end tag.

endpoint In SOAP terminology, the final destination of a SOAP message. *See also* intermediary.

envelope The root element of a SOAP envelope, identified by the Envelope tag.

ERP (Enterprise Resource Planning) A term that is broadly used to describe the systems that focus on back-end operations; popular ERP packages include SAP and JD Edwards.

fault In SOAP terminology, an exception that is raised.

find In a service-oriented architecture, the act of a requester locating a provider of one or more specified services.

framework A set of closely related classes designed to facilitate application development. J2EE consists of a number of frameworks.

FTP (File Transfer Protocol) A popular protocol for uploading and downloading files.

header In SOAP terminology, the element that is defined by the Header tag. Many SOAP systems use the header to provide extensions and value-added features such as security and versioning.

HRXML An XML standard that is specific to the human resources (HR) industry.

HTML (Hypertext Markup Language) A tag-based language that is used to create Web pages; a major limitation is that the data and display tags are intermingled. *See also* XML.

HTTP (Hypertext Transfer Protocol) The protocol used by browser and Web servers to communicate and transfer information (resulting in Web pages). This is probably the most popular transport protocol for Web Services for the foreseeable future.

HTTPR (Hypertext Transfer Protocol Reliable) An emerging protocol proposed by IBM to provide reliability to HTTP.

HTTPs (Hypertext Transfer Protocol Secure) A secure version of HTTP.

IDL (Interface Definition Language) A platform and programming language-independent syntax used in CORBA development to declare the operations that can be invoked on a CORBA server.

integration broker Usually built on MOMs, an integration broker provides additional services including data transformation and message warehousing. A popular integration broker is MQSeries Integrator.

intermediary A system or organization that, if properly authorized, may act on a SOAP message as it travels to its final destination. For example, in the retail environment, an intermediary may be a firm that provides a credit check of an incoming customer request (via SOAP) before forwarding the SOAP message to the retailer.

interoperability A subjective term to describe the level of effort required for two or more systems to effectively exchange data and/or share application functionality. *See also* EAI *and* Web Service.

J2EE (Java 2 Enterprise Edition) A set of specifications from Sun Microsystems for building enterprise-level applications and Web Services. Many firms, including IBM, BEA Systems, Iona, and SilverStream, have licensed the specifications. The most notable exception is Microsoft, which provides .NET as its Web Services platform. These specifications include, among other things, RMI, JMS, and JCA. *See also* JCA, JMS, *and* RMI.

Java A popular platform-independent object-oriented language predominantly for writing server-side applications. It is OS independent through the use of a Java virtual machine (JVM) and intermediate byte-codes.

JAXM (Java API for Messaging) A J2EE API for XML messaging using SOAP.

JAXP (Java API for XML Processing) A J2EE API for providing a parser-independent way of parsing XML. It supports DOM, SAX, and XSLT.

JAXR (Java API for XML Registries) A J2EE API for connecting to and manipulating registries. The API currently provides support for ebXML and UDDI registries.

JAX-RPC (Java API for RPC) A J2EE API for performing remote procedure calls (RPCs) using XML-RPC, a predecessor to SOAP.

JCA (Java Connector Architecture) A J2EE API that defines a package-independent manner for connecting to and manipulating enterprise information systems including ERP, CRM, and legacy systems. Each package requires the use of a specific adapter.

JCP (Java Community Process) An open organization of Java developers, licensees, and customers who collaborate on changes and additions to the Java platform.

JDBC (Java Database Connectivity) A J2EE API that defines an API for connecting to data sources, independent of the underlying data source. JDBC provides support for relational databases and flat files.

JMS (Java Message Service) A J2EE API that defines an API for connecting to various message-oriented middleware packages, independent of the underlying package.

JSP (Java Server Pages) A J2EE technology that works with servlets to display Web-based content.

JSR (Java Specifications Request) A mechanism for identifying and tracking extensions or additions to the Java specifications.

JVM (Java Virtual Machine) A runtime environment that provides an OS-independent layer on which Java applications execute.

loose coupling A subjective term that describes the level of effort required to change one system and the ripple effect of the changes to the systems to which it is connected. Systems that are loosely coupled are more resilient to change than systems that are tightly coupled.

metalanguage A language that can be used to create other languages. XML is an example of a metalanguage: it is used to create other languages such as WSDL and UDDI.

middleware A term to broadly describe the set of technologies for connecting otherwise disparate systems. Examples include CORBA and DCOM. Middleware is often used with CBD.

MOM (Message-Oriented Middleware) A specialized version of middleware that provides support for loose coupling, messaging, and related services; examples include MQSeries from IBM and SonicMQ from Sonic Software. *See also* integration broker.

namespace A mechanism in SOAP for qualifying element names. An element name needs to be unique only for a given namespace.

.NET Microsoft's Web Services platform, which provides support for multiple languages (including VB.NET, C++, and C#) via the Common Language Interface (CLI) and Common Language Runtime (CLR).

OMG (Object Management Group) A worldwide consortium whose focus is promoting interoperability. The OMG was primarily responsible for the CORBA specifications.

OOT (object-oriented technology) A development and modeling approach where problems are decomposed into objects. An object is a software abstraction that includes identity, state, and operations. Languages that support OOT concepts are called object-oriented languages and include C++, Java, and C#. *See also* CBD.

PKI (public key initiative) The architecture, organizations, practices, and technologies that are necessary to support a certificate-based public-key cryptographic system.

point-to-point integration An integration model that connects one system directly to another system. While effective, it can create tight coupling between the two systems and can become unmanageable when integrating a large number of systems. *See also* publish-subscribe integration.

proxy The local representation of a remote object. *See also* stub *and* skeleton.

publish In a service-oriented architecture, the act of advertising the availability of a service in a repository (private or public).

publish-subscribe integration An integration model where clients can subscribe to available topics; clients are then notified via broadcast when a server provides any updates to the topic. It provides looser coupling than point-to-point integration.

repository In a service-oriented architecture, the collection of available services that providers have published and clients can search.

reuse A term that defines using an existing asset such as code or requirements. Reuse and interoperability have been two goals that have existed since the early days of computing.

RMI (Remote Method Invocation) A J2EE technology that provides distributed computing to Java applications through the use of proxies. It can be used only if the client and provider are both Java-based systems. *See also* CORBA.

RPC (Remote Procedure Call) A mechanism for supporting distributed computing. For example, a procedure (or function or method) calls a procedure (or function or method) on a remote server. RPC has historically been used only for integrating systems that were running on the same OS and/or using the same language. *See also* CORBA.

SAAS (Software as a Service) A billing and deployment model of selling software like a utility similar to electricity or voicemail, so that the revenue is recurring rather than a lump sum. Adopting firms would not incur the costs of operating and updating the software since all costs (operations, development, etc.) are outsourced to the provider.

SAX An event-based API for parsing XML documents in a read-only manner. Because the parsing is read-only, a SAX parser cannot modify the XML document. *See also* DOM.

servlet A Java technology for providing server-side functionality.

servlet engine A program that compiles and executes servlets. Many application servers have built-in servlet engines, although there are standalone servlet engines including JRun from Allaire and Servlet-Exec from NewAtlanta.

skeleton A server-side proxy that represents the remote client. *See also* CORBA, proxy, RMI, *and* stub.

SMTP (Simple Mail Transfer Protocol) A popular protocol for email.

SOA (software-oriented architecture) An architecture that includes three roles: client broker and provider. *See also* bind, find, *and* publish.

SOAP (Service-Oriented Access Protocol, previously Simple Object Access Protocol) An XML-based protocol that supports both synchronous and asynchronous messaging in a platform-, OS-, and language-independent manner. The requester invokes an operation on the server, passing in a SOAP document, which the receiver can then populate with the return values.

stub A client-side proxy that represents the remote server. *See also* proxy, skeleton, RMI, *and* CORBA.

tight coupling A subjective term that describes the level of effort required to change one system and the ripple effect of the changes to the systems to which it is connected. Generally speaking, tight coupling is not desirable because it implies a high level of effort for even minor changes. *See also* loose coupling.

UDDI (Universal Description, Discovery and Integration) A protocol for allowing services to be searched and registered. IBM and Microsoft also operate public UDDI registries on which firms can register their businesses.

URL (Uniform Resource Locator) A mechanism for uniquely identifying a resource (a Web page, a file, etc.). It is most commonly used by a browser to locate a Web page.

valid An XML document is said to be valid if it is well formed and can be validated against a DTD or XML schema.

VB.NET The .NET version of the popular programming language Visual Basic. It is now a fully object-oriented language and is markedly different from Visual Basic.

W3C (Worldwide Web Consortium) An international standards body created in 1994 to adopt specifications and help ensure interoperability of Web technologies (HTML, XML, etc.).

Web Service A piece of software functionality that can be registered, described, and invoked over a network. *See also* SOAP, UDDI, *and* WSDL.

well formed Containing no errors. For example, a well-formed XML document is one that contains no syntax errors.

WSDL (Web Services Definition Language) An XML-based protocol for describing the characteristics of a Web Service (the available operations, its location, etc.).

WSFL (Web Services Flow Language) An XML-based grammar invented by IBM for describing workflow and orchestration of Web Services.

XML (Extensible Markup Language) A metalanguage that can be used for describing data, application functionality (SOAP), and creating new languages (WSDL, UDDI, etc.).

XML parser A program that decomposes an XML document into its individual elements. XML parsers are either DOM based or SAX based.

XML schema An external document against which an XML document can be validated. An XML schema is itself an XML document and provides validation features such as type enforcement and range checking. Schemas address many shortcomings of DTDs.

XSLT (Extensible Stylesheet Language Transformation) A language for transforming XML documents from one format to another.

Index

X

XML (Extensible Markup Language),
31–37, 113, 250, 256, 279–80, 282–84
   defined, 31
   document object model (DOM) parser
     34, 250
   document type definition (DTD),
     35–36
   encryption, 113
   JDOM, 34
   namespace, 36

   performance concerns, 256, 258–59
   schemas, 35–36
   simple event API (SAX), 34
   valid, 35
   well-formed, 35
   XML-RPC, 279–80, 282–84
XMLBus 7, 268–69, 285–91 (*See also*
J2EE vendors)
   CD-ROM, 7
   review, 285–91

About the Author

Alex Nghiem is the president of Blue Samba Solutions (*www.bluesamba.com*), a solutions provider that specializes in helping clients reduce integration costs and reach new markets through Web Services. He occasionally collaborates with Giga Information Group and InfoWorld to perform strategic IT assessments.

Nghiem previously founded Global Objects (1993), a consulting firm that focused on application server and middleware development, and later sold it to a leading CRM solutions firm (2000). After the sale, he became the firm's CTO and VP of Engineering and managed over 80 engineers in three offices.

He is a member of Young Entrepreneurs Organization (YEO), the premier peer-to-peer networking group of entrepreneurs under age 40. He is the founding member of Rueda de Amigos, a salsa dance troupe that performs at charity functions.

His previous textbook on object-oriented technologies, *NextStep Programming: Concepts and Applications* (Prentice Hall, 1993), was translated into Japanese in 1995.

In his spare time, he enjoys dancing, snowboarding, traveling abroad, watching good movies, and reading comic books and novels.

Blue Samba Solutions helps clients manage integration costs and open new markets by leveraging technologies such as Web Services and wireless technologies. Our team has helped clients map out their businesses and delivered mission-critical solutions in multiple domains including telecommunications, financial, logistics, and insurance.

SERVICE	BENEFITS
• IT strategy (ROI studies, corporate governance, succession planning, etc.)	• Ensure that the IT solution is in alignment with business objectives
• Product evaluation and selection	• Obtain objective third-party feedback
• Systems integration	• Reduce risk and development schedule
• Training	• Enable development staff and reduce delivery schedule

Sample testimonial from CheckFree (a publicly traded firm that currently offers online billing and payments for hundreds of companies on the Web).

"Blue Samba Solutions quickly integrated with our team and helped us scale and deploy our mission-critical application without impacting our original schedule while saving significant dollars from our original estimates. CheckFree and our customers have been delighted with the work so far and look forward to working with Blue Samba Solutions again."

VP of Engineering, CheckFree

Contact us to see how we can help you.

Blue Samba Solutions, LLC
3340 Peachtree Rd NE #1000
Atlanta, GA 30326
404.869.9131
info@bluesamba.com

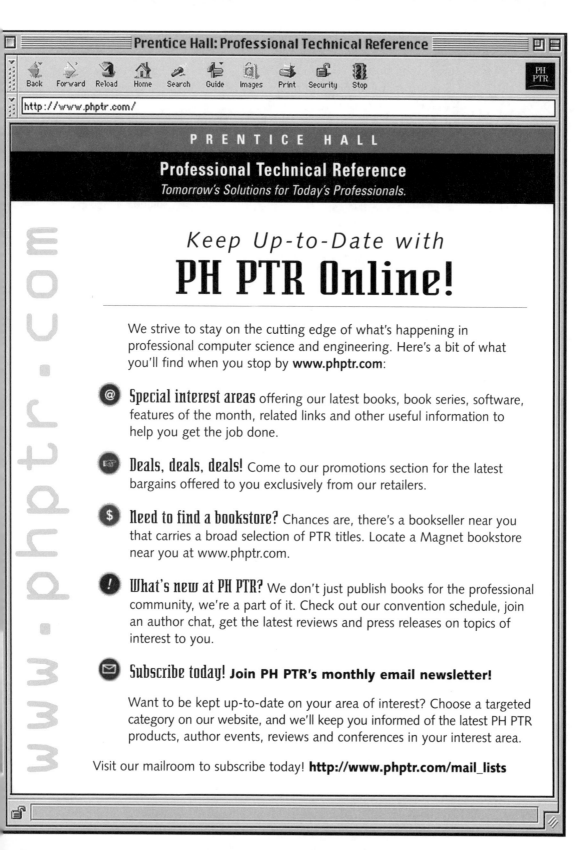

LICENSE AGREEMENT AND LIMITED WARRANTY

READ THE FOLLOWING TERMS AND CONDITIONS CAREFULLY BEFORE OPENING THIS SOFTWARE PACKAGE. THIS LEGAL DOCUMENT IS AN AGREEMENT BETWEEN YOU AND PRENTICE-HALL, INC. (THE "COMPANY"). BY OPENING THIS SEALED SOFTWARE PACKAGE, YOU ARE AGREEING TO BE BOUND BY THESE TERMS AND CONDITIONS. IF YOU DO NOT AGREE WITH THESE TERMS AND CONDITIONS, DO NOT OPEN THE SOFTWARE PACKAGE. PROMPTLY RETURN THE UNOPENED SOFTWARE PACKAGE AND ALL ACCOMPANYING ITEMS TO THE PLACE YOU OBTAINED THEM FOR A FULL REFUND OF ANY SUMS YOU HAVE PAID.

1.   **GRANT OF LICENSE:** In consideration of your payment of the license fee, which is part of the price you paid for this product, and your agreement to abide by the terms and conditions of this Agreement, the Company grants to you a nonexclusive right to use and display the copy of the enclosed software program (hereinafter the "software") on a single computer (i.e., with a single CPU) at a single location so long as you comply with the terms of this Agreement. The Company reserves all rights not expressly granted to you under this Agreement.

2.   **OWNERSHIP OF SOFTWARE:** You own only the magnetic or physical media (the enclosed software) on which the software is recorded or fixed, but the Company retains all the rights, title, and ownership to the software recorded on the original software copy(ies) and all subsequent copies of the software, regardless of the form or media on which the original or other copies may exist. This license is not a sale of the original software or any copy to you.

3.   **COPY RESTRICTIONS:** This software and the accompanying printed materials and user manual (the "Documentation") are the subject of copyright. You may not copy the Documentation or the software, except that you may make a single copy of the software for backup or archival purposes only. You may be held legally responsible for any copying or copyright infringement which is caused or encouraged by your failure to abide by the terms of this restriction.

4.   **USE RESTRICTIONS:** You may not network the software or otherwise use it on more than one computer or computer terminal at the same time. You may physically transfer the software from one computer to another provided that the software is used on only one computer at a time. You may not distribute copies of the software or Documentation to others. You may not reverse engineer, disassemble, decompile, modify, adapt, translate, or create derivative works based on the software or the Documentation without the prior written consent of the Company.

5.   **TRANSFER RESTRICTIONS:** The enclosed software is licensed only to you and may not be transferred to any one else without the prior written consent of the Company. Any unauthorized transfer of the software shall result in the immediate termination of this Agreement.

6.   **TERMINATION:** This license is effective until terminated. This license will terminate automatically without notice from the Company and become null and void if you fail to comply with any provisions or limitations of this license. Upon termination, you shall destroy the Documentation and all copies of the software. All provisions of this Agreement as to warranties, limitation of liability, remedies or damages, and our ownership rights shall survive termination.

7.   **MISCELLANEOUS:** This Agreement shall be construed in accordance with the laws of the United States of America and the State of New York and shall benefit the Company, its affiliates, and assignees.

8.   **LIMITED WARRANTY AND DISCLAIMER OF WARRANTY:** The Company warrants that the software, when properly used in accordance with the Documentation, will operate in substantial conformity with the description of the software set forth in the Documentation. The Company does not warrant that the software will meet your requirements or that the operation of the software will be uninterrupted or error-free. The Company warrants that the media on which the software is delivered shall be free from defects in materials and workmanship under normal use

for a period of thirty (30) days from the date of your purchase. Your only remedy and the Company's only obligation under these limited warranties is, at the Company's option, return of the warranted item for a refund of any amounts paid by you or replacement of the item. Any replacement of software or media under the warranties shall not extend the original warranty period. The limited warranty set forth above shall not apply to any software which the Company determines in good faith has been subject to misuse, neglect, improper installation, repair, alteration, or damage by you. EXCEPT FOR THE EXPRESSED WARRANTIES SET FORTH ABOVE, THE COMPANY DISCLAIMS ALL WARRANTIES, EXPRESS OR IMPLIED, INCLUDING WITHOUT LIMITATION, THE IMPLIED WARRANTIES OF MERCHANTABILITY AND FITNESS FOR A PARTICULAR PURPOSE. EXCEPT FOR THE EXPRESS WARRANTY SET FORTH ABOVE, THE COMPANY DOES NOT WARRANT, GUARANTEE, OR MAKE ANY REPRESENTATION REGARDING THE USE OR THE RESULTS OF THE USE OF THE SOFTWARE IN TERMS OF ITS CORRECTNESS, ACCURACY, RELIABILITY, CURRENTNESS, OR OTHERWISE.

IN NO EVENT, SHALL THE COMPANY OR ITS EMPLOYEES, AGENTS, SUPPLIERS, OR CONTRACTORS BE LIABLE FOR ANY INCIDENTAL, INDIRECT, SPECIAL, OR CONSEQUENTIAL DAMAGES ARISING OUT OF OR IN CONNECTION WITH THE LICENSE GRANTED UNDER THIS AGREEMENT, OR FOR LOSS OF USE, LOSS OF DATA, LOSS OF INCOME OR PROFIT, OR OTHER LOSSES, SUSTAINED AS A RESULT OF INJURY TO ANY PERSON, OR LOSS OF OR DAMAGE TO PROPERTY, OR CLAIMS OF THIRD PARTIES, EVEN IF THE COMPANY OR AN AUTHORIZED REPRESENTATIVE OF THE COMPANY HAS BEEN ADVISED OF THE POSSIBILITY OF SUCH DAMAGES. IN NO EVENT SHALL LIABILITY OF THE COMPANY FOR DAMAGES WITH RESPECT TO THE SOFTWARE EXCEED THE AMOUNTS ACTUALLY PAID BY YOU, IF ANY, FOR THE SOFTWARE.

SOME JURISDICTIONS DO NOT ALLOW THE LIMITATION OF IMPLIED WARRANTIES OR LIABILITY FOR INCIDENTAL, INDIRECT, SPECIAL, OR CONSEQUENTIAL DAMAGES, SO THE ABOVE LIMITATIONS MAY NOT ALWAYS APPLY. THE WARRANTIES IN THIS AGREEMENT GIVE YOU SPECIFIC LEGAL RIGHTS AND YOU MAY ALSO HAVE OTHER RIGHTS WHICH VARY IN ACCORDANCE WITH LOCAL LAW.

ACKNOWLEDGMENT

YOU ACKNOWLEDGE THAT YOU HAVE READ THIS AGREEMENT, UNDERSTAND IT, AND AGREE TO BE BOUND BY ITS TERMS AND CONDITIONS. YOU ALSO AGREE THAT THIS AGREEMENT IS THE COMPLETE AND EXCLUSIVE STATEMENT OF THE AGREEMENT BETWEEN YOU AND THE COMPANY AND SUPERSEDES ALL PROPOSALS OR PRIOR AGREEMENTS, ORAL, OR WRITTEN, AND ANY OTHER COMMUNICATIONS BETWEEN YOU AND THE COMPANY OR ANY REPRESENTATIVE OF THE COMPANY RELATING TO THE SUBJECT MATTER OF THIS AGREEMENT.

Should you have any questions concerning this Agreement or if you wish to contact the Company for any reason, please contact in writing at the address below.

Robin Short
Prentice Hall PTR
One Lake Street
Upper Saddle River, New Jersey 07458

About the CD

The CD-ROM included with *IT Web Services: A Roadmap for the Enterprise* contains the following:

Orbix E2A Web Services Integration Platform XMLBus, Edition 5.0.

The CD-ROM can be used on Microsoft Windows NT/2000/XP and UNIX. On a UNIX machine, the user has to click on the index.html file. The UNIX platforms that are supported include Solaris, Tru64, Linux, and HP-UX 11.

License Agreement

Use of the software accompanying *IT Web Services: A Roadmap for the Enterprise* is subject to the terms of the License Agreement and Limited Warranty, found on the previous two pages.

Technical Support

Prentice Hall does not offer technical support for any of the programs or third-party software on the CD-ROM. However, if the CD-ROM is damaged, you may obtain a replacement copy by sending an email that describes the problem to *disc_exchange@prenhall.com*.